KNOW IT ALL, FIND IT FAST

An A–Z source guide for the enquiry desk

Bob Duckett
Peter Walker
Christinea Donnelly

facet publishing

© Bob Duckett, Peter Walker and Christinea Donnelly, 2002

Published by
Facet Publishing
7 Ridgmount Street
London WC1E 7AE

Facet Publishing (formerly Library Association Publishing) is wholly owned by
CILIP: the Chartered Institute of Library and Information Professionals

Bob Duckett, Peter Walker and Christinea Donnelly have asserted their right under
the Copyright, Designs and Patents Act, 1988, to be identified as Author of this
work.

First published 2002

British Library Cataloguing in Publication Data

A catalogue record for this book is available from the British Library

ISBN 1-85604-434-3

Typeset in 10/14 pt Aldine 721BT and Dax by Facet Publishing.
Printed and made in Great Britain by MPG Books Ltd, Bodmin, Cornwall.

Contents

KNOW IT ALL, FIND IT FAST

INTRODUCTION

Answering questions from its users is one of the most important services undertaken by a library's staff. Yet it is also one of the most difficult, least understood, and most neglected of subjects. Despite years of working in reference libraries, information units and subject departments, the lack of help we frontline staff get to assist people with their enquiries is a constant source of amazement and irritation. And puzzlement. How *do* you train staff to answer questions? Manuals on question-answering techniques – the social and psychological aspects – there are a-plenty. Lists of recommended reference books are also common. Courses on government publications, law reports, online searching and other specialist literatures and search techniques exist. These can help, of course they can, but all too frequently the questions fired at us out of the blue have not been covered on a course. And the majority of staff on enquiry desks do not have formal qualifications and have not been on courses. And there is a queue, the phone is ringing unanswered, the photocopier has jammed, and your inquisitor is waiting impatiently for an answer. You are stressed and you can feel the panic rising. Few outsiders can understand the terror experienced by staff newly placed on public enquiry counters. Few of us who have been there will ever forget those early experiences. Some of us *never* get over them!

What is needed is a guide that staff can use to know where to find the answers, and quickly! Hence this book. We hope it will help.

This book is intended as a first point of reference for library staff unfamiliar with the subject of the enquiry. It is aimed at general library staff and no prior knowledge is assumed. It is an A to Z because this is the quickest way to find a subject. Some typical questions are given to indicate the nature of the subject. Then follow a few background comments that will assist the member of staff to clarify the nature of the enquiry; before one can find an answer it is important to have asked the right follow-up question or questions to make sure the questioner and the questioned understand each other. Then come a few of the more commonly available sources that may help to answer the question. These include printed sources, electronic sources (mostly free websites), and some useful contacts for referral purposes. Finally we include some of the more common tips and pitfalls. A general, non-specialist service is assumed. This is not a book for the specialist.

The sources that can be used to find information are vast; the ones listed in this book are merely a few that the compilers have, themselves, found useful. Your own library will have others, and maybe better ones. The volumes of *Walford's guide to reference material*, published by Library Association Publishing (now Facet Publishing), are an annotated guide to resources compiled for librarians and researchers seeking further sources, and there are other guides similar in character. An important tip is to get to know and use the sources that you *already* have to hand. It is amazing how many enquiries can be answered by an intelligent use of the local telephone directory, *Whitaker's almanack*, a dictionary and a set of encyclopedias.

Our aim is to provide a handbook that will help the hard-pressed member of staff serving the public to find a source that may contain the answer, or at least go some of the way to finding it. No book can ever provide the answer to everything, and obviously specialist or more experienced help will often be needed, but we hope that this little guide will help some of the time. All of us, the compilers, spend most of our time on enquiry counters and work with others who do likewise. We have tried to avoid jargon and to base this book on the reality of everyday enquiries. We hope you find it useful. We wish we had had such a guide when we started!

Our thanks go to our many colleagues who have helped us answer enquiries over the years, and to the publisher's reader who gave much useful advice and positive support.

Bob Duckett, Pete Walker and Christinea Donnelly

ABBREVIATIONS & ACRONYMS

See also Dictionaries

Typical questions
- What do the letters NACRO stand for?
- What does *ibid.* mean?

Considerations

Abbreviations are shortened forms of a word or phrase, such as 'Tel.' for Telephone or 'fax' for facsimile. *Ibid.* is short for *ibidem* (Latin for 'in the same place'). Acronyms are groups of letters made up of some or all of the first letters of a name such as BL for British Library, NACRO for the National Association for the Care and Resettlement of Offenders, or CAMRA for the Campaign for Real Ale. Both abbreviations and acronyms are common in text and speech. They do cause difficulty for people unfamiliar with them. They are particularly common in technical or specialist writing where they are useful as a form of shorthand.

Where to look
Printed sources

There are numerous dictionaries of abbreviations and acronyms. They are usually shelved with dictionaries. Examples are:

De Sola, R. (1994) *Abbreviations dictionary*, 9th edn, CRC Press
Paxton, J. (2001) *Dent dictionary of abbreviations*, Dent
The Oxford dictionary of abbreviations (1992) Oxford University Press

Many general dictionaries include the more common abbreviations and acronyms, either in the main sequence or as appendices. Specialist subject dictionaries and handbooks often contain them, though obviously the subject area needs to be known first. An example is

Ramsay, A. (2001) *Eurojargon: a dictionary of European Union acronyms, abbreviations and sobriquets*, Fitzroy Dearborn

Electronic sources

The World Wide Web Acronym and Abbreviation Server
www.ucc.ie/info/net/acronyms

Acronym Finder **www.acronymfinder.com**
    180,000 definitions.

Other sources
This is one of the areas where just asking colleagues may result in the answer.

Tips and pitfalls
Ask the enquirer for the context in which the abbreviation or acronym was heard or read. This will help narrow the search. Is it in current use? Was it in a newspaper or a book? If so, what was the subject? Is it a technical term? Or literary?

Beware the many abbreviations and acronyms that have more than one meaning. JSC can stand for Joint Stock Company and Joint Staff Council; BL for British Library or British Leyland.

ABSTRACTS *see* ARTICLES IN JOURNALS

ACCOUNTS, AUDITING & BOOKKEEPING

See also Companies – Accounts

Typical questions
- I need help keeping my accounts
- Can you give me details of a local accountant?
- What does ... mean in accountancy?

Where to look
Books
French, D. (1985) *Dictionary of accounting terms*, Croner Publications

Beattie, V., Brandt, R. and Fearnley, S. (2001) *Behind closed doors: what company audit is really about*, Palgrave

Flower, J. and Ebbers, G. (2001) *Global financial reporting*, Palgrave
    This provides an analysis of the financial reporting practices of five major countries, it proceeds to an examination of the International Accounting Standards Committee.

Directories

Association of Chartered Certified Accountants directory of members
> **www.accaglobal.com**

Institute of Chartered Accountants of England and Wales list of members and firms,
> Waterlow Specialist Information Publishing **www.icaewfirms.co.uk**
> This has a free searchable directory of chartered accountants by location or
> area of specialism. It offers worldwide coverage.

Journals

There are a number of journals that are excellent for keeping up to date with
accountancy practice. These are only a selection, it is best to check *Willings press
guide* for further titles. *See* Publishing.

Accountancy
> Institute of Chartered Accountants
> Tel: 020 7833 3291 Fax: 020 7833 2085
> Monthly
> Covers everything to do with accountancy and auditing.

The Accountant
> Lafferty Publications
> Tel: 020 7563 5700 Fax: 020 7563 5701
> Monthly
> Looks at the development of accountancy standards and practices
> worldwide.

Associations and websites

There are numerous associations dealing with accountancy and auditing. Refer
to *Directory of British associations and associations in Ireland*. *See* Associations & Organizations.

Accountancy Glossary **www.bized.ac.uk/glossary/accountglos.htm**
> Excellent, not only giving definitions of terms but where applicable, related
> diagrams to explain terms further. It is aimed primarily at students but it
> would be suitable for anyone to clarify accounting terminology.

Association of Chartered Certified Accountants **www.accaglobal.com**

Audit Commission **www.audit-commission.gov.uk**

1 Vincent Square, London SW1P 2PN

Tel: 020 7828 1212

Looks at the use of public money.

Business Bureau UK: Small Business Information Resource
www.businessbureau-uk.co.uk/accounting/book-keeping/index.htm
Offers a simple guide to what records to keep and defines the important accountancy terms.

Chartered Institute of Public Finance and Accountancy (CIPFA)
www.cipfa.org.uk
This organization is the authority on accountancy and financial management for the public services. It has an excellent website that includes the annual report, accounting issues and CIPFA for the Regions. Each region has its own web pages full of news, jobs, events and information.

Institute of Chartered Accountants of England and Wales **www.icaew.org.uk**

International Accounting Standards Committee. **www.iasc.org.uk**
This provides details of standards in force and current projects designed to develop an understandable and clear global accounting standards. It also gives details of publications.

National Audit Office **www.nao.gov.uk**
157–197 Buckingham Palace Rd, London SW1W 9SP
Tel: 020 7798 7000
Monitors central government spending.

ACRONYMS *see* ABBREVIATIONS & ACRONYMS

ACTORS & ACTRESSES

See also Awards & Prizes, Films & Cinema, Theatre

Typical questions
- Who starred as Barry in the 1980s TV series *Auf Wiedersehen Pet*?
- What films has Johnny Depp starred in?
- Have you a biography of Marilyn Monroe?

- Where and when was Emmanuelle Béart born?
- Which character did Nicholas Cage play in the film *Leaving Las Vegas*?

Considerations

Questions in this category can cover film, theatre and television, so a wide variety of sources can be used. There can also be many types of questions, as can be seen from the examples above.

Where to look

Printed sources

Walker, J. (ed.) (1999) *Halliwell's who's who in the movies*, 13th edn, HarperCollins
This covers actors, directors, producers and writers involved in film making.

Lewis, J. E. and Stempel, P. (1999) *Ultimate TV guide*, Orion
Thousands of TV programmes from 1946 to the present day are covered.

Evans, J. (1995) *Guinness television encyclopedia*, Guinness Publications
This includes hundreds of programmes, actors and presenters.

For general biographies, check your library catalogue.

If your library holds copies of the *TV Times* and/or *Radio Times*, these can sometimes come in useful for recent TV films or programmes. Both magazines usually list casts.

Electronic sources

A useful site on the internet is the *Internet Movie Database* (**www.imdb.com**). This includes cast listings for every imaginable film.

If you are searching for an actor or actress on the internet, simply type their name into a good search engine.

ACTS & REGULATIONS

Typical questions

- Have you got the Dangerous Dogs Act?
- When did the Human Rights Act come into force?

Considerations

All major libraries should have copies of acts. Most will keep Statutory Instruments and Command (Green and White) Papers too. The arrival of the world wide web has made these available to everyone, even the smallest branch library.

Where to look
Electronic sources

For government acts from 1988 and Statutory Instruments from 1987, go to the following site:

> **www.legislation.hmso.gov.uk**

For Green and White Papers try:

> **www.official-documents.co.uk/menu/uk.htm**

For Bills before Parliament try:

> **www.parliament.uk**

For debates on acts try *Hansard*:

> **www.parliament.the-stationery-office.co.uk/pa/cm/cmhansrd.htm**

ADDRESSES & POSTCODES

Typical questions
- I want to find the address of Mr ... in Hull.
- What is the postcode for ... Street in Wishaw?
- Who lives at no. 12 ... Street in Tilehurst, Reading?

Considerations

Finding addresses can be tricky, especially ones that are out of your local area. Finding postcodes, though, could not be easier.

Where to look
Printed sources

One of the first places you should look is in the telephone directory. If you have a full set then you can search the whole of the country. Obviously, if a person is ex-directory, then this is no use. You could also check the elctoral register for your local area. However, you can only check addresses with these and not people's names.

For postcodes, see if you have a local postcode directory, where you can look up an address and find its postcode.

Electronic sources

Using the internet can save you mounds of time when looking for addresses. You can search telephone directories worldwide, check electoral registers in other parts of the country, and check postcodes at the touch of a button.

To look at the UK telephone directories, try:

www.ukphonebook.com/

For telephone directories around the world:

www.teldir.com/

To combine a telephone directory and electoral register search in the UK try:

www.192.com

This service lets you search by name or address in a particular area. You do have to register and there is a charge if your search becomes wider. If you are simply trying to find Mr Smith in Brighouse then you should not have a problem.

The Royal Mail postcode finder lets you type in a street name and town and gives you the postcode. Alternatively, type in a postcode and it will give you the house number and street name.

www.royalmail.co.uk/paf/

AGRICULTURE *see* FARMING

AIRCRAFT & AIRLINES

Typical questions
- What is the national airline of Belgium?
- What speed can a Boeing 757 reach?
- Can you give me the telephone number for Easyjet?

• I would like to know times of flights from Leeds/Bradford to London.

Considerations

There are several types of questions you could receive when dealing with this subject. Some may be about aircraft and their specifications. Others may be about flight schedules. The range is quite large. It is probably worth splitting airlines and aircraft into two separate sections in order to answer questions more effectively.

There are many sources of information for identifying aircraft and looking at their specifications: Jane's is the world leader in this subject. Larger reference libraries should have a copy of their aircraft book and if not, they should consider buying one.

As regards airlines and schedules, most major carriers are now represented on the world wide web and the information there may be more up to date than any directories you may have.

Where to look
Printed sources – Aircraft

Jane's all the world's aircraft, Jane's Information Group. Annual
> This is the guide to both civil and military aircraft of the world. Every country with air potential is considered. It is now available online. There is a subscription fee.

Your library may have some books about individual aircraft, such as Concorde or Spitfire. These 'in-depth' histories will be useful for more serious research.

If you receive any enquiries about aircraft terminology, the following are good references:

Gunston, B. (1989) *Jane's aerospace dictionary*, Jane's Information Group

Hall, R. J. and Campbell, R. D. (1991) *Dictionary of aviation*, Blackwell Scientific Publications

Printed sources – Airlines

When dealing with queries regarding airlines, the following publications are essential:

Ginsberg, M. (1999) *Directory of British aviation 1999/2000*, Aviation Directories Ltd
> This lists all airports in the UK as well as all the UK and main international operators.

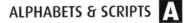

World airways guide, OAG
> This is the complete guide to air travel. It gives flight schedules, airline codes and information, airport codes and websites of operators.

Top world airlines, Avinar Data Ltd
> This gives details of the main airline companies, along with brief histories.

Electronic sources

Most of the world's major airlines now have a presence on the internet. You can find them simply by typing their name into a search engine. There is also a useful listing of airlines, with schedules, prices and online booking facilities at:

http://flyaow.com/frames.htm

Tips and pitfalls

When dealing with enquiries about airline schedules and prices, it would be more prudent to direct the enquirer to a travel agent, especially if you do not have any up-to-date information at your disposal.

ALPHABETS & SCRIPTS

See also Languages & Translating; Signs & Symbols

Typical questions

- Have you got the Russian alphabet?
- I'm trying to read an old document, but having difficulty with some of the letters.
- I want to learn how to write old-fashioned script.
- Should I look under 'The', or 'B' for the address 'The Beeches'?
- I can't find this word in the index!

Considerations

Much will depend on how much the enquirer knows. Most enquiries about alphabets come from people with poor language skills who do not realize how complex scripts can be. A particular difficulty, especially with languages from the Middle East, India and Pakistan, is that a single language can be written in more than one script. Another difficulty can be that a single letter, or combination of letters, can be pronounced differently in different languages (think of the difficulty that Welsh presents to non-Welsh speakers). Some languages do not have vowels in their printed form (e.g. Hebrew); some scripts are read right to left, or even alternately upwards and downwards. Other languages do not use letters but pictograms and ideographs.

Old print can cause difficulty. In English, 'ss' was printed 'ff', and the letters 'j' and 'u' did not exist before printing developed in the 16th century. (Be careful when using old indexes and catalogues: even the 1965 version of the British Museum catalogue often uses 'i' and 'v' for 'j' or 'u'.) In German, the ß is still commonly used for 'ss'.

Old handwriting (manu script), is a more difficult problem, and the enquirer is best referred to someone with archival skills, or to a book on the subject.

Where to look

Alphabets

Brief descriptions of alphabets, often with a tabular presentation, can be found in the larger encyclopedias, dictionaries and teach-yourself-type grammars of the language concerned. Many general books on languages such as the *Dictionary of languages: the definitive reference to more than 400 languages*, Bloomsbury, 1998, also have tables. Probably best is Volume 2 of Diringer, D. (1968) *The alphabet: a key to the history of mankind*, 3rd edn, Hutchinson. This volume consists entirely of plates.

Calligraphy

For calligraphy, the art of fine writing, see, for example:

Wilson, D. (1991) *The encyclopedia of calligraphy techniques*, Headline Press

Calligraphy is a subject sometimes taught at evening classes, or even features in kits that can be purchased at the bigger stationers or craft and artists' shops. Also contact local Asian communities who often teach calligraphy.

Old writing (palaeography)

Avrin, L. (1991) *Scribes, script and books: the book arts from antiquity to the Renaissance*, American Library Association/British Library
A good all-round account.

Hector, D. (1991) *The handwriting of English documents*, 2nd edn, Edward Arnold

Archivists have training in reading old scripts and deciphering old documents. They may be able to advise.

Filing and indexes

Filing, or the order in which letters and words are arranged, is a seriously under-rated skill. Does 'Social Work' come before or after 'Socialism', for example? Users of indexes and directories need to be aware how such things as hyphenated names are presented (by first or second element of the name?), how names that are the same are distinguished, and whether or not the definite and indefinite articles (the, a, an) are used to influence order. Sophisticated filing rules do exist, but are frequently ignored. When someone complains they can't find something in an index, it may be that they are not aware of alternative methods of filing. Two British Standards are:

BS 1749: 1985 (1991) Recommendations for alphabetical arrangement and the filing of numbers and symbols

BS 6478: 1984 (1990) Guide to filing bibliographic information in libraries and documentation

Other sources

Society of Archivists **www.archives.org.uk**
40 Northampton Rd, London EC1R 0HB
Tel: 020 7278 8630 Fax: 020 7278 2107
E-mail: societyofarchivists@archives.org.uk

Society of Indexers **www.socind.demon.co.uk**
Globe Centre, Penistone Rd, Sheffield S6 3AE
Tel: 0114 281 3060 Fax: 0114 281 3061
E-mail: admin@socind.demon.co.uk

Tips and pitfalls

Beware non-Roman scripts that have been put into a Roman script phonetically. Many of the older dictionaries use systems of transliteration (correspondences between sounds and letters, or one system of letters into another) no longer understood by those whose languages are being transliterated. Russian and Chinese are two that can cause confusion. Thus Tchaikovsky can also be spelt Chaikovskii, and Peking is now generally spelt Beijing (Pinyin characters replaced the Wade-Giles system in the mid-1950s, though both use the Roman alphabet). Beware classic and modern versions of the same language, e.g. Arabic, Greek.

ANIMALS & PETS

See also Birds

Typical questions

- I think my pet is ill. Have you a book that will help?
- I want to learn about looking after animals.
- What are the qualities to look for in a pedigree dog?
- What is the difference between a stoat and a badger?

Considerations

Pets, and animals in general, often mean a great deal to people and the library staff have to be particularly sensitive. While there are many good cheap books about on pets, there are occasions when the resources of the library are sought.

Be careful not to be give advice about pets. All staff can do is to refer people to sources.

Where to look

Printed sources

There are many encyclopedias of animals, e.g. *Larousse encyclopedia of animal life* (1969), Hamlyn. Most encyclopedias will have useful articles on animals. Other books include:

Allaby, M. (ed.) (1997) *The dictionary of zoology*, 2nd edn, Oxford University Press
Boden, E. (2001) *Black's veterinary dictionary*, 20th edn, A & C Black

The latter is frequently revised – a standard reference dictionary for vets, students and journalists. Covers topical issues such as BSE and foot and mouth disease.

To find vets, try the Yellow Pages and other local directories.

Individual animals

HarperCollins do an excellent series of Field Guides on a wide range of animals, e.g.: Bellman, H. (1985) *A field guide to the grasshoppers and crickets of Britain and Northern Ireland*.

Important for dog lovers are: Kennel Club (1990) *The Kennel Club's illustrated breed standards*, 2nd edn, Ebury Press and Fogle, B (2000) *The new encyclopedia of the dog*, 2nd edn, Dorling Kindersley. Others include:

Fogle, B. (2001) *The new encyclopedia of the cat*, 2nd edn, Dorling Kindersley

Morris, D. (1996) *Cat world: a feline dictionary*, Ebury Press

Axelrod, H. R. (1997) *Atlas of freshwater aquarium fishes*, 9th edn, TFH
Over 3500 photographs.

Flade, J. E. (1987) *The complete horse*, David & Charles

Animal rights

Clough, C. and Kew, B. (1993) *Animal welfare handbook*, Fourth Estate
Kistler, J. M. (2000) *Animal rights: a subject guide, bibliography and internet companion*, Greenwood Press
Animal Life (quarterly) is the official journal of the RSPCA.

Dinosaurs

Brett-Surman, M. K. (ed.) (2000) *Dinosaurs; the ultimate guide to prehistoric life*, Collins
Svarney, T. E. and P. (2000) *The handy dinosaur answer book*, Visible Ink

Electronic sources

BBC **www.bbc.co.uk/nature**

ARKive **www.arkive.org.uk**
Endangered species.

Natural History Museum **www.nhm.ac.uk**
Includes details of the Museum's collections and contacts.

Other sources

The Royal College of Veterinary Surgeons **www.rcvs.org.uk**
Belgravia House, 62–64 Horseferry Rd, London SW1P 2AF
Tel: 020 7222 2001 Fax: 020 7222 2004

RSPCA (Royal Society for the Prevention of Cruelty to Animals)
www.rspca.org.uk
Wilberforce Way, Southwater, Horsham, West Sussex RH12 9RS
Tel: 01403 264181

The Kennel Club **www.the-kennel-club.org.uk**

1 Clarges St, London W1J 8AB
Tel: 0870 606 6750 Fax: 020 7518 1058

Tips and pitfalls

Sometimes people bring in their pets. This can make for interesting anecdotes!

ANNIVERSARIES

See also Dates

Typical questions

• What item is associated with your fifth wedding anniversary?
• When is the anniversary of D-Day?
• How many years is a diamond jubilee?

Considerations

The main types of questions regarding anniversaries are like the examples above: which items are associated with which wedding anniversary, or what are the anniversaries of important events.

Where to look

Printed sources

There is a list of wedding anniversaries in:

Whitaker's pocket reference almanac, The Stationery Office
    Check under wedding anniversaries in the index. If you have not got a copy, try a good encyclopedia.

Dates: by day within a year, i.e. arranged 1 January–31 December

Beal, G. (1992) *The Independent book of anniversaries*, Headline
Beeching, C. L. (1997) *A dictionary of dates*, 2nd edn, Oxford University Press
Frewin, A. (1979) *The book of days*, Collins

Dates: by event

Butler, A. (1985) *Dent's dictionary of dates*, 7th edn, Dent
    A–Z by event.

General encyclopedias will feature noteworthy events. Also the newspaper indexes

such as those to the *Guardian* and *The Times*.

Dates: by year divided by event; chronologies

The annual register: a record of world events. 1758 to the present, Keesings World
Wide, Annual

This year-by-year record of world events provides information with
historical context, perspective and biographical information. Large
libraries may have the full set. Also available as a subscription website.

Facts on file. Weekly with cumulating indexes and annual binders

'World news digest with index.' This major news service indexes events
within each year.

The Chronicle series of heavyweight books published by Chronicle Communications such as *Chronicle of the World*, *Chronicle of America*, *Chronicle of Britain*, etc.
give newspaper-type accounts with illustration to events. They are very popular
with children.

Electronic sources

If you have access to the internet, try the following page for wedding
anniversaries:

www.hintsandthings.co.uk/library/anniversary.htm

This site also has a useful section for birthstones.

Tips and pitfalls

Wedding anniversaries can be frustrating to find, so if you do discover a list, it
may be worth photocopying and leaving in a useful place.

ANTIQUES

Typical questions

- I have some old porcelain vases. How much are they worth?
- Have you any information on old Corgi toys?
- I have a collection of old cigarette cards. Are they worth anything?

Considerations

There are several points to consider here. Is the enquirer simply wanting to know how much an item is worth, or are they wanting more detailed information about a particular piece? Some enquirers may be wanting to read up about collecting as a hobby. Whatever the scenario, if you do get a lot of enquiries regarding antiques, it may be worth subscribing to a journal or magazine on the subject. They can keep you up to date with prices, auctions and fairs and will be more 'current' than many books.

Where to look

Printed sources

One of the best journals is *Antique Dealer and Collectors Guide*, Statuscourt Ltd (Bimonthly). This magazine is excellent for listing countrywide auctions and antique fairs. It also includes features on different types of antiques and is up to date with its prices.

There are so many books about antiques and collectibles that you could probably start your own collection! Books may date and prices may be years out of date, but descriptive information should still be good. Ensure that you have a current price guide though. These can be invaluable.

Miller, J. and Miller, M. (2000) *Millers antique price guide*, Octopus
This annual guide lists prices for thousands of different types of antiques.

Another similar title is:

Curtis, T. (ed.) (2000) *Lyle antiques price guide*, Lyle Publications

These are two of the most popular price guides. There are also guides to different categories of antiques and collectibles, e.g. toys, porcelain, watches. Check your shelves for availability.

If you are looking for antique shops, check the Yellow Pages or see if you have the following publication:

Adams, C. (2001) *Daily Telegraph guide to the antique shops of Britain 2001–2002*, Antique Collectors Club

Sotheby's and Christies auction catalogues can be useful guides to prices if you have any of them.

Electronic sources

An excellent gateway site to the subject is

LAPADA www.lapada.co.uk

This is the website of the Association of Art and Antiques Dealers, and gives useful advice and links.

Another good site is the BBC's Antiques Roadshow site:

www.bbc.co.uk/antiques

There are useful sections here on caring for antiques and tips on how to identify your item.

Tips and pitfalls

Never tell an enquirer whether an item is worth anything. Simply guide them in the direction of an antique specialist. Also, be careful not to endorse a particular antique specialist as this can also cause problems.

Local museums can also be useful contacts, especially as regards objects relevant to the locality.

ARCHAEOLOGY *see* HISTORY & ARCHAEOLOGY

ARCHITECTURE

See also Construction

Typical questions

- Have you got details of famous buildings?
- How can I find out if a particular building is listed?
- Where can I find a plan of my house?
- How do I get planning permission?
- What's a corbel? And dressed stone?

Considerations

Architecture and building design is a huge subject and users are best referred to specialist libraries, but many of the more common practical questions can be dealt with in smaller libraries.

 **ARCHITECTURE**

Where to look
General

There are numerous dictionaries of architectural features; most general encyclopedias will give information. Use their indexes. Three useful books are:

Maliszewski-Pickart, M. (1998) *Architecture and ornament: an illustrated dictionary*, McFarland

Curl, J. S. (1999) *A dictionary of architecture*, Oxford University Press

Speaight, A. and Stone, G. (2000) *Architect's legal handbook: the law for architects*, 7th edn, Architectural Press

Lists of buildings

The fullest list of descriptions of architectually important buildings is the Buildings of England series of books (Yale University Press) by Nikolaus Pevsner. The Victoria County History series is also important, especially for older buildings. Most libraries will have these, at least the volumes for their locality. There are several other popular sources, e.g.:

Orback, J. (1987) *Blue guide to Victorian architecture in Britain*, A & C Black

Tjack, G. and Brundle, S. (1994) *Country houses of England*, Blue Guides, A & C Black

Listed buildings

Lists of protected buildings in a particular area may be consulted in the local authority's planning departments. Library local studies departments may also have lists. The full English national list is kept (in some 300 folders) by English Heritage at the National Monuments Record, Kemble Drive, Swindon SN2 2GZ.

The standard text on the law of listed buildings is:

Suddards, R. W. and Hargreaves, J. H. (1996) *Listed buildings: the law and practice of historic buildings, ancient monuments and conservation areas*, Sweet & Maxwell

Planning

Armour, M. (1988) *Home plans*, 4th edn, PRISM Press
Standard plans and fittings for the home builder.

Moore, V. (2000) *A practical approach to planning law*, 7th edn, Blackstone Press

Willman, J. (1990) *The Which? guide to planning and conservation*, Consumers
   Association and Hodder & Stoughton

Plans of local houses rarely exist, but local large-scale maps will give outlines to
property for most areas. Try the local studies library or planning department. Old
Ordnance Survey maps can be of value for highlighting unusual features.

Electronic sources

For listed buildings see:

English Heritage **www.heritage.co.uk/apavilions/glstb.html**
   This gives frequently asked questions including the grading criteria, advice
   on listing, and grants and loans.

Royal Commission on Historic Monuments
   www.rchme-gov.uk/homepage.html

Images of England **www.imagesofengland.org.uk**
   Photographs every one of England's 370,000 listed buildings.

Other sources

The Listed Buildings Information Service (Tel: 020 7208 8221) will fax a copy of
the listing for one particular building.
   Advice on listing and related matters may be had from The Department of Culture, Media and Sport, 24 Cockspur St, London SW1Y 5DH.

English Heritage **www.english-heritage.org.uk**
   The UK government statutory adviser on England's built heritage.
   Concerned with every building, monument and site in England that is of
   architectural significance. Tel: 0870 333 1181

National Monuments Record **www.english-heritage.org.uk**
   Kemble Drive, Swindon SN2 2GZ
   Tel: 01793 414600
   The public archive of English Heritage. Holds more than 10 million
   photographs.

Royal Institute of British Architects (RIBA) **www.riba.org**
   66 Portland Place, London W1B 1AD
   Tel: 020 7580 5533

A ARCHIVES

Most tourist offices will have information and handouts on historically and architecturally important buildings.

Local history societies and local publications can also be helpful.

ARCHIVES

See also Family History & Genealogy

Typical questions
- Where are your archives? I want to trace my family tree
- Where can I find original records of a firm?

Considerations

'Archives' is a word that is often used loosely. It is popularly used to refer to old documents, particularly if handwritten (manu script), but it is also used of modern typed and printed records which are the result of the work of an organization, such as memos, reports, letters and minutes of meetings. ('Records management' is a phrase frequently used in this context.) A rule of thumb is that an archive is any document that has not been published, that is, not produced in quantities for public use. It is necessary to ask exactly what the enquirer has in mind. Many of the enquiries for archives in libraries may well be answered by using printed, microfilmed and electronic sources.

Warn readers that archives, being unique documents, are subject to strict rules of access and use. Archive departments and Record Offices often work on an appointment system, and material located through indexes and 'calendars' needs to be fetched from stores rather than being made openly available on public shelves. Some archives may be 'embargoed' or have other restrictions on their use. Users need to be precise in what they want and to give themselves plenty of time, both for the material to be fetched, and to consult it.

Where to look
Printed sources

Forster, J. and Sheppard, J. (eds) (1999) *British archives: a guide to archive resources in the United Kingdom*, Palgrave
Some 1500 locations described.

Aldridge, T. M. (1993) *Directory of registers and records*, 5th edn, Longman
Particularly strong on current social records.

Royal Commission on Historical Manuscripts (1999) *Record repositories in Great Britain*, 11th edn, Public Record Office

Electronic sources

Many record offices have their own websites, often with catalogues and indexes. These are usually linked to local authority websites.

Public Record Office **www.pro.gov.uk**
> The PRO website lists national archives and gives other useful information. It also has the text of numerous leaflet guides that can be printed out.

Historical Manuscripts Commission **www.hmc.gov.uk**

Other sources

Many firms and other organizations keep their own archives and records and may even have their own archivist. Apply direct to the organization to find out.

Churches and cathedrals are often in people's minds when they use the term archives, but it is usually best to refer the enquirer to the local archive or record office first.

Society of Archivists **www.archives.org.uk**
> 40 Northampton Rd, London EC1R 0HB
> Tel: 020 7278 8630 Fax: 020 7278 2107
> E-mail: societyofarchivists@archives.org.uk

NIDS (National Inventory of Documentary Sources in the United Kingdom and Ireland)
> This serial publication reproduces on microfiche guides to the archives and manuscript holdings of many document repositories. An index to the material reproduced is available on microfiche, CD-ROM and the world wide web, and there is an occasional newsletter. Contact: Proquest,The Quorum, Barnwell Rd, Cambridge CB5 8SW Tel: 01223 215512

Tips and pitfalls

Since archives may not have been published, it is necessary to warn the enquirer to check about copyright in case they want to make copies.

Do beware of the vague idea people have of what an 'archive' is and the loose way in which the word is used.

Beware, also, the school child who insists on consulting 'primary sources' as

the National Curriculum asks him or her to do! 'Primary sources' can be published sources such as newspapers.

ARMED FORCES

See also Battles & Battlefields; Medals & Decorations; Uniforms

Typical questions

- How many aeroplanes do the RAF have?
- I want a book about the history of the RAF.
- How many soldiers does Britain have?
- What are the names of Britain's aircraft carriers?

Where to look

Printed sources

Both *Whitaker's almanack* and the *Statesman's yearbook* have statistics for different countries' air forces, armies and navies, listing numbers of aircraft, naval vessels, armoured vehicles, personnel, etc. *Whitaker's* has a more detailed section on all three armed forces, including the number and type of aircraft and naval vessels owned, numbers of officers, names of ships, army divisions, etc. The *Statesman's yearbook* goes into more detail for countries other than the UK. The *NATO yearbook* is the best for NATO armies.

The following publications are both useful:

Brassey's defence yearbook, Centre for Defence Studies. Annual
International Institute for Strategic Studies, *Strategic survey annual*, Oxford University Press

Both of these list the major military- and security-related events of the year.

Air Force

For more detail on the RAF, its history and its squadrons try:

Jefford, Wing Commander C. G. (1988) *RAF squadrons*, Airlife

There is a more detailed description of all the world's air forces in the following:

Taylor, M. J. H. (1988) *Encyclopedia of the world's air forces*, Patrick Stephens Publications

This lists all the major air forces, showing all their aircraft, the air force symbol and its history.

Army

Chandler, D. (ed.) (1994) *Oxford illustrated history of the British army*, Oxford University Press
Covers British armed forces from 1485 to the present day. Excellently illustrated.

Makepeace-Warne, A. (1998) *Brassey's companion to the British army*, Brassey's
An essential reference book for anyone seeking information on any matter relating to the British army since 1660.

Navy

Thomas, D. A. (1988) *A companion to the Royal Navy*, Harrap
Covers the development of the Royal Navy for over three centuries to the present day.

Personnel

The Stationery Office brings out a list of all armed forces personnel every year. These can be useful for tracing records of former personnel.

The Army list
Ministry of Defence Officers' Publications, Officers' Record of Service, Army Personnel Centre, Room 3322, Kentigern House, 65 Brown Street, Glasgow G2 8EX

The Navy list
Ministry of Defence, 2SL/CNH, Centurion Building, Grange Road, Gosport, Hampshire PO13 9XA

The Air Force list
Ministry of Defence, PMA(CS)2a(RAF), RAF Personnel Management Agency, Room 9, Building 248a, Royal Air Force Innsworth, Gloucester GL3 1EZ

Websites

Army **www.army.mod.uk/**
Royal Navy **www.royal-navy.mod.uk/**

RAF **www.raf.mod.uk/rafhome.html**
NATO **www.nato.int**

ART

See also Museums & Galleries

Typical questions
* Who painted 'The Kiss'?
* I want some information about the artist Paul Delvaux.
* I have a painting by someone called Atkinson Grimshaw. Do you know how much it is worth?
* I want some information about the Pont Aven School.

Considerations
This is a huge and often troublesome area, but can frequently be broken down into more manageable concepts like sculpture, graphic art, design, etc. Enquirers often expect libraries to have information about every artist that ever lived, famous or otherwise. The range of art-related questions can be mind boggling. This section aims to help you find your way around this 'minefield'.

Where to look
Printed sources
Encyclopedias and dictionaries can be used to gather a brief history of artists and art movements.

For general art try:

Osborne, H. (1970) *Oxford companion to art*, Oxford University Press
Chilvers, I., Osborne, H. and Farr, D. (1988) *Oxford dictionary of art*, Oxford
    University Press
Murray, P. and Murray, L. (1997) *Penguin dictionary of art and artists*, Penguin

There are also texts and dictionaries for specific art movements. For example:

Richard, L. (1978) *Concise encyclopedia of expressionism*, Chartwell
Alexandrian, S. (1985) *Surrealist art*, Thames and Hudson

You may also have dictionaries for art materials and techniques, for example:

Mayer, R. (1969) *A dictionary of art terms and techniques*, 2nd edn, HarperCollins

Bibliographies and indexes can cover many different subjects and can be useful in finding books and articles on a subject. Check for bibliographies in individual works or biographical works. The *British humanities index* lists journal articles and newspaper indexes like *The Times* or Clover list articles in newspapers (*see* Articles in Journals).

You may have books on individual artists or on the artists of a specific period, country, style or movement. Check your library catalogue.

Finding a painting

If you are searching for information on a specific painting but the artist or title is unknown, there are several sources you could use. One of the best is:

Monro, I. S. and Monro, K. (1956) *Index to reproductions of European paintings*, H W Wilson

Valuations

Hislop, D. (ed.) *Art Sales Index*, Art Sales Index Ltd, annual, contains price and details of oil paintings, watercolours, drawings, miniatures, photographs, prints and sculptures sold at public auction throughout the year.

Locations of works

Wright, C. (1976) *Old master paintings in Britain*, Philip Wilson
Lists Continental old master paintings in British public collections.

Catalogues of paintings in British collections are also available, e.g. National Gallery, National Portrait Gallery, Tate.

Electronic sources

Jones, L. S. (1999) *Art information and the internet: how to find it, how to use it*, Fitzroy Dearborn
Try and get a copy of this if you have serious art researchers in your library. It will help guide them through the maze of art information on the web.

There are many useful resources available for free. Try the following:

www.artcyclopedia.com
www.artsguide.org
www.world-arts-resources.com

Many of the major galleries around the world have good websites. *See* Museums & Galleries for more information.

Tips and pitfalls

Don't panic if you get an enquiry you cannot deal with. You may be able to pass on the enquiry to your local art gallery or even to an expert association. Check the *Directory of British associations* to see if there are any relevant bodies. Examples include art societies, art libraries, art galleries and museums, even government bodies.

ARTICLES IN JOURNALS

Typical questions

- Have any articles been published on ...?
- Where can I get this journal article?

Considerations

Sometimes somebody may have details of a particular article from a magazine or journal they want to read. More usually they want information on something and suggest that there might be something in a journal. Often it is the librarian that suggests there may be an article on a subject, particularly when they have failed to find a book on a subject. It is often the case that an article in a journal, magazine or newspaper may exist when no book has been written on a topic. Millions of articles are written every year: one of the traditional skills of the librarian is to trace these.

This skill is more applicable to academic and research libraries and there will often come a point at which it will be sensible to refer the enquirer to such a library which may have large holdings of journals and indexing and abstracting sources.

An important preliminary point is to be aware that obtaining articles will often incur expense and will take time. There may be local policy guidelines on this matter. It is best to treat such enquiries in two stages: 1) to seek articles the library has in stock and that the enquirer can consult or photocopy immediately; 2) to broaden the search using indexes to journals the enquirer will have to consult elsewhere, or obtain through interlibrary lending. (*See* Journals and Periodicals.)

The availability of journals on the internet (usually via subscription) is changing the way in which librarians access material. Do check your local resources.

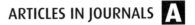

Printed sources

Some journals will have their own indexes. Examples are *New Scientist*, *New Statesman* and *Nation*. Newspapers such as *The Times* and the *Guardian* also have printed indexes (as well as indexes on the internet). Check that your library has these, and where. Are they with the journal or filed in a separate index sequence?

British humanities index, Bowker. Monthly and annual cumulations
> This easy-to-use A–Z index, available in most large libraries, indexes articles in 360 journals and periodicals. Articles are indexed by subject, source, authors and title. Includes economics and politics as well as the traditional humanities. About 15,000 articles a year. Useful general purpose source. CD-ROM and web versions are also available.

Applied social sciences index, Bowker. Monthly and annual cumulations
> Includes sociology and psychology. 600 journals indexed. CD-ROM and web versions are also available.

Clover index, Clover Publications. Fortnightly with annual volumes
> Covers over 100 popular journals and magazines. CD-ROM and web versions are also available.

For older journals see:

The Wellesley index to Victorian periodicals, 1824–1900 (1989), 5 vols, University of Toronto Press
> Volumes 1–4 give contents pages of 43 UK journals. Volume 5 is the index.

Poole, W. F. (1882–1908) *Index to periodical literature 1802–1906*, 6 vols, Osgood (Boston), Turner (London).

Electronic sources

Apart from the many subscription websites offering access to journal articles, some journals have their own websites, while some may be wholly electronic e-journals. Use a good search engine to find these. The downside to these is that they tend to lack back files.

Tips and pitfalls

If possible, get the enquirer to search the indexes for themselves. Not only can such searches become time consuming and open ended, but it is often best for the enquirer to decide for themselves whether or not items are worth pursuing.

Guidance may be needed to interpret the cryptic references and advice given on where to locate the journals.

Note the difference between indexes (which give only bibliographic details plus a subject entry), abstracts (which give, in addition, an indication of what an article is about) and full text. These differences are particularly important in electronic databases. Many users will only want full text.

ASSOCIATIONS & ORGANIZATIONS

Typical questions
- Is there an organization that deals with …?
- Is there a professional body responsible for …?

Considerations
It is important to ask the enquirer whether they believe the association/organization is local, national or international. Local associations/organizations are often the hardest to locate. Your library may keep a list of local societies and associations/organizations; if it does, it is essential to keep this up to date. It is worth also checking Telephone Directories for local contacts in professional or trade associations/organizations.

Where to look
Directories

Directory of British associations and associations in Ireland, CBD Research
> With a coverage of 6800 associations this publication provides information on national associations, societies and institutes that have a voluntary membership. It also includes regional and local organizations concerned with industries and trades. In addition, it has chambers of commerce and county agricultural, archaeological, historical, natural history and sports bodies. It is arranged alphabetically by group name. There is a subject index at the back, providing a list of relevant groups. There is also an abbreviations index. Also available on CD-ROM. Priced at £293 from CBD Research (tel: 020 8650 7745, fax: 020 8650 0768).

It is worth trying also:

Adams, R. (ed.) *Centres and bureaux: a directory of UK concentrations of effort, information and expertise*, CBD Research

The majority of centres listed in this directory are associated with universities and their constituent colleges. It is arranged alphabetically by centre name. There is both a subject index and abbreviations index.

Councils, committees and boards including government agencies and authorities, CBD Research

This directory provides information on the advisory bodies, executive bodies and tribunals (all known as non-departmental public bodies; includes authorities, commissions and royal commissions and councils). It is arranged alphabetically. There is both a subject index and abbreviations index.

Key organizations, Carel Press

This has an A–Z listing of 3000 organizations and groups throughout the UK. In addition, it has a thematic guide to organizations, which is useful for those looking for a particular subject. It is also available on CD-ROM and online; for details contact Carel Press (tel: 01228 538928 or **www.carelpress.com**).

The directory of UK associations, 2nd edn, Hollis Publishing

This covers 6000 organizations, including, among others, pressure groups, institutes, unions, medical support groups, trade bodies and societies. It has an A–Z list of organizations, keyword index, activity index, location index and a master index.

Whitaker's almanack, A & C Black

This covers details of some named associations/organizations. Try also the website **www.acblack.com**

International organizations

World directory of trade and business associations (2000), Euromonitor

This covers 5000 industry bodies and named contacts. It has extensive country and sector coverage.

Try also:

Encyclopedia of associations: international organizations (2002), 39th edn, Gale Group. Annual

Directory of European professional and learned societies (2001), CBD Research

The London diplomatic list, Foreign and Commonwealth Office. Bi-annual
This incorporates the *Directory of international organizations*.

Many trade directories will include details of trade and professional associations, including international ones.
For European groups try:

Directory of 9300 trade and professional associations in the European Union, Blue Book, The Stationery Office

Websites
Trade Association Forum **www.taforum.org.uk**

Tips and pitfalls
A lot of the larger associations/organizations now have websites (addresses can be found in the above directories) which may have information or links to related associations/organizations, including international groups. This can often help when looking for some of the smaller or more obscure groups.

ASTROLOGY *see* THE UNEXPLAINED

ASYLUM *see* NATIONALITY & IMMIGRATION

ATLASES & GAZETTEERS

See also Countries; Geography; Maps

Typical questions
- Where is Ansdell?
- There is a town called Coudes in France. Where is it exactly?
- What is the OS grid reference for Newquay?

Considerations
This subject area should not cause too many problems. Most enquirers will simply be asking where specific places are, or planning routes on an atlas. Every

reference library should have an atlas of the UK. Most will have one of Europe and the world too. All these atlases will have indexes.

Gazetteers provide more in-depth coverage. They are simply a list of place names and locations, some with grid references.

Where to look
Printed sources

There are many good atlases available. Your library should have some of them.

The Times produce a very good range of atlases, e.g.:

The Times comprehensive atlas of the world 2000 (1999) Times Books

For gazetteers, these are two 'essentials':

Ordnance Survey gazetteer of Great Britain (1999) Macmillan Reference
Every name from the 1:50,000 Landranger series is included here. Ordnance Survey sheet numbers are included, as well as grid references and longitude and latitude.

Cohen, S. B. (1998) *Columbia gazetteer of the world*, Columbia University Press
By far the best for world coverage.

Electronic sources

There are many maps and atlases available on the internet. These range from town plans to suggested route plans.

For UK maps, try the following:

www.multimap.com

For Europe:

www.mappy.com

and for route plans:

www.theaa.co.uk
www.rac.co.uk
www.mappy.com

For gazetteers, the *Getty thesaurus of geographic names* is worth a look:

http://shiva.pub.getty.edu/tgn_browser

Tips and pitfalls

Make sure you have a current atlas. The changes in the post-Soviet world have made immense differences to countries and you should have an atlas that covers these.

AUCTIONS

Typical questions

* Can you give me a list of local auctions?
* When is the next auction for catering equipment?

Considerations

It is not always easy to track down where and when an auction is going to be held. The Yellow Pages can provide lists of the local auction houses, which the enquirer can ring to find out their next sale date. Many of the large auction houses operate catalogue-only sales that require either a subscription or purchase of the catalogue before the sale takes place. Your local paper may have a day for advertising auctions, usually listed in the classified section; it is worth making a note of this. These will probably be mostly of a general nature such as household items, antiques and paintings; sometimes they may include industry equipment, car and property sales. Auctions can also be known as liquidation sales and disposal of stock. In addition to local newspapers, many of the national daily and Sunday newspapers advertise auctions. For details of auctions taking place abroad take a look at some of the established auction house websites, which are listed below.

Where to look
Printed sources

Daily Telegraph guide to the antique shops of Britain, Antiques Collectors' Club
   This has a very good chapter on auctioneers arranged by area.

Household items

National and local newspapers, trade and industry journals.

Industry equipment

National and local newspapers, trade and industry journals.

For cars
National and local newspapers.

For property
National and local newspapers, *Estates Gazette*.

Journals
Auction Insider
> Meteor Press,
> Tel: 020 7353 5998
> Ten issues per year
> Everything to do with auctions including auction listings.

Government Auction News
> Wentworth Publishing
> Tel: 020 8597 0181 Fax: 020 7353 6533
> **www.ganews.co.uk**
> Monthly
> Provides auction news and UK listings.

Electronic sources
Auction Net **www.auctions.co.uk**
> Internet resource for UK auctions. This covers art and antiques, cars and motor vehicles, catering equipment, computer, general and property. Both bankruptcy and insolvency auctions are listed. In addition, there are links to relevant publications.

Car Auctions UK **www.carauctionsuk.com**

Christies **www.christies.com**

Phillips **www.phillips-auctions.com**

Sothebys **www.sothebys.com**

UK Classic Car Online Auctions **www.classic-car auctions.co.uk**

Tips and pitfalls
Don't try to give advice on whether goods are acceptable for auction or a likely price they would fetch; neither can you advise on a buying price. It is best to refer

the enquirer to one of the many price guides available. See the relevant subject sections in this directory.

AUTHORS *see* BIOGRAPHIES; LITERATURE; PSEUDONYMS; WRITERS & WRITING

AWARDS & PRIZES

Typical questions
- Who won last year's Booker Prize?
- Have you a list of Nobel Prize winners?
- What is The Alan Ball Award given for?

Considerations
Awards and prizes are a feature of everyday life. Unfortunately they are not always easy to find out about. If you unfamiliar with the award, find out from the enquirer what the subject of the award is (literature? civic service?), the country it is awarded in, and the date for which the information is required. If they know any of these it will make finding easier. If a specific subject is known, it may be quicker to go to a subject source rather than a general one.

Where to look
Printed sources
For recent awards, newspapers and news services are a good source. Some books to consult are:

Cook, C. (ed.) (1994) *Pears book of winners and champions*, Pelham Books
Marshall, A. (1994) *The Guinness book of winners*, Guinness Publications
Siegman, G. (ed.) (1990) *World of winners: a current and historical perspective on awards and their winners*, Gale Research

Good general reference books will list the main prizes e.g. Oscars, Booker, Nobel, etc. Try:

Crystal, D. (ed.) (1998) *Cambridge factfinder*, Cambridge University Press

Whitaker's almanack lists current holders only but covers a wider range of awards, e.g. BAFTAs, Pulitzer Prize.

The *London Gazette* covers Honours Lists and military awards.

Electronic sources

Previous Oscar winners:

www.filmsite.org/oscars.html

For current Oscars, BAFTAs, Brits, Emmys, Golden Globes, etc.:

www.niata.net/awards/index.html

There is a useful site for literature awards, with links to sites giving previous winners:

www.literature-awards.com/

For Nobel prizes:

http://almaz.com/nobel/nobel.html

BANKS & BANKING

Typical questions
- I need to know the address for a bank in Italy.
- I have a complaint against my bank; who do I write to?
- Where's the nearest branch of the Halifax?

Considerations
The majority of enquiries about banks and building societies will relate to contact details both home and abroad. Most of these can be answered using the excellent *Bankers almanac* or the *Building societies yearbook*. The disgruntled bank user is best contacting the Banking Ombudsman. Finally, there are those who want to know more about either their bank or the banking industry in general. For these you can't beat the bank's own annual report. If your library doesn't keep annual reports you could look at Carol (Company Annual Reports OnLine). In addition you can use one of the banking websites now available (see below). These can also be useful for those going for job interviews or for students with projects covering the banking industry.

Where to look
Printed sources
Directories

Bankers almanac, 6 vols, Reed Business Information
>   Information on 4500 major international banks of the world and details of 23,000 other authorized banks.

Also available is the *Bankers almanac BANKbase CD-ROM* (£840 per year) or, via the internet, **www.bankersalmanac.com** which is a subscription service (£1650 per year) from Bankers Almanac (tel: 01342 335962).

Building societies yearbook, Building Societies Association, PBI Newmedia
>   Provides a complete alphabetical listing of building societies' details and balance sheets. This includes branch details.

Tracing dormant accounts

Both the British Bankers Association **www.bba.org.uk** and the Building Societies Association **www.bsa.org.uk** offer a free tracing service for people who have lost track of accounts. Claim forms are available from all banks and building societies or via the associations' websites.

Electronic sources
Market research

Bank for International Settlements **www.bis.org/cbanksl.htm**
   This gives a list of world central banks' websites. Excellent.

Bank of England **www.bankofengland.htm**
   Excellent site for banking statistics.

British Bankers Association **www.bankfacts.org.uk**

Banks and annual reports

Barclays Bank **www.barclays.co.uk**
Halifax **www.halifax.co.uk**
HSBC **www.hsbc.co.uk**
Lloyds TSB **www.lloydstsb.co.uk**
National Westminster Bank **www.natwest.co.uk**
Royal Bank of Scotland **www.royalbankofscotland.co.uk**
Carol (Company Annual Reports OnLine) **www.carolworld.com**
   Select Reports – Europe – then Banks – Retail

Associations

The Office of the Banking Ombudsman
   70 Gray's Inn Rd, London WC1X 8NB
   Tel: 020 7404 9944

The Office of the Building Societies Ombudsman
   Millbank Tower, Millbank, London SW1P 4XS
   Tel: 020 7931 0044

Tips and pitfalls

Avoid comment on the merits or problems of individual banks or building societies. Don't be drawn into calculations of overcharging, etc. Suggest the enquirer contacts the Banking or Building Society Ombudsman if the issue cannot be resolved with the bank itself.

BATTLES & BATTLEFIELDS

Typical questions
- I am doing a project on the Battle of Waterloo. Have you any information?
- How many lives were lost at the Battle of Marston Moor?
- Where is Stamford Bridge, the site of the famous battle?

Considerations
This subject is always very popular, especially the battlefield's area. Relations often want to know about where their loved ones fought or perished. Many even want to visit the battlegrounds.

Where to look
Printed sources
There may be detailed histories of certain battles available on your shelves, but for quick enquiries, encyclopedias and the following reference books should be sufficient:

Laffin, J. (1986) *Brassey's battles: 3500 years of conflict, campaigns and wars, from A–Z*, Pergamon

An encyclopedia of battles: accounts of over 1560 battles from 1479 BC to the present (1985) Dover Publications

Other useful sources of information include the Imperial War Museum and the Ministry of Defence.

Imperial War Museum
   Lambeth Rd, London SE1 6HZ
   www.iwm.org.uk

Ministry of Defence
   Tel: 0870 607 4455
   www.mod.uk

Battlefields
If you are trying to find battlefields in the UK, try the excellent:

Smurthwaite, D. (ed.) (1984) *Ordnance Survey complete guide to the battlefields of Britain*, Webb and Bower

There are useful guides to the more recent battlefields of World Wars 1 and 2 in Northern Europe:

Holmes, R. (1995) *Army battlefield guide: Belgium and Northern France*, HMSO

Electronic sources

The Commonwealth War Graves Commission publish lists of the burial places of the war dead of World Wars 1 and 2, as well as other items relating to battles and battlefields. You can get more information, as well as free access to their huge database of war dead at **www.cwgc.org**.

BEERS & BREWING

Typical questions
- Who brews a certain brand of lager?
- Can you give me a list of breweries?
- What is the most popular beer?
- I'm doing a project on the beer industry.

Considerations

Questions on this subject area fall into two categories: those that are asking about brands and company information, which require contact details, and those that are asking about the industry itself, which requires market research and statistical information. There are a number of directories produced that will give you company and product details (listed below) and there is a plethora of market research available. For those without access to market reports there are some great sources on the internet.

Where to look
Directories

Yeo, A. (ed.) *The brewery manual*, PJB Publications. Annual
> An invaluable directory which provides analysis of the UK drinks market. It gives contact details and the latest financial details for British brewing companies and pub chain operators.

The Grocer directory of manufacturers and suppliers (2001) William Reed
> Publishing. Annual

This provides information on 8000 companies, 700 products and over 16,000 brand names. It covers primary producers, agents and brokers, export and import, wholesalers and distributors.

The BFBI directory, Brewing, Food and Beverage Industry Suppliers Association
Provides details of products and services, UK brewers, smaller independent brewers and pub operating groups, and a directory of trade names.

CAMRA (Campaign for Real Ale) good beer guide (2002) Camra Books. Annual

Journals
Brewers' Guardian
PJB Publications
Tel: 020 8948 3262 Fax: 020 8332 8993
Monthly
An international journal covering technological developments and market trends.

Market intelligence
Mintel market reports, Mintel International Group
Provides in-depth research into the alcoholic drinks industry. Looks at market factors, market segmentation, the consumer and the future. Also available on CD-ROM. For details visit **www.mintel.co.uk** or tel: 020 7606 4533, fax: 020 7606 5932.

Key Note reports, Key Note
For free executive summaries of report titles listed under drinks and tobacco visit **www.keynote.co.uk**. For details of obtaining full reports, contact Key Note (tel: 020 8481 8750, fax: 020 8783 0049).

British Beer and Pub Association statistical handbook, Brewing Publications.
Annual
www.beerandpub.com
This provides a wealth of information on the industry and beer.

Websites
BDI Brewing and Distilling International (includes a trade directory)
www.bdinews.com

Beer Info Source **www.beerinfo.com**
　For beer rating list.

Brewing, Food and Beverage Industry Suppliers Association **www.bfbi.org.uk**

CAMRA (Campaign for Real Ale) **www.camra.org.uk**

BENEFITS

See also Social Welfare

Typical questions
- Have you details on the Jobseekers Allowance?
- I've just been made redundant; what benefits am I entitled to?
- What's the address of the local social services?

Considerations
General information
Enquiries about benefits can be difficult and distressing. Difficult, not because benefit regulations are complex and difficult to understand, although they are, but because you are dealing with a socially, politically and psychologically charged topic. Sometimes the enquirer will be calm and objective and used to using library materials; more usually the enquirer will be emotional and demanding, asking, insisting even, that you give them advice and tell them what to do. It requires considerable skill on the part of the librarian to remain calm and objective.

As with all such legal and financial enquiries, one must be careful not to give advice on interpreting regulations. To do so could invite all sort of complications, from being sued for losing someone benefits to inviting crowds of other benefit seekers seeking free advice!

The role of the librarian here is twofold. First, to provide text-based sources giving the statutory and legal regulations and related commentary. Secondly, to provide details of places the enquirer should go to to get advice and further information. A complication may be that the enquirer has tried the Benefits Office or Citizens' Advice Bureaux and *they* have been unhelpful (or so the enquirer says). One can only stick to one's job, which is providing information, not giving legal advice.

BENEFITS

Where to look
Printed sources
Standard sources are:

Welfare Benefits Handbook. Annual. CPAG (Child Poverty Action Group)
This provides comprehensive coverage of all social security benefits.

Zebedee, J. and Ward, M. (2001) *Guide to housing benefit and council tax benefit 2001–2002*, Shelter
An authoritative overview of the rules in Great Britain.

Findlay et al. (2001) *CPAG's housing benefit and council tax benefit legislation, 2001–2002*, CPAG

CANS digest of social legislation, CANS Trust
Available in a three-volume loose-leaf publication or as a CD-ROM. Provides legal information on all the social legislation of Great Britain written in plain English. Includes nationality, consumer protection, employment, housing, discrimination and social security.

Social services year book
Also available on CD-ROM. Over 50,000 contact details for all social services related organizations in the UK. Includes voluntary, charitable and private organizations.

Essential information
Child support handbook, CPAG. Annual
Council tax handbook, CPAG, 4th edn, 2000
Debt advice handbook, CPAG, 4th edn, 2000
Disability rights handbook, CPAG, 26th edn, 2001–2
Fuel rights handbook, CPAG, 12th edn, 2001
Guide to training and benefits for young people, CPAG, 6th edn, 2001
Housing rights guide, Shelter, 2001. Annual
New deal handbook, CPAG, 4th edn, 2001-2
Paying for care handbook, CPAG, 2nd edn, 2001
Welfare rights bulletin, CPAG
Issued six times a year.

There are numerous leaflets available giving information about a whole range of benefits obtainable from local agencies. Libraries generally make these freely available. Often these will provide the information required.

Electronic sources

A vast amount of information is freely available on the internet. Try the government website for a list of all the departments.

> **www.open.gov.uk**

Other sources

Referral is generally the best option here. The local DWP Benefit Office and Citizens' Advice Bureaux are obvious places. See Yellow Pages, etc. for Legal Aid.

CANS Trust
> 89 Albert Embankment, London SE1 7TP
> Tel: 020 7820 3456 Fax: 020 7820 7890
> E-mail: canstrust@aol. com
> **www.cans.org.uk**

Shelter (the national campaign for homeless people)
> 88 Old Street, London EC1V 9HU
> Tel: 020 7505 2000 Fax: 020 7505 2169
> **www.shelter.org.uk**

Child Poverty Action Group
> 94 White Lion Street, London N1 9PF
> Tel: 020 7837 7979 Fax: 020 7837 6414
> E-mail: staff@cpag.demon.co.uk
> **www.cpag.org.uk**
> A campaigning group with an active publishing programme

Tips and pitfalls

Never underestimate the amount of knowledge about state benefits that seemingly unsophisticated enquirers may have. They have probably spent a lot more of their life reading the leaflets, talking to experts, and sharing experiences with other seekers than you have! And they are more motivated.

Be aware, in the most tactful way possible of course, of whom among your work colleagues has experience of which benefits. Answering enquiries is all about shared experience and teamwork. Many of your regular users might volunteer their expertise! If they should not be giving advice, they may understand the question.

While some enquirers will be demanding and intrusive, others may be shy and embarrassed. Make sure there is plenty of relevant material on open access and notices giving the addresses of local offices.

Many libraries have formal links to appropriate advisory bodies – these are worth cultivating. A list of emergency contacts to the DWP local offices, shelters and social services is worth having and keeping up to date. Currency of publications is essential.

BIBLOGRAPHIES, REFERENCES & CITATION

See also Theses & Dissertations; Writers & Writing

Typical questions

- My tutor has asked me to prepare a bibliography. How do I do that?
- I've been given this reference, but I don't understand it.
- How should this report be cited?
- What is the Harvard system?

Considerations

As librarians, we are used to how books are described in catalogues and we groan when someone hands us incomplete or garbled details about a book they want. Accuracy about book details is something we soon learn, but people who are not bookish do not always realize the need for such precise details. And which details?

A bibliography is simply a list of books; references and citations mean the same thing and refer to how details of a book or other source of information are described. Sometimes, especially in technical and specialist subjects, it is difficult to understand citations. Law is one such common area of confusion.

Most books on how to write dissertations and reports (*see* Writers and Writing) have a section on preparing a bibliography. Since there are so many styles of bibliography, it is important to seek the views of the tutor or publishers. Many publishers have their own style manuals.

In the Numeric or Vancouver style of citing, sources quoted or referred to in the text are indicated by a running number. Full details are given in numerical order in the bibliography at the end of the article or chapter.

The Harvard or Short Author style of citing indicates the source referred to in the text by using the author's surname followed by the date of publication. Full details are given in the bibliography in alphabetical order of surname.

Where to look

Two style guides in popular use are:

Modern Humanities Research Association (1996) *MHRA style book: notes for authors, editors and writers of theses*, 5th edn, Maney Publishing

Butcher, J. (1992) *The Cambridge handbook for editors, authors and publishers*, 3rd edn, Cambridge University Press
A popular and detailed handbook.

BS 5605: 1990 (1997) Recommendations for citing and referencing published material

Tips and pitfalls

It may seem obvious, and librarians are sometimes ashamed to be seen doing so, but do check the prefatory matter of a book or index for information on how the author has set out his or her listings. Often abbreviations have been used that are not obvious.

Sometimes numbers refer to columns not pages, for example in *Halsbury's laws of England*; sometimes letters are used to indicate columns, and sometimes parts of a page, for example in the *Index to the Times*.

BIOGRAPHIES

Typical questions

- Can you tell me something about Lord Healey of Riddlesden?
- I'm trying to find out about the life of Elvis Presley.

Considerations

This section concentrates mainly on general British biographies and lists some of the more valuable resources. Biographies of specific individuals will appear under the relevant subject heading, e.g. SPORTS, ART.

Where to look

Printed sources

First stop if you are looking for a brief biography should be a general biographical dictionary or even an encyclopedia:

B BIOGRAPHIES

Crystal, D. (ed.) (1994) *Cambridge biographical encyclopedia*, Cambridge
University Press
This gives basic information for over 16,000 people, describing their life
and achievements. Obviously, this is not suitable for detailed research, but
it can be an ideal starting point. For more detailed information, the
Dictionary of national biography is a must.

Dictionary of national biography (1938–81), 22 vols, Oxford University Press
This covers British notables who lived prior to 1950. There is also a concise
biographical dictionary which covers notables who died before 1970.

Who's who (1849–), A & C Black. Annual
This covers prominent living people, principally British.

Debrett's people of today, Debrett's. Annual
Some 32,000 leading figures in British society.

Who was who (1897–2000), A & C Black, 10 vols plus index
This is a companion to *Who's who* and contains biographies of those who
have died during this period. It is published every ten years. Also available
on CD-ROM.

Current biography (1940–), H W Wilson
This has articles about living leaders in all fields of human accomplishment
the world over.

Dictionary of international biography, Melrose Press. Bi-annual
Over 5000 men and women in all professions and fields of interest
worldwide. Back-files now cover 200,000 people.

There are also numerous specialist biographical dictionaries, e.g.:

Who's who in international affairs (1997), Europa Publications
Crockfords clerical directory 2002/2003 (2001), 97th edn, Church House
Publishing
Marshall, C. (2002) *Cricketer's who's who*, Queen Anne Press

Books covering the history of a subject, or giving an introduction to a subject, may
also contain information about people associated with that subject.

Obituaries are also useful. If you have newspaper indexes (e.g. *The Times, Telegraph*), check them to see if you can find the date of an obituary for the person
you are interested in.

Electronic sources

The excellent biography.com is worth a look:

www.biography.com

Or type in the name of the individual into a search engine.

Tips and pitfalls

Some local studies or local history libraries keep cuttings from local newspapers and publications about local worthies. These can be incredibly useful if the subject is local.

BIRDS

Typical questions

- What is the average wingspan of a golden eagle?
- Have you got any books for identifying birds?

Considerations

The most common questions about birds concern the identification of certain types. Make sure your library has some type of guide for identifying birds.

Where to look

Printed sources

One of the most complete and definitive resources is:

Cramp, S. et al. (eds) (1977–) *Handbook of the birds of Europe, the Middle East and North Africa*, Oxford University Press
This seven-volume set describes all the species of birds in this area and shows habitats, populations, movement, voices, plumage, etc.

Beaman, M. and Madge, S. (1998) *The handbook of bird identification for Europe and the Western Palearctic*, Christopher Helm

A much more concise, though still useful guide is:

Peterson, R. et al. (1983) *A field guide to the birds of Britain and Europe*, Collins

For birds worldwide, a good reference is:

Sibley, C. G. and Monroe Jr, B. L. (1990) *Distribution and taxonomy of birds of the world*, Yale University Press

Electronic sources

Sometimes the best way to find information about a specific bird is to simply use the internet. Type the bird's name into a good search engine. There is also a very good section of websites on birds in the Internet Public Library:

www.ipl.org/ref

Also try the RSPB website:

www.rspb.co.uk

Tips and pitfalls

Ornithology is a complex subject, but you should get by in most cases with a good book for identifying birds. For more information about specific types of bird, the internet can be a good option.

BOOKKEEPING *see* ACCOUNTS, AUDITING & BOOKKEEPING

BOOKS

See also Journals & Periodicals; Libraries; Newspapers; Writers & Writing

Typical questions
- Has a book been published on …?
- Where can I get this title?
- I have an old book. Is is valuable?
- Can you give me advice on looking after old books?

Considerations

Tens of thousands of books are published every year. Millions of different books exist. And the public expect librarians to know them all!

Although some library users are book experts, the majority are not, so library staff will generally have the advantage. One problem is that the field is so vast and complex, yet the public will not appreciate this. So, as always, progress carefully, step by step, taking nothing for granted. Another problem encountered is that many people have a touching faith in the value of books, both monetary and intrinsic, and often we have to deflate high expectations, particularly the monetary!

Where to look

Books in general

Bookseller, Whitaker. Weekly
> A good source of information about new and forthcoming publications. Indexed.

Publisher's Weekly, Publisher's Weekly
> A similar magazine for the USA.

Peters, J. (ed.) (1983) The *bookman's glossary*, 6th edn, Bowker

Books in print

For books in print, that is, available in standard bookshops and by mail order see: *Books in print* (for US books), *Whitaker's British books in print*, *International books in print* and other national trade bibliographies. Many of these services are available in fiche, CD-ROM and online format on subscription.

British National Bibliography, British Library. Weekly with cumulations
> This national bibliography records all books and new serials deposited at the Legal Deposit Office of the British Library. Also published monthly on CD-ROM. This is usually available in larger public libraries.

Electronic sources

Bowker/Whitaker Global Books in Print Plus on CD-ROM (Subscription)
> The largest database.

BookFind-Online **www.bookfind-online.com**
> A subscription web-based UK or global bibliographic service.

Most bookshop chains have their stock holdings online, and often on their (free) websites. Examples are:

WH Smith's International Bookshop **www.bookshop.co.uk**
Waterstones **www.waterstones.co.uk**

Blackwells **www.blackwell.co.uk**

Most popular is Amazon Books **www.amazon.co.uk**, which has the largest listing. A multimedia source is:

BOL (Books OnLine) **www.bol.co.uk**
    An international media and entertainment store on the internet offering books, music, DVD and video.

These are free services and are a good first place to look, but the detail may need to be supplemented by other sources.

Similarly, most publishers have details of their books on their websites. Often these will give more information about the books than is available in bibliographies. Examples are:

www.galegroup.com
www.macmillan.com
www.butterworths.co.uk

Book reviews

Some of the bookshop sites contain book reviews. Others are:

Times Literary Supplement **www.the-tls.co.uk**
Independent **www.independent.co.uk/books**
Daily Telegraph **www.booksonline.co.uk**
Yahoo! **www.yahoo.co.uk/Arts/Humanities/Literature/Reviews**
Amazon Bookshop **www.amazon.co.uk**
BOL Internet Bookshop **www.uk.bol.com**

Government publications

UKOP (United Kingdom Official Publications), The Stationery Office and Proquest
    A good source for British government publications, both in and out of print. It is held by larger public libraries and most academic libraries. There are fiche, CD-ROM and internet versions.

Microfilms

Guide to microfilms in print, K G Saur. Annual

Reprints

Guide to reprints, K. G. Saur. Annual

Old books

National catalogues such as the *National Union catalogue* and the *British Library catalogue* have comprehensive listings of books. *See* Libraries.

New Cambridge bibliography of English Literature, 5 vols, Cambridge University Press
In process of being revised. Good for books on authors and types of literature.

For book values, see, for example:

Connolly, J. (1993) *Modern first editions: their value to collectors*, 4th edn, Little, Brown and Co.
An A–Z author guide.

Book auction records (1924–), Dawson. Annual
This is useful for the more valuable books and will give an idea of top prices.

Annual register of book values, The Clique. Annual
This selects details from booksellers' catalogues.

For rare books in libraries see:

Bloomfield, B. C. (ed.) (1997) *A directory of rare book and special collections in the United Kingdom and the Republic of Ireland*, 2nd edn, Library Association Publishing

Most dealers produce their own printed catalogues, with the larger dealers and booksellers having their own websites.

Antiquarian Book Review. Monthly
Gives news of book auctions and feature articles, and a useful web directory.

Book and Magazine Collector. Monthly
Gives useful price lists.

Electronic sources

The internet has seen a revolution in the marketing of antiquarian books, thus:

UK Book World **www.ukbookworld.com**
This lists half a million books, old, rare and out of print from 400 British

BOOKS

bookshops and booksellers.

Alibris **www.alibris.com**
> This provides free searching for the old and out-of-print books from over 1550 secondhand and antiquarian booksellers.

The Register of British Internet Bookdealers **www.clique.co.uk/bibfind.htm**
> Gives the contact details of some 2100 British internet bookdealers handling old and out-of-print books, with links to individual bookdealer websites and their holdings.

Bibliofind **www.bibliofind.com**
> Lists some 20 million used and rare books, periodicals and ephemera offered for sale by booksellers around the world.

Directory of UK Bookfairs **www.inprint.co.uk/fairs**

Directory of Secondhand Bookshops **www.clique.co.uk/bookshops.htm**
> Lists some 275 UK bookshops selling old, rare and secondhand books.

The *Antiquarian Book Monthly* has a regular selection of bookdealers' websites, multi-dealer databases and auction house websites.

Description

Note also books on the precise description of books, e.g.:

Bowers, F. (1994) *Principles of bibliographical description*, Oak Knoll

Care of books

Barnes-Cope, A. D. (1989) *Caring for books and documents*, 2nd edn, British Library
> A brief layman's guide.

Shep, R. L. (1991) *Cleaning, repairing and caring for books*, 4th edn, Richard Joseph

Other sources

Seek assistance from your library's bibliographic, cataloguing and ordering departments. Many of the sources that will be useful for answering book enquiries are also those which are the tools of the job and may be sitting on their desks!

Many library colleagues will be knowledgeable about books. Seek their help.

Do refer people to the specialist bookshops and dealers – they are the experts – but be careful when recommending particular ones as this may be seen as promotion.

Tips and pitfalls

It may seem obvious, and librarians are sometimes ashamed to be seen dong so, but do check the prefatory matter of a book or index for how the author has set out his or her listings. Often abbreviations have been used that are not obvious.

Sometimes numbers refer to columns not pages (e.g. *Halsbury's laws of England*); sometimes letters are used to indicate columns, sometimes quarters of a page (e.g. *Index to The Times*).

The book market is quite volatile and printed sources, in particular, may be out of date. With older material, most (non-bookish) enquirers will have an inflated idea of the value of their books. Most books that are brought into libraries have little or no value. Be prepared to let the enquirer down gently. You will be doing them, and your colleagues, a favour.

The condition of a book influences its value. Prices quoted in the price guides tend to be for books with dust wrappers and in good condition.

Never give a judgement on a book's monetary value. This is a job for experts, and even they will be cautious. Get it wrong and you could be sued! Just give advice on general points such as condition, whether it could be a first edition (surprisingly few people look at the back of a title page or can understand Roman numerals) and give the location of the nearest specialists.

Whitaker's almanack has a good section on Roman numerals.

BREWING *see* BEERS & BREWING

BRITISH STANDARDS

Typical questions

- Which British Standard do I need to look at for …?

Considerations

You may not be lucky enough to have the full collection of British Standards at your disposal but the *British Standards catalogue* and British Standards Institution website will allow you to look up by subject and by BS number any British Standard. For those trying to set up in business use *Business opportunities profile*, Cobweb Information Ltd, to find out the British Standards that need to be consulted:

www.cobwebinfo.com

Where to look

Directories

British Standards catalogue (2001), BSI

Websites

British Standards Institution **www.bsi-global.com**
> This has an excellent site with an explanation as to what a standard is. It includes a whole section devoted to education. In addition, it includes a search facility to find out a BS number using a keyword or vice versa. It includes both European and international standards. For the full British Standard document it is necessary to subscribe to British Standards Online **www.bsonline.techindex.co.uk** or in hard copy.

BROADCASTING *see* ACTORS & ACTRESSES

BUILDING *see* CONSTRUCTION

BUILDING SOCIETIES *see* BANKS & BANKING

BUILDINGS *see* ARCHITECTURE; HISTORIC HOUSES & CASTLES

BUSINESS – SETTING UP

Typical questions
- I want to start a business and need help preparing my business plan.
- Are there any organizations who can help me start a business?

• Who can help me finance my new business?

Considerations

There is so much to consider when starting a new business, from the initial idea to putting together a business plan. Normally, the idea bit is easy; the hard part is demonstrating on paper how the business could work. It is easier to break the business plan down into small parts. The main part, which you, as an information worker, will find yourself involved in, is probably providing statistics and market research that will back up the idea. There are numerous sources of information that can be used, many of which are listed below. It is also an area in which a little bit of lateral thinking goes a long way.

Where to look
Directories

Small business briefings, Gee Publishing. Annual loose-leaf manual

These provide an overview and definition of seven different sectors within 40 briefings. Market trends are looked at to highlight the future of the sector. The structure of the market is defined with statistics provided to indicate its value and size. Sources of further information, relevant associations, some legal considerations and a list of publications, which may be of further use, are also provided. Updated throughout the year.

Business opportunity profiles, Cobweb Information
www.cobwebinfo.com
Tel: 0191 261 2853 Fax: 0191 261 1910
This provides an introduction to the market, its potential customers and possible competitors. It indicates start-up costs and legal considerations. Also includes further reading and useful addresses of relevant associations and organizations. Updated throughout the year.

Market research

A full guide to market research resources can be found under Market Research. *See also* Statistics.

Refining the business idea and developing the unique selling point (USP)

Use trade directories to find suppliers, competitors or business-to-business customers within the industry on both a regional and national basis. *See* Companies for general directories.

Trade journals can provide overviews of the industry, providing statistics on the latest trends and developments. They can highlight the need for a service or help to refine the unique selling point. Although most will be national in coverage, many of these journals are important sources of industry/service information and will be widely read.

Most industries and services will have associations and professional bodies. *See* Associations and Organizations for relevant directories. Some offer information on the market and include relevant statistics, trends and developments. Increasingly you will find this information available on the internet.

Local market research information

Whereas the above provide excellent coverage of the national market, in reality it will be research using local information that will be the best support to any business idea and/or indicate whether or not it is viable.

Local sources

Local newspapers provide a wealth of information for market research. One of the best places to find out about local competitors is in the advertisements section. As well as the names of local businesses, information relating to services and products offered may be available, including in some cases prices. This type of information will enable identification of major competitors. As well as competitors, local newspapers can be used to locate suppliers and potential business-to-business customers.

Local directories provide local company information. See Companies.

Statistics and Census data

Not only are statistics useful to show trends and developments in the market sector but they also provide a valuable source of local information with regard to the local population, age groups and ethnic mix. This type of information is useful for planning the location of a business and to build up a profile of potential customers. The best source of local statistical data is the Census. Most libraries will keep Census data for the local area even if they do not subscribe to the full hard copy set. However, if you do require local data for outside your area, use the Neighbourhood Statistics site from National Statistics **www.statistics.gov.uk/neighbourhood**

Books

There are simply hundreds of books published that deal with setting up in business. Here are a few recommended titles:

Barrow, C. (1995) *The complete small business guide: sources of information for new and small businesses*, 4th edn, BBC Books
Despite being due for revision, this is still a useful reference for anyone thinking of starting a business. It is packed with useful advice and considerations, and details of contacts and where to get help.

Williams, S. (2001) *Lloyds TSB small business guide*, 15th edn, Continuum Publishing Group

Organizations and websites

Barclays Small Business Site **www.smallbusiness.barclays.co.uk**

Business Link **www.businessadviceonline.org/businesslink**

British Chambers of Commerce **www.britishchambers.org.uk**
Excellent for business advice, guides, exporting and much more. It has a section to find your nearest chamber. Well worth a visit.

British Franchise Association **www.british-franchise.org.uk**

Department of Trade and Industry **www.dti.gov.uk**

Enterprise Zone **www.enterprisezone.org.uk**
A gateway to business information that includes business start-up.

Information Society Initiative **www.isi.gov.uk/isi/**
Good for information on grant schemes. It is sponsored by the DTI.

Inland Revenue **www.inlandrevenue.gov.uk**
This has a section for starting up in business covering the main tax and NI issues you need to understand when you are running a business.

National Westminster Bank **www.natwest.co.uk**
This has a good small business and starting in business site.

Prince's Trust **www.princes-trust.org.uk**

Shell LiveWIRE **www.shell-livewire.org**
Freepost NT 805, Newcastle upon Tyne NE1 1BR

Tel: 0845 757 3252
Provides lots of free publications on setting up in business.

Small Business Gateway **www.sbgateway.com**
Small Business Portal **www.smallbusinessportal.co.uk**
Excellent for a wide range of resources.

Tips and pitfalls

Use a variety of sources. If you can, instill in the enquirer that time taken to do desk research is well worth it, for producing a good business plan. If you can take the time yourself to know exactly what needs to go into a business plan and other considerations for starting a business, then you will be in a better position to advise and assist.

CALENDARS *see* DATES, EVENTS, CHRONOLOGIES & CALENDARS

CALLIGRAPHY *see* ALPHABETS & SCRIPTS

CAREERS

See also Employment; Jobs

Typical questions
- What qualifications do you need to be a policeman?
- I am interested in joining the army. What careers do they offer?

Considerations
Many libraries have small careers sections, but more comprehensive information can be found at the local careers office. The specially trained staff there can offer you better advice too.

Where to look
Printed sources
One of the best references available, if your library has it, is:

Davies, K. (2000) *Occupations*, Careers and Occupational Information Centre
> This book has entries for most careers and offers guidance on what qualifications you may need to enter the profession, the work involved, pay and conditions, training courses and addresses for further information.

Electronic sources
The world wide web can be useful for finding out information on professional organizations, e.g. Royal College of Nursing, Institute of Electrical Engineers, etc.

There are some useful careers websites available now. There is a useful gateway to all these sites at:

www.aiuto.net/uk.htm

Tips and pitfalls

Never offer any careers advice to enquirers. Suggest that they visit their local careers office for more information and specialist advice.

CARS & THE MOTOR INDUSTRY

See also Repair Manuals

Typical questions

- I want to know how much my old car is worth.
- Can you give me the address of ... car manufacturer?
- How many cars are produced in the UK per year?
- I'm doing an assignment on the car industry.
- How many people own a car in the UK?

Considerations

Queries about used car prices can be quickly answered using *Parkers*, now only available freely on the internet (**www.parkers.co.uk**). For queries relating to car manufacturers either use *Kompass* or *Key British enterprises* (*see* Companies) or one of the more specialized directories listed below. Local car dealers can be tracked down using Yellow Pages or **www.yell.com**. If it's the motor industry you are searching for, it is best to home in on exactly what the enquirer wants: it is a huge industry. Listed below are some useful sites for statistics and market research.

Where to look

Directories

The UK motor industry directory, Society of Motor Manufacturers and Traders
This directory is invaluable for answering queries related to car parts/accessories manufacturers. It includes details of 4000 companies supplying products and services to the motor industry. It provides an A–Z listing of companies with contact details. In addition it has a supplier list arranged by category such as passenger vehicles, motor goods vehicles, special purpose vehicles and trailers. Also available is the *The UK motor industry directory CD-ROM* from SMMT (tel: 020 7344 1612/1661).

European vehicle manufacturers, IMS Ltd
This provides detailed company profiles of the major European vehicle

manufacturers arranged alphabetically. The data includes vehicle sales and market share.

Motor Trader buyers' guide, Reed Business Information
An excellent directory providing four sections of information: wholesalers and distributors by county, wholesalers and distributors A–Z, buyers' guide (divided into 400 categories of products and services) and a company A–Z listing.

Worldwide automotive supplier directory, Automotive Engineering International
This covers the Americas, Europe and the Pacific. It has both a supplier index and a product index.

Beaulieu encyclopaedia of automobile coachbuilding, The Stationery Office
An excellent reference work on the automobile.

Beaulieu encyclopaedia of the automobile, The Stationery Office
A comprehensive book covering the history and social significance of private motoring. Gives details on every make and type of car ever built.

For motorcycles try:

Motorcycle trader directory 2000, Seven Kings Publications
This provides an alphabetical listing of all organizations supplying goods and services to the trade. These are cross-referenced with detailed product locators. There is also an alphabetical listing of nearly 1000 brand names of clothing, accessories and spare parts.

Journals

Motor Trader
Reed Business Information
Tel: 01342 326972 Fax: 01342 335612
www.motortrader.com
47 issues per year
Covers news and information on the latest developments within the automotive industry.

Market intelligence

Key Note reports, Key Note
For free executive summaries of report titles listed under transport and

motor goods visit **www.keynote.co.uk**. For details of obtaining full reports contact Key Note (tel: 020 8481 8750, fax: 020 8783 0049).

Mintel reports, Mintel International Group
For details visit **www.mintel.co.uk**

Refer also to sources and websites mentioned in Market Research.

Statistics

World automotive statistics, Society of Motor Manufacturers and Traders (SMMT)
This looks at car and commercial vehicle production in the UK and overseas. Also provides a survey of motor-producing countries.

Mitchell, K. and Lawson, S. (1998) *The great British motorist*, AA

Websites for used car prices

Parkers OnLine **www.parkers.co.uk**
This replaces the monthly publication from Emap. The website is updated daily. It offers advice on buying a car and includes prices, reviews and road test reports.

Glass's Information Service **www.glass.co.uk**
Includes a range of Glass's Guides. One of the most popular is *Glass's guide to part-exchange values and purchase prices*.

Automobile Association (car data check) **www.theaa.com**

Autohit **www.autohit.co.uk**

Autotrader **www.autotrader.co.uk**

Direct Line (car-buying site) **www.jamjar.com**

Websites for market research

Association of Car Fleet Operators (ACFO) **www.bizjet.com/fleet**
Society of Motor Manufacturers and Traders **www.smmt.co.uk**

Websites for technical information

Society of Automotive Engineering **www.sae.org**
An international one-stop resource for technical information used in designing, building, maintaining and operating self-propelled vehicles for

use on land or sea, in air or space. It offers access to SAE standards to purchase. Details and content of standards offered free. Also available is *Ground vehicles standards on CD-ROM*. Price on application to SAE (sales rep **e-mail: elecpubs@sae.org**).

Road Tax Calculator **www.theaa.com/allaboutcars/index.html**

Tips and pitfalls

Don't be drawn into commenting on the value of someone's old car; once you have referred them to sources let the user make their own decision about how accurate it is.

CASTLES *see* HISTORIC HOUSES & CASTLES

CATALOGUES *see* BOOKS; LIBRARIES

CATERING

See also Cookery

Typical questions

- Are there any recommended restaurants in …?
- How much does the average person spend on eating out?
- Where can I buy specialist catering equipment?
- Do you know the address of any catering schools?

Considerations

The catering industry looks after the business of preparation and cooking of food for others through restaurants, sandwich bars, cafés, work canteens, hospitals and schools. The type of enquiries can range from restaurant recommendations and how much we spend on eating out to how to start a business in catering. For local restaurants and cookery schools you can use the Yellow Pages or **www.yell.com**. Your library or local tourist office may also produce local eating-out guides.

 **CATERING**

Where to look

Directories

Caterer and hotelkeeper directory, Reed Business Information

Ainsworth, J. (2001) *The Which? good food guide*, Which? Books
  Lists 1200 establishments from top hotels to cafés and pubs.

AA restaurants guide (2001), Automobile Association
  Lists 1800 restaurants in the UK with an AA rosette.

Journals

Caterer and Hotelkeeper
  Reed Business Information
  Tel: 01342 326972 Fax: 01342 335612
  www.caterer.com
  Weekly
  Covers all aspects of the hospitality industry.

Statistics

National food survey 1999, The Stationery Office
  This has a section devoted to eating out: expenditure, consumption and
  nutrient intakes.

Consumer Trends, The Stationery Office. Quarterly

Websites

British Hospitality Association (BHA) **www.bha-online.org.uk**
  This provides a list of titles of surveys, statistics and journals that are useful
  to the hotel and catering industry. For those setting up a business it produces
  guidance notes which the association will e-mail free of charge or post for
  £20. This site is packed with information and links. It is well worth a visit.

Restaurant Association **www.ragb.co.uk**

CENSUS DATA *see* FAMILY HISTORY &
GENEALOGY; LOCAL HISTORY; POPULATION

CHARITABLE ORGANIZATIONS

Typical questions
- Can you give me a list of childrens' charities?
- Can you tell me which charities offer grants for ...?
- How does my group/organization gain charitable status?
- I would like to know more about the financial status of ... charity.

Considerations
Many people associate charities with names they have seen on high street charity shops or collection days; however, there are thousands of charitable organizations and they come in many shapes and sizes. When people are referring to charities they can also mean voluntary groups, trusts and foundations. The directories listed below will define each of these. However, before embarking on an enquiry try to clarify what the 'charity' does and where. National and international organizations are, of course, easier to find than local ones and many produce annual reports. These are excellent for financial information. The internet can also be a great help, especially as more and more local charities have web pages.

With regard to the term 'charitable status' the *Charities digest* has a section on setting up a charity which should answer this query or you can refer to:

Phillips A. (1994) *Charitable status: a practical handbook*, Directory of Social Change

or

Cairns E. (1996) *Charities: law and practice*, 3rd edn, Sweet & Maxwell

However, do bear in mind that these are probably due for revision.

Where to look
Directories
Charities digest: selected charities and voluntary organizations, Waterlow Professional Publishing
Provides an alphabetical list of national charities and key local organizations. Information given includes name, date of foundation, charity registration number, contact details and the type of activities of the organization. There is a subject index. In addition, it is excellent for

providing a list of Citizens' Advice Bureaux and Volunteer Bureaux.

Bevan, O., Davis, J. and Moncrieff, D. (eds) *Directory of grant making trusts*, 3 vols, Charities Aid Foundation

An invaluable reference source for details of charitable grant makers in the UK. Volume 1 contains three indexes, covering trusts by geographical areas, field of interest and grant type. Volume 2 is an alphabetical listing of trusts with an income of £13,000-plus which make grants to charities and voluntary organizations. Volume 3 contains details of the major grant-making trusts.

Dresdner RCM top 3000 charities, CaritasData Ltd

This publication is not only excellent for listing details of charities but is very useful for charity trends and data. In addition there are some excellent articles included under the section Charity Focus. Also available is the *Top 10,000 Charities CD-ROM*. Priced £1350 from CaritasData Ltd (tel: 020 7250 1777, fax: 020 7250 3050).

Voluntary agencies directory, National Council for Voluntary Organizations

An alphabetical listing of 2500 organizations, providing contact details and descriptions for each. There is a classified index at the back. In addition it has a section of useful addresses which includes some European contacts.

Whetter, L. and Rybus, V., *International directory of voluntary work*, Vacation Work

This covers organizations worldwide in need of volunteers with a wide range of skills. It provides contact details and a description of the work and organization.

International foundation directory, Europa Publications

This directory, covering well over 100 countries, is invaluable for international foundations. For the purpose of this directory, foundations must be recognized as charitable or for public benefit. They are listed alphabetically within countries with a full index provided.

Journals

Charity Times

Perspective Publishing Ltd

Tel: 020 7426 0424 Fax: 020 7426 0042

www.charitytimes.com

Six issues per year

Third Sector
> Third Sector Arts Publishing International
> Freepost LON6577, London E2 9BR

Market research

Key Note reports, Key Note
> For free executive summaries of report titles listed under financial services (charity funding), visit **www.keynote.co.uk** For details of obtaining full reports contact Key Note (tel: 020 8481 8750, fax: 020 8783 0049).

Statistics

For key facts, figures, analysis and trends:

Pharoah, C. and Smerdon, M. *Dimensions of the voluntary sector*, Charities Aid Foundation. Annual

Awareness days

Awareness Campaign Register **www.awareness.com**
> A register of UK charities' awareness days, weeks and campaigns.

The Year Ahead **www.yearahead.co.uk**
> This consists of a complete calendar of over 5000 events.

Websites

Charity Choice **www.charitychoice.co.uk**
> Provides a listing of registered charities in the UK and their objectives.

Charity Commission **www.charity-commission.gov.uk**
> Also produces a loose-leaf file of information which is updated.

Charity Net **www.charitynet.org**

Voluntary Services Overseas (VSO) **www.vso.org.uk**

CHEMICALS & THE CHEMICAL INDUSTRY

See also Drugs

Typical questions
- I need the chemical formula for ... .
- I have an assignment on the chemical industry.
- Can you tell me the manufacturer of ...?

Considerations
The chemical industry and the pharmaceutical industry are often confused. The chemical industry relates to the raw chemical materials used in drug making and other industries such as fertilizers. It also includes equipment used within the industry. It is necessary, therefore, to think around this subject area when answering enquiries and establish exactly what the user wants. Directories can be used to find both company details and/or product and service information. Don't rule out using some general directories such as *Kompass* or *Dun & Bradstreet's key British enterprises. See* Companies section.

Where to look
Chemical data

CRC handbook of chemistry and physics: a ready reference book of chemical and physical data 2001–2002, 82nd edn, CRC Press
Excellent reference book covering the whole subject area.

Dean, J. A. (1998) *Lange's handbook of chemistry*, 15th edn, McGraw-Hill
This is a comprehensive handbook of chemistry and chemical data.

Directories

Chemical industry Europe, Miller Freeman Information Services
An invaluable directory that provides a list of chemical and plant products and services. It has an alphabetical list of brand and trade names together with manufacturers' names and brief descriptions of the products. The Company Data section gives contact details, product/service details, quality assessment and export/import indicators. It also has an excellent country index to companies which also indicates whether the company is a chemical manufacturer or a plant and equipment supplier. It includes a list of

chemical organizations and a table of the top European chemical companies.

Market intelligence

Mintel industrial reports, Mintel International Group

For details visit **www.mintel.co.uk** or tel: 020 7606 4533, fax: 020 7606 5932.

Key Note reports, Key Note

For free executive summaries of report titles listed under chemical and allied industries visit **www.keynote.co.uk**. For details of obtaining full reports, contact Key Note (tel: 020 8481 8750, fax: 020 8783 0049).

Statistics

PRODCOM quarterly industry reports, Office for National Statistics

Excellent source of UK manufacturer sales, imports and exports statistics. Available to download free of charge from

www.statistics.gov.uk/OnlineProducts/default.asp

Journals

Chemical Week

Chemical Week Associates

Tel: 020 7436 7676 Fax: 020 7436 3749

www.chemweek.com

Weekly

Worldwide coverage of the global chemical industry.

Websites

British Agrochemical Association **www.baa.org.uk**

Chemical Industry **www.chemical-industry.org.uk**

Excellent site offering a wealth of information on all aspects of the chemical industry.

Chemical Industries Association **www.cia.org.uk**

69

CHILDCARE

Typical questions
- Have you a list of childminders/nurseries?
- How do I set up a nursery/day care centre, etc.?

Considerations
It is usually the case that the local council will maintain lists of registered childminders and nurseries. It is best to suggest that the user talks to the relevant department for this type of information because of the strict checks that they carry out on people included on their lists. You will find the number in your local telephone book or contact details may be available on the council's website. You may want to keep a copy of the list for your library but remember to keep it up to date.

Where to look
British opportunity profiles, Cobweb Information
Tel: 0191 261 2853 Fax: 0191 261 1910
These are very good for those thinking of setting up a childcare service. They provide an introduction to the market, its potential customers and possible competitors. They indicate start-up costs and legal considerations. They also include further reading and useful addresses of relevant associations and organizations. Look for 'Childminding Service' and 'Children's Day Nursery'.

Market intelligence
Mintel reports (childcare facilities and children's holiday clubs), Mintel International Group
For details of reports visit **www.mintel.co.uk** or contact Mintel International Group (tel: 020 7606 4533, fax: 020 7606 5932).

Key Note reports, Key Note
For free executive summaries of report titles listed under healthcare and medical (childcare) and lifestyle (working women) visit **www.keynote. co.uk**. For details of obtaining full reports, contact Key Note (tel: 020 8481 8750, fax: 020 8783 0049).

Organizations

Daycare Trust
> 21 St George's Rd, London SE1 6ES
> Tel: 020 7840 3350 Fax: 020 7840 3355
> **www.daycaretrust.org.uk**
> This produces a great little booklet called *Your guide to choosing childcare*.

Kids Club Network
> Bellerive House, 3 Muirfield Crescent, London E14 9SZ
> Tel: 020 7512 2112 Fax: 020 7512 2010
> **www.kidsclubs.co.uk**

National Childminding Association
> 8 Masons Hill, Bromley, Kent BR2 9EY
> Tel: 020 8464 6164 Fax: 020 8290 6834
> **www.ncma.org.uk**

National Family and Parenting Institute
> 430 Highgate Studios, 53–79 Highgate Rd, London NW5 1TL
> Tel: 020 7424 3460 Fax: 020 7485 3590
> **www.nfpi.org**
> This produces an excellent booklet, which provides a quick guide to the law
> on childcare: *Is it legal? a parents' guide to the law*.

Websites

Childcare careers **www.dfes.gov.uk/childcarecareers**

Childcare Link **www.childcarelink.gov.uk**
> Lots of information available.

Flametree **www.flametree.co.uk**
> For child-care issues.

Childline **www.childline.org.uk**

CHRONOLOGIES *see* DATES, EVENTS, CHRONOLOGIES & CALENDARS

CINEMA *see* FILMS & CINEMA

CITATION *see* BIBLIOGRAPHIES, REFERENCES & CITATION

CLASSICAL MUSIC *see* MUSIC

CLOTHES & CLOTHING

See also Costumes & Fashion, Textiles

Typical questions
- I need to know who makes this brand of sportswear.
- Have you got a list of dress manufacturers?
- Can you tell me who makes ...?

Considerations

Do not take for granted that the name given by the user is definitely a company name: it could well be a brand (trade) name or vice versa. The clothing industry is riddled with brand names. Most of the directories mentioned below are good for looking up both company names and/or brand names. Also bear in mind that some users may be interested in wholesalers as well as manufacturers. *Kompass*, *Kelly's* and *Dun & Bradstreet's key British enterprises* (*see* Companies) are all good sources to use but for more details and a more comprehensive coverage of the clothing industry the directories listed below would be useful.

Where to look
Directories

Kemps British clothing industry yearbook, Kemps Publishing Ltd
An excellent starting point for many queries. This directory provides an alphabetical list of companies, a classified list of products (product lists are provided in a number of European languages), and a trade names section. The products section is further subdivided within categories.

The fashion index (incorporating Shoe trades directory), Emap Fashion
Another excellent starting point for many queries. This directory provides an alphabetical listing of companies, trade names, fashion agents and a classified list of merchandise listed alphabetically within categories. As well

as giving full contact details, brand names and product details for each company, the *Fashion index* now provides (where possible) web addresses.

Market research

Mintel reports, Mintel International Group
> For details visit **www.mintel.co.uk** or tel: 020 7606 4533, fax: 020 7606 5932. There is a wide selection of clothing reports.

Key Note reports, Key Note
> For free executive summaries of report titles under clothing and personal goods visit **www.keynote.co.uk** For details of obtaining full reports, contact Key Note (tel: 020 8481 8750, fax: 020 8783 0049).

Journals

There are a number of journals that are excellent for keeping up to date with the world of fashion. These are a selection of the most useful, but it is best to check *Willings press guide* for further titles.

Company Clothing
> Hemming Group
> Tel: 020 7973 4638 Fax: 020 7233 5057
> Ten issues per year
> Covers all aspects of corporate and work clothing.

Drapers Record
> Emap Fashion
> Tel: 020 7520 1500 Fax: 020 7837 4699
> **www.drapersrecord.co.uk**
> Weekly
> Covers all aspects of the clothing/fashion industry.

Fashion Forecast International
> Benjamin Dent and Co
> Tel: 020 7637 2211 Fax: 020 7637 2248
> Published in December and August.

FW
> Emap Fashion
> Tel: 020 7520 1500 Fax: 020 7520 1646
> Published in February and August.

Covers men and women's fashion.

Menswear
  Emap Communications
  Tel: 020 7841 6600 Fax: 020 7841 6605
  Monthly
  Covers all aspects of men's clothing including retail.

Statistics

PRODCOM quarterly industry reports, Office for National Statistics
  Excellent source of UK manufacturer sales, imports and exports statistics.
  Available to download free of charge from **www.statistics.gov.uk/
  OnlineProducts/default.asp**.

Electronic sources

Fashion Websites **www.fashionwebsites.co.uk**
  Provides a list of websites.

COATS OF ARMS *see* HERALDRY & COATS OF ARMS

COINS & STAMPS

See also Medals & Decorations

Typical questions

- How much is this old coin worth?
- I have an old coin which I think may be Roman. Can you help me identify it?
- I have a stamp from 1920. What is it worth?
- Have you any books with stamps from Turkey in?

Considerations

Most questions regarding coins and stamps will be about their value and/or identification.

Where to look

Coins

There are many books available on coins. Check your shelves to see what you have. The following texts, or ones similar to these, should help you answer most enquiries.

Krause, C. L., Mishler, C. and Bruce, C. R. (eds) (2000) *Standard catalog of world coins*, Krause Publications
> This provides full details of coins with current values and identification keys.

Spinks standard catalogue of British coins: coins of England and the United Kingdom, Spink. Annual
> **www.spink-online.com**
> This lists coins from Celtic times to the present day. It is an invaluable publication for identifying British coins and finding their values.

Stamps

The stamp collector's 'bible' is the collection of Gibbons catalogues, e.g.:

Stamps of the world, 4 vols

British Commonwealth, 2 vols

The catalogues are annual and are published by Stanley Gibbons Ltd.
> There is a useful 'gateway' site for stamp collectors at:

> **www.ukphilately.org.uk**

Other sources

Keen coin collectors may wish to join the Royal Numismatic Society:

The Royal Numismatic Society
> c/o The British Museum, Department of Coins and Medals, Great Russell St, London WC1B 3DG
> **www.rns.dircon.co.uk**

Local museums can also be a useful source of information if they have coin collections.
> Stamp collectors also have their own national society:

The Royal Philatelic Society London
41 Devonshire Place, London W1G 6JY
www.rpsl.org.uk

COLLEGES *see* UNIVERSITIES & COLLEGES

COMPANIES

See also Job Interviews

Typical questions
- Have you got the address of ...?
- Who owns ...?
- Have you got the telephone number for *x* firm in Manchester?
- Can you give me a list of companies who make steel rods?

Considerations

It is certainly useful to know what constitutes the various types of registered company. The following are brief descriptions annotated from Company Law Club

www.companylawclub.co.uk

(1) **Private Companies Limited by Shares** – These will have the word 'Limited' or 'Ltd' at the end of the name. They are usually small or medium-sized and therefore need only file 'small' accounts at Companies House. A private company cannot offer shares or debentures to the public.

(2) **Public Limited Companies** – Despite our familiarity with the term PLC, there are, in fact, only a small proportion of companies that are public companies. The company name will end in the words 'Public Limited Company' or 'PLC'. They are large businesses with shares available to the public. Public companies have greater legal requirements than private companies, filing full accounts at Companies House.

(3) **Property Management Companies** – This is a type of private limited company. It is set up to own the freehold of a property that is divided and owned in parts by individuals, e.g. flats.

(4) **Companies Limited by Guarantee** – A company limited by guarantee is a private company, very like a private company limited by shares but it does not have a share capital. It is widely used for charities, clubs,

community enterprises and some co-operatives. Such companies are registered at Companies House and are subject to the requirements of the Companies Acts. There are no shares and therefore no shareholders but they do have members, who control each company through general meetings. The directors are often called a management committee but in law are still company directors and subject to the rules.

(5) **Unlimited Companies** – It is possible to register at Companies House a private company which is unlimited, i.e. the members accept complete liability for the company's debts. It is not required to register annual accounts at Companies House.

Sole traders and partnerships are not strictly companies.

For company information it is advisable to make sure you are familiar with at least two good directories. There are a number listed below. If you do not have any of these available in your library, you may want to bookmark a few of the excellent online directories listed below.

Where to look
Directories

Kompass, vols 1–4, Reed Business Information
www.reedbusiness.com
This provides details of 40,000 products and services and 47,000 companies. Further volumes provide details of parent companies and their subsidiaries and industrial trade names.

It is worth also trying:

Kompass OnLine **www.kompass.co.uk**
This is an excellent site that is free to search and provides product/services and company details for UK and international companies. Subscribers can view the full list of results; otherwise a selection is provided free.

Key British enterprises UK, 5 vols, Dun & Bradstreet
Provides contact, financial, operational and corporate details for the 50,000 companies covered.

Try also:

Dun & Bradstreet Online **www.dnb.com**
This offers a free directory of over 1.8 million UK businesses. It gives

contact details, business activity and a location map via multimap.com.

Kelly's, Reed Business Information
Provides both company and products and services information. For each company the address, telephone, fax and business activity are given. Also use **www.kellysearch.com**.

Sell's products and services directory, 2 vols, United Business Media
This provides information on 60,000 companies and 8900 products and services, a buyers' guide and trade/brand names. It is also available on CD-ROM.

Who owns whom UK and Ireland, 2 vols, Dun & Bradstreet
This is indispensible for finding out company ownership.

Waterlow stock exchange yearbook, Waterlow Specialist Information Publishing
This provides information on all companies and securities listed on the London and Dublin stock exchanges and all those traded in the Alternative Investment Market. Companies in administration, liquidation and receivership are also included as well as a section on dealing with government, corporation and provincial stocks and bonds.

Directory of directors, 2 vols, Reed Business Information
Volume 1 provides names of 50,000 directors of major British companies. Volume 2 gives details of 14,000 major companies and their 120,000 board members listed in alphabetical order. All FTSE companies are included as well as smaller and harder-to-find businesses.

Dun & Bradstreet business registers, 32 vols, Dun & Bradstreet
www.dnb.com.uk
This is a set of 30-plus regional directories. The listing includes businesses with five or more employees, or an annual sales turnover in excess of £250,000, and their branches.

Online services

Companies House **http://ws4.companieshouse.gov.uk**
Companies House provides information on 1.5 million registered companies. Information available includes company reports, company director details, dissolved companies and disqualified directors, document images. The basic company and director details are free. The other

information can be paid for either by credit card or by subscription.

ICC – Juniper

For more details contact **www.icc.co.uk** or tel: 020 8481 8800. ICC covers credit and business information for 6.5 million UK companies. Juniper is an internet subscription-based service providing access to financial information, directors and major shareholders for all 1.4 million limited companies in the UK. It is updated daily. The service also provides credit risk scores and access to an image bank of all director reports, accounts and annual returns since March 1995. There is also a database of unincorporated businesses.

Finding out more about a company

International directory of company histories, St James Press, Gale Group

A multi-volume work which provides histories of the major and influential companies of the world.

European intelligence wire CD-ROM, Lexis Nexis Europe, Proquest

This is a monthly subscription service. It contains business-related articles from over 50, mainly UK and some overseas, newspapers and business journals. You can search by company name, industry or keyword.

Websites

Annual Reports Library **www.global-reports.com**

Annual reports and documents for 1.5 million American companies. Brilliant site.

Applegate Company Information **www.applegate.co.uk**

Covers the following sectors: agribusiness, electronic, engineering, oil and gas, plastics and rubber, and recruitment.

Bized **www.bized.ac.uk**

Business Network **www.countyweb.co.uk**

Carol (Company Annual Reports OnLine) **www.carolworld.com**

Companies House **www.companieshouse.gov.uk**

Corporate Information **www.corporateinformation.com**

Free company and industry reports.

Financial Times **www.ft.com**

Hemmington Scott Ltd **www.hemscott.co.uk/hemscott**

Hoover's Online (UK) **www.hoovers.co.uk**
    Provides information on 50,000 companies worldwide.

Northcote: The LINK to annual reports **www.northcote.co.uk**

Northern Ireland Top 100 **www.belfasttelegraph.co.uk/tops/laypot/home.html**

Tips and pitfalls

Always check the spelling of companies with the enquirer. If they have a letter from the company, ask if you can look at it: it may well give you some leads. Company information is expensive but there is a lot of free information on the internet. Don't be frightened of searching, for example, **google.com** with a company name. A lot of companies are developing websites which include company information and trade catalogues.

COMPANIES – ACCOUNTS

Typical questions
- Have you got the annual report for ...?
- Can you tell me the turnover for ...?
- Have you got a credit rating for ...?

Considerations

In the main, company financial information does not come cheap, especially if further analysis has been carried out by the supplier. The best source of free company financials is the annual report. If your library does not keep annual reports, the enquirer can either contact the company directly for the annual report (*see* Companies) or use one of the websites such as Carol (Company Annual Reports OnLine).

Where to look

Reid, W. and Myddelton, D. R. (2000) *The meaning of company accounts*, Gower

Online Services

Companies House **http://ws4.companieshouse.gov.uk**

> Companies House provides information on 1.5 million registered companies. Information available includes company reports, company director details, dissolved companies and disqualified directors, document images. The basic company and director details are free. The other information can be paid for either by credit card or by subscription.

ICC – Juniper

> For more details visit **www.icc.co.uk** or tel: 020 8481 8800. ICC covers credit and business information for 6.5 million UK companies. Juniper is an internet subscription-based service providing access to financial information, directors and major shareholders for all 1.4 million limited companies in the UK. It is updated daily. The service also provides credit risk scores and access to an image bank of all director reports, accounts and annual returns since March 1995. There is also a database of unincorporated businesses.

Dun & Bradstreet's Company Documents Online

> For more details visit **www.dnb.com**. This service downloads images from Companies House via its internet site. These include accounts and annual returns.

Websites

Carol (Company Annual Reports OnLine) **www.carolworld.com**

Companies House **www.companieshouse.gov.uk**

Corporate Information **www.corporateinformation.com**

> This offers free company and industry reports for countries worldwide. It provide financial information and analysis.

Northcote: The LINK to annual reports **www.northcote.co.uk**

COMPANIES – DEFUNCT

Typical questions
- Can you tell me if this company still exists?
- When did this company go into liquidation?

Considerations

Firstly, let us clarify what all these terms mean. 'Liquidation' (or 'winding up') means that the assets of a company are sold off and the money shared among its creditors according to their position in the payment queue. 'Voluntary liquidation' is the result of a resolution by the shareholders and 'compulsory liquidation' is the result of a court order. At the end of liquidation the company will be 'dissolved'. 'Administration' is a court-based procedure under which a company may be reorganized or its assets realized under the protection of statutory moratorium. 'Administrative receivership' and 'receivership' are not strictly insolvency proceedings but are available to a secured creditor (usually the bank) allowing realization of assets which are subject to security, e.g. the bank lends money, the company offered a warehouse as security, the bank then sends in receivers to get what is due. The difference between the receiver and the administrator is basically the 'Receiver' looks after whoever appoints him, the 'Administrator' looks after creditors.

In the majority of cases, enquirers don't know that the company they are looking for no longer exists. You may find you have to go through the full search process using the sources mentioned under Companies before you actually find this out. When you are actually faced with someone who is trying to find out about a dissolved company you will probably be limited in the amount of information you can offer. The best advice is for the enquirer to contact Companies House.

Where to look

Defunct companies

Companies that have gone into liquidation, amalgamated or changed their name can be traced using one of the following:

Companies House **http://ws4.companieshouse.gov.uk**
> Companies House provides information on 1.5 million registered companies. Information available includes company reports, company director details, dissolved companies and disqualified directors, document images. The basic company and director details are free. It also provides company change of name with the date it took place or the date a company was dissolved. This service is also available via the telephone. The other information can be paid for either by credit card or by subscription.

Waterlow stock exchange yearbook, Waterlow Specialist Information Publishing www.waterlowfinancial.com

This provides lists of companies in administration, receivership and liquidation. Also has a register of defunct and other companies.

London Gazette

www.london-gazette.co.uk

This daily publication lists petitions and resolutions for winding up, appointments of liquidators, meetings of creditors, final meetings and bankruptcies.

Websites

Companies House **www.companieshouse.gov.uk**

Insolvency Service (DTI) **www.insolvency.gov.uk**

COMPANIES – INTERNATIONAL

Typical questions

- Have you got the address of …?
- Who owns …?
- Have you got the telephone number for a company in Rome?
- Can you give me a list of companies who make clocks in Spain?

Considerations

Enquirers may not always know the nationality of a company and neither will you. It is difficult to offer assistance without having at least a few of the resources listed below. However, you could use one of the free internet databases.

Where to look

Directories

World business directory, 4 vols, Gale Group

Information on 140,000 companies within the global market place.

The top 5000 global companies, Gale Group

This provides details on the world's 5000 largest manufacturing and service companies by size of sales revenue, the 500 largest banks by size of assets and the 100 largest insurance companies by size of premium income.

Try also other titles from the Gale Group:
www.galegroup.com/world

Major companies of the Arab world

Major companies of the Africa south of the Sahara

Major companies of central and eastern Europe and the Commonwealth of Independent States

Major companies of Europe

Major companies of the Far East and Australia

Major companies of Latin America and the Caribbean

Major companies of Southwest Asia

Ward's business directory of U.S. private and public companies

D & B Europa, Dun & Bradstreet

The first three volumes provide an alphabetical list of 60,000 companies arranged within countries. Volume 1 covers Belgium, Switzerland, Germany, Denmark and Spain. Volume 2 covers France, Greece, Iceland, Ireland, Israel and Italy. Volume 3 covers Luxembourg, the Netherlands, Norway, Austria, Portugal, Finland, Sweden, Turkey and the UK. Volume 4 provides indexes, rankings, statistics and tables. Further details of arrangement can be found in the introduction in Volume 1. Volume 4 provide company rankings by sales in ecu (millions), bank rankings by total assets in ecu (millions), rankings by employees and top companies by business activity by annual sales in ecu. It also provides various other statistical profiles.

Kompass **www.kompass.co.uk**

Kompass produces directories for a large number of countries. They are arranged and organized in a similar way to the UK Kompass. Try also Kompass Worldwide on the internet.

Who owns whom continental Europe, Dun & Bradstreet

This directory provides corporate family trees of parent companies registered in Austria, Belgium, Switzerland, Germany, Denmark, Spain, France, Greece, Italy, Luxembourg, Norway, Netherlands, Portugal, Sweden and Finland. In addition it provides parent companies worldwide with those of their subsidiaries or associates incorporated within continental Europe. The second volume provides an alphabetical index to subsidiaries and associates of parent companies listed in the first volume.

Who owns whom USA and Canada, Dun & Bradstreet

Europe's 15,000 largest companies, The Stationery Office
Lists the top companies in Europe ranked by turnover and, in the case of banks, assets. It provides tables on Europe's 500 largest companies, the largest industrial companies in Europe and the largest service companies in Europe along with an alphabetical index of all companies. This is also available as a CD-ROM.

Europages: the European business directory **www.europages**
This covers 18 sectors of activity, listing companies for each of the 22 countries covered. It includes a market analysis of each sector. This can be very useful for an overview of the sector. There is an alphabetical index of suppliers at the back of the publication.

Websites
Carol (Company Annual Reports OnLine) **www.carolworld.com**

Corporate Information **www.corporateinformation.com**
This is the sort of site we all dream of. It offers free company and industry reports for the Americas, Europe and Oceania. The reports include financials, analysis and competitor comparisons. Well worth a visit and one to bookmark.

Tips and pitfalls
Don't rule out using the world telephone directories for basic contact details. Look at

www.teldir.com

COMPANIES – LAW

See also Employment – Law; Law

Typical questions
- What are the legal obligations of a company director?
- Can you give me a guide to the Companies Acts?

Considerations
This is a huge area and for many queries specialist help may be required. However, for information purposes there are a number of reference books that are

excellent. Company law is constantly being updated and it is important to check the date of the information offered.

Where to look
Books

For a general reference book try:

Dine, J. (2001) *Company law*, Palgrave Law Masters, Palgrave
This is an excellent publication, providing a concise yet comprehensive introduction to the subject without oversimplifying the complex issues involved. It is very readable.

Also:

Mayson, S., French, D. and Ryan, C. (2001) *Mayson, French and Ryan on company law*, Blackstone Press

French, D. (2001) *Statutes on company law*, Blackstone Press
This brings together statutes relating to company law in one volume. Primarily aimed at students it is excellent for answering enquiries regarding this area.

Don't rule out using publications such as:

Rose, F. (2001) *Company law nutshells*, Nutshells, Sweet & Maxwell
This presents the essentials of law in clear and straightforward language.

Also, for a guide to the duties and liabilities of company directors:

The company director's guide: your duties, responsibilities and liabilities (2001), Institute of Directors

Health and safety

This is an important aspect of company law.

Croners' health and safety at work, Croner CCH Group
This is an excellent publication for reference to the Acts, Regulations, and Codes of Practice and Guidance currently in force in the UK for the control of health and safety at work.

Hsedirect **www.hsedirect.com**
Hsedirect was developed by the Health and Safety Executive (in

partnership with Butterworths) and provides health and safety legislation and guidance. It is also available on CD-ROM.

Websites

Company Law Club **www.companylawclub.co.uk**
You will need to register but it is well worth it.

Delia Venables' site **www.venables.co.uk**
This is good for links

Infolaw **www.infolaw.co.uk**

International Centre for Commercial Law **www.icclaw.com**

Law Commission **www.lawcom.gov.uk**

LawZone **www.lawzone.co.uk**

LegalPulse **www.legalpulse.com**
Provides free legal information for small businesses. After free registration you are given access to the Documents Library, which cover all aspects of business including forming a company, developing a business, employment matters, etc. There is also a legal dictionary.

Social Science Information Gateway (SOSIG) **www.sosig.ac.uk/law**

COMPOSERS *see* BIOGRAPHIES; MUSIC

COMPUTERS *see* INFORMATION TECHNOLOGY

CONFERENCES & EXHIBITIONS

Typical questions
- Can you tell me the organizers of ...?
- Where and when will the next ... conference be held?

Considerations
This is a subject area well covered by the internet and most professional journals

will give relevant conference details.

Where to look

Directories

Conference blue and green, United Business Media

These are the leading directories for the conference industry in the UK, distributed free of charge. They cover nearly 6000 companies and are available in hard copy, CD-ROM or at **www.venuefinder.com**.

The white book, Inside Communications

This is an essential reference book for event organizing with contact information for conferences and events both in the UK and overseas. It can also be searched online via **www.whitebook.co.uk**.

Journals

Exhibition Bulletin

Tarsus Group PLC

Tel: 020 8846 2700 Fax: 020 8846 2801

Monthly

Provides details of exhibitions both in the UK and abroad.

Websites

e-bulletin **www.e-bulletin.com**

The online companion to *Exhibition Bulletin*. Subscribers to the bulletin can have full access, others have limited period access.

FT Conferences **www.ftconferences.com**

Trade Fairs and Exhibitions UK **www.exhibitions.co.uk**

The official website for the UK exhibition industry, sponsored by Trade Partners UK, providing a free listing of all consumer and trade exhibitions. Highly recommended.

TSNN Global Network **tsnn.co.uk**

Contains data on more than 15,000 exhibitions and conferences and more than 30,000 seminars.

Venuefinder **www.venuefinder.com**

this is for meeting and event organizers and is particularly good for links.

CONSTRUCTION

Typical questions
- Can you give me the address of a housebuilding firm?
- Who makes a certain branded product for construction?
- Can you tell me what products this firm makes?
- I'm interested in statistics related to the construction industry.

Considerations
There are numerous specialist directories for the construction industry but if you don't have access to any of the following don't rule out using *Kompass* or *Dun & Bradstreet's key British enterprises*. *See* Companies. Contracts within the construction industry are listed in both *Building* and *Construction News* (see below).

Where to look
General
MacLean, J. H and Scott, J. S. (1993) *The Penguin dictionary of building*, 4th edn, Penguin Books

Defects in buildings: symptoms, investigation, diagnosis and care (2001), 2nd edn, Carillion Series
Covers common defects in all the principal types of construction.

Directories
RIBA product selector, RIBA Information Services
An indispensable two-volume directory. It contains product and company information on 7400 manufacturers and suppliers of building products and services, 20,000 trade names and 1100 advisory organizations. It is worth also looking at the RIBA Information Service website **www.ris.gb.com**. This provides a link to Sweet's Product Marketplace™ **www.sweets.com** for those involved in the European and/or American construction industry.

Barbour index: building product compendium, Barbour Index PLC
Contains details of over 6000 UK manufacturers and suppliers, 3000 product categories and features over 1600 product ranges in full colour. Visit the Barbour website **www.barbour-index.co.uk** for information on other resources available and to access building and construction journals.

Spon's price books and landscape projects are invaluable guides to the construction industry. Titles available include:

Spon's architects and builders' price book
Spon's civil engineering and highway works price book
Spon's landscape and external works price book
Spon's mechanical and electrical services price book

All now available with free CD-ROM. Other titles are available also. Spon also produce international price books. Titles available include:

Spon's African construction costs handbook
Spon's Asia and Pacific construction costs handbook
Spon's European construction costs handbook
Spon's Irish construction price book
Spon's Latin American construction costs handbook
Spon's Middle East construction costs handbook

For more details visit **www.efnspon.com**

Building restoration and conservation

Building conservation directory, Cathedral Communications
Provides work specialists for historic buildings, their contents and surroundings, a starting point in the search for appropriate products and services and expert advice. It is also useful to look at the website **www.buildingconservation.com** which provides a gateway to the building conservation and restoration industry.

Building regulations

Building regulations are government-approved specifications relating to health and safety, energy conservation, and the welfare and convenience of disabled people. A useful compilation of these is:

Knight's building regulations 2000, with approved documents, Charles Knight Publications
A two-volume loose-leaf publication. Covers England and Wales.

Construction Knowledge Bank
An online subscription service providing key regulatory information. This includes building regulations, health and safety, and Acts of Parliament. It

covers England, Wales, Northern Ireland and Scotland and is regularly updated. Subscription details can be found at **www.clicktso.com**

Market intelligence

Key note reports, Key Note
> For free executive summaries of report titles listed under construction visit **www.keynote.co.uk**. For details of obtaining full reports, contact Key Note (tel: 020 8481 8750, fax: 020 8783 0049).

Journals

Building
> Builder Group PLC
> Tel: 020 7560 4000 Fax: 020 7560 4014
> Weekly
> Covers major developments in the industry.

Construction News
> EMAP Construct
> Tel: 020 7505 6600 Fax: 020 7713 7164
> Weekly

There are numerous journals for the construction industry, details of which can be found in *Willings press guide* (*see* Journals & Periodicals).

Statistics

Construction statistics annual brings together statistics previously included in the annual *Digest of data for the construction industry and housing and construction statistics*. Published by the Department of Trade and Industry. It is available to download free of charge or to view at **www.dti.gov.uk/construction/stats/index.htm**, or contact DETR Publications Sales (tel: 01709 891319).

Monthly statistics of building materials and components
> This is a subscription publication but back copies are available to download free of charge at **www.dti.gov.uk/construction/stats/materials.htm**

Other price and cost indices are available. Details can be found on the DTI website.

PRODCOM annual industry reports, Office for National Statistics
> Excellent source of manufacturer sales, imports and exports statistics. Available to download free of charge from **www.statistics.gov.uk/**

OnlineProducts/PRODCOM2000_annual.asp

Quarterly State of Trade Survey, Federation of Master Builders
www.fmb.org.uk
Free statistical publication.

Websites

Automated Builder Magazine **www.automatedbuilder.com**
Online to the Built Environment **www.barbourexpert.com**
Building Conservation **www.buildingconservation.com**
Building Information Warehouse **www.biw.co.uk**
Building Products Index Online **www.bpindex.co.uk**
Careers in Construction **www.careersinconstruction.com/**
Chartered Building Company Scheme **www.cbcscheme.org.uk**
Chartered Institute of Building **www.ciob.org.uk**
Construction Confederation **www.constructionconfederation.co.uk**
Construction Industry Council **www.cic.org.uk/index.htm**
ConstructionNet **www.constructionnet.net/**
FERL Construction Sources
    www.ferl.becta.org.uk/resource.cfm?IngLoc=12
House Builders Federation **www.hbf.co.uk**
Institution of Civil Engineers **www.ice.org.uk**
International Council for Research and Innovation in Building and
    Construction **www.cibworld.nl**
National Federation of Builders **www.builders.org.uk**
RUDI (Resource for Urban Design Information) **www.rudi.net/**
RICS Online **www.rics.org.uk**
UK Construction **www.ukconstruction.com/builders.htmI**

CONSULATES *see* EMBASSIES & CONSULATES

CONSUMER INFORMATION

See also Retailing & Consumer Spending

Typical questions

• Who do I complain to about a product?

- Have you got a guide to consumer law?
- Have you got a survey on the best microwave to buy?

Considerations

The consumer is someone who buys a product or service. Consumers are either seeking information because they want to purchase something or because they have a grievance about a product or service, which they cannot resolve with the seller. Advice on the purchase of goods can only be limited to providing good product surveys such as those done by *Which?* or *What to Buy for Business*. Consumers with a complaint in the main want to know who can help with the problem.

Where to look

For surveys

What to Buy for Business
    Reed Business Information
    Tel: 01342 326972 Fax: 01342 335612
    Monthly

Which? Magazine
    Consumers Association
    Tel: 020 7830 6000 Fax: 020 7770 7600
    Monthly
    Contains product tests and campaigns for improvements in goods and services.

Legislation

A useful book to refer to is:

Lowe, R. and Woodruffe, G. (1999) *Consumer law and practice*, Sweet & Maxwell

Try also:

Miles, R. (2001) *Blackstone's sale and supply of goods and services*, Blackstone Press
    This offers a one-volume guide to the legislation relating to the sale and supply of goods, together with a background to the law of contract.

C CONSUMER INFORMATION

Associations and organizations

Use your local telephone directory for your local Trading Standards Department or use the Trading Standards website **www.tradingstandards.gov.uk** to locate it for you by entering your postcode.

Department of Trade and Industry
  Corporate and Consumer Affairs Directorate
  Location 4.G.25, 1 Victoria St, London SW1H 0ET
  Tel: 020 7215 0344
  www.dti.gov.uk/capc/ca/default.htm
  Excellent site packed with publications and links.

Office of Fair Trading
  Field House, 15–25 Bream's Buildings, London, EC4A 1PR
  Tel: 0345 224 499
  www.oft.gov.uk
  Excellent site packed with information and advice.

National Consumer Council
  20 Grosvenor Gardens, London, SW1W 0DH
  Tel: 020 7730 3469 Fax: 020 7730 0191

Websites

Consumer Gateway **www.consumer.gov.uk**

Which? Online **www.which.net**
  E-zine covering consumer interest articles from *Which?* magazine.

Trading Standards Institute **www.tradingstandards.gov.uk**
  Excellent site packed with information and publications for consumers and businesses.

Tips and pitfalls

Avoid comment on individual problems. Equally, you cannot recommend goods and services, merely present the information.

COOKERY

See also Food & Drink

Typical questions
- I want to find a recipe for tripe.
- What recipes were popular during World War 2?

Considerations
From experience, most questions regarding cookery are about specific recipes. There are also questions about histories of certain dishes and cuisines.

Where to look
Printed sources
There are one or two 'classic' cookbooks, which most libraries should have. For example:

Mrs Beeton's cookery and household management (1980), revised edn, Ward Lock Ltd

Grigson, J. (ed.), (1974) *The world atlas of food*, Mitchell Beazley
This useful book includes recipes and descriptions of cuisine from all over the world.

There is also a wealth of specialized cookbooks. For example, there are books on regional cookery, cooking for special occasions, cooking with specific appliances (e.g. microwave ovens, food processors, etc.), and cooking for different diets or medical conditions. Check the library shelves for availability.

There is an excellent book which concentrates on the English and their food:

Drummond, J.C. and Wilbraham, A. (1991) *The Englishman's food: five centuries of English diet*, revised edn, Pimlico
This shows in great detail what we have eaten from Tudor times to the 20th century. There are no recipes as such, but the book provides a fascinating history.

The following titles are also useful:

Davidson, A. (1999) *Oxford companion to food*, Oxford University Press

McGee, H. (1984) *On food and cooking*, Unwin

Electronic sources

There are literally thousands of cookery sites on the web. The best way to find them is to use a popular search engine and type in your key words e.g. recipes AND tripe.

A useful gateway site is

The Kitchen Link **www.kitchenlink.com**

> This is a comprehensive, organized listing of recipes and food-related resources.

COPYRIGHT

Typical questions

- Can I photocopy this?
- How can I take out copyright on my work?
- Someone told me I've got to send a copy of my book to the British Library. Is this true?
- How can I get money from people borrowing my book from libraries?

Considerations

Concerns about copyright, particularly photocopying material, are frequent. It is important that library staff provide correct advice. This is particularly so since it is usually library material that is being copied, and on library equipment. It is an offence to infringe copyright, and unlike most of the other subjects covered in this book, this is one where library staff should be able to give (qualified) advice. Guidelines, such as books listed below, and notices by copying equipment, should be readily available to the staff and public.

Every library will have its own procedures and guidelines relating to copying and it is important that staff have access to those. Thus some subscription services will have licensing restrictions and many libraries will be registered with the Copyright Licensing Agency. Despite the somewhat fraught, complex and often unclear law on copyright, the general principle is clear – that copying done in quantity, or for a commercial purpose, must have the permission of the author or copyright owner. If in doubt, ask the person requesting the copies to get written permission from the publisher, or to sign a declaration that the material is to be used for the purposes of private study. Better to say 'No' than break the law.

Visual, audio and digital material, as well as printed, is covered by copyright.

We concentrate here on copyright and copying, but copyright extends into other areas such as patent and design law, intellectual property and designation. Refer to the library catalogue for these heavyweight subjects. *See also* Inventions & Patents.

As for taking out copyright, there are no special requirements needed apart from being able to prove that you did, in fact, produce the work.

Where to look
Printed sources

Cornish, G. P. (2001) *Copyright: interpreting the law for libraries, archives and information services*, 3rd edn, Library Association Publishing
A popular guide by the then Copyright Officer of the British Library.

Norman, S., (ed.) (1999) *Copyright in further and higher education libraries*, 4th edn, Library Association Publishing

Norman, S. (ed.) (1999) *Copyright in health libraries*, 3rd edn, Library Association Publishing

Norman, S. (ed.) (1999) *Copyright in industrial and commercial libraries*, 4th edn, Library Association Publishing

Norman, S. (ed.) (1999) *Copyright in public libraries*, 4th edn, Library Association Publishing

Norman, S. (ed.) (1999) *Copyright in school libraries*, 4th edn, Library Association Publishing

Norman, S. (ed.) (1999) *Copyright in voluntary sector libraries*, 3rd edn, Library Association Publishing

Pedley, P. (2000) *Copyright for library and information service professionals*, 2nd edn, ASLIB/IMI

The following Statutory Instruments are basic to the subject:

SI 89/816 Copyright, Design and Patent Act 1988

SI 89/1212 The Copyright (Librarians and Archivists) (Copying of Copyright Material) Regulations 1989

SI 96/2967 The Copyright and Related Rights Regulations 1996

Electronic sources

Intellectual Property **www.intellectual-property.gov.uk**
A Patent Office website which gives a wide range of copyright and intellectual property issues. There is a Frequently Asked Questions page.

C COPYRIGHT

US Copyright Office **www.loc.gov/copyright**

Other sources

Authors' Licensing and Collecting Society (ALCS)
  Marlborough Court, 14–18 Holborn, London EC1N 2LE
  Tel. and Fax: 020 7395 0600
  E-mail: alcs@alcs.co.uk
  www.clcs.co.uk

Copyright Licensing Agency
  90 Tottenham Court Rd, London W1P 9HE
  Tel: 020 7436 5931 Fax: 020 7436 3986
  E-mail: cla@cla.co.uk
  www.cla.co.uk

HMSO Copyright Section
  St Clements, Colegate, Norwich NR3 1BQ
  Tel: 01603 521000 Fax 01603 723000
  www.hmso.gov.uk/copy.htm

Ordnance Survey
  Copyright Branch, Romsey Rd, Maybush, Southampton SO9 4DH
  Tel: 01703 792706 Fax: 01703 792535
  www.ordsvy.gov.uk

Performing Right Society
  29/33 Berners St, London W1P 4AA
  Tel: 020 7580 5544 Fax: 020 7306 4740
  www.prs.co.uk

Legal deposit

This is a legal requirement that a publisher must send a copy of every publication to the British Library, and further copies to the other Copyright Libraries on demand. Legal deposit used to be a condition of copyright. Contact:

The Legal Deposit Office
  British Library, Boston Spa, West Yorkshire, LS23 7BY
  Tel: 01937 546267

Public Lending Right (PLR)

PLR is a scheme whereby an author can register his or her book and get paid for the estimated number of times that it is borrowed from public libraries. Contact:

The Registrar, PLR Office, Sorbonne Close, Stockton on Tees TS17 6DA
  Tel: 01642 604699
  www.plr.uk.com

Tips and pitfalls

Generally, the public are lax and cavalier about copying material and may regard the library staff as ridiculously authoritarian and bureaucratic when insisting that regulations are observed. Tough! Better unpopular than in prison! Make it clear that you are merely carrying out the law, not making it up. Besides, you wouldn't want *them* to get into trouble!

COSTUME & FASHION

See also Clothes & Clothing; Uniforms

Typical questions

* What did a policeman wear in Victorian times?
* I need a picture of a traditional Bulgarian folk costume.
* What men's clothes were fashionable in the 1930s?

Considerations

Costume and fashion are two separate, but related subjects. Costume tends to deal with the clothing and dress of particular groups or occupations. Fashion deals with what type of dress is popular at a particular time. Most questions regarding these two subjects will be historical – what costumes used to be worn or what fashions used to be like. You may also receive enquiries about modern-day fashion, or fashion terms and types.

Where to look

Printed sources

An excellent source for costumes around the world is:

Yarwood, D. (1978) *The encyclopedia of world costume*, Batsford
  This is in simple A–Z order with over 2000 line drawings and colour

illustrations.

If you are looking for occupational or work costumes, the following book is useful:

Cunnington, P. and Lucas, C. (1976) *Occupational costume in England: from the eleventh century to 1914*, A & C Black

Fashions can be more difficult to pinpoint. A good starting point for recent fashions is:

Mendes, V. and de la Haye, A. (1999) *20th century fashion*, Thames and Hudson

Tips and pitfalls

Find out from the enquirer exactly what they are looking for. They may ask for a book on Victorian costume and really they just want a picture of a Victorian policeman. It may be just as quick to find a book on the history of the police force as to check through all your costume books.

A useful place to check for fashions is in old magazines. Check to see if your library has back-runs of any suitable titles, e.g. *Vogue* or *Cosmopolitan*. *Picture Post* and *Illustrated London News* can be useful for older fashions. Some libraries may even have copies of old mail order catalogues, and these can be most useful for looking at past fashions.

COUNCIL TAX *see* TAX

COUNTRIES

See also Atlases & Gazetteers; Geography; Maps; Travel

Typical questions
- What is the population of Moldova?
- What is the capital of Sierra Leone?

Considerations

This is such a large subject area that you will need to quiz the enquirer somewhat to find out exactly what they are looking for. A typical scenario is the following. A member of the public comes to the enquiry desk and asks for some information on Bulgaria. This information alone is usually not sufficient. Are they intending to go on holiday there, to go on a business trip, doing a project, or simply answering a quiz question? Once you have found out what type of information they are looking for, your task should be that much easier. You may have to extend your search further by looking under other relevant headings in this guide, e.g. History & Archaeology, Timetables, etc.

Where to look

Printed sources

For general information, e.g. capital cities, populations, areas, currency, etc., *Whitaker's Almanack* is a good bet, as is any decent encyclopedia. For more detailed information, the *CIA world factbook* or *Statesman's yearbook* go into much more depth. They include sections on geography, people, government, economy, communications, transport and the military.

CIA world factbook, Central Intelligence Agency. Annual
> This is a 700-page compendium of information. It is in A–Z order by country, and includes maps.

Statesman's yearbook, Macmillan Reference. Annual
> This is a useful and concise annual reference.

Europa world yearbook, Europa Publications. Annual
> This provides detailed facts and statistics giving a political and economic survey of over 200 countries. Also excellent are the Europa Regional Guides, published bi-annually. These include:

> *Eastern Europe, Russia and Central Asia*
> *Central and South Eastern Europe*
> *The Middle East and North Africa*
> *Africa, south of the Sahara*
> *The Far East and Australia*
> *South America, Central America and the Caribbean*
> *The USA and Canada*
> *Western Europe*

Electronic sources

The *CIA world factbook* is also available online:

www.cia.gov/cia/publications/factbook/

Most countries have an official website. Simply type their name into a good search engine. Embassies and consulates can also be useful sources of information. For a full list try:

www2.tagish.co.uk/Links/WesternEurope/UK/Embin.htm

Tips and pitfalls

Questions regarding countries should be quite straightforward once you have found out exactly what your customer wants.

CRAFTS

Typical questions

- Can you give me a list of craft fairs in the region?
- Have you got the address of a ... manufacturer?
- I'm interested in weaving; are there any groups I can join?

Considerations

There are hundreds of crafts with hundreds more products. Craft also spills over into many other areas such as textiles, clothing, ceramics, jewellery, clock-making and metalwork to name but a few. The directory below is highly recommended for covering lots of products and services for the craft industry. However, depending on the area you may want to use additional directories as well. Local newspapers can give details of local craft fairs to be held. Also use your local Yellow Pages or **www.yell.com** for local organizations.

The craft industry is also a popular one for start-up businesses. Not only will these people require directory information but market information too, especially when they are preparing their business plan.

Where to look

Directories

Craftworkers Yearbook, The Write Angle Press

This directory has three main sections of information. Firstly, it lists craft shows, fairs, festivals and exhibitions, arranged chronologically by date. Secondly, it provides details of organizers. For each record the name of the company is given, address, telephone and fax, contact name, cost per day for event space and the selection policy. Thirdly, it has a classified list of suppliers of products and services to the craft industry. In addition, there are contact details of craft associations, societies, guilds and other relevant organizations.

The Essential Craft and Art Guide, Craftsman Magazine Publications
A guide to craft events. Also provides contact information for event organizers and craft suppliers.

The textile directory 2002: a guide to what's on in creative textiles, Word4Word
www.thetextiledirectory.com
Includes details of courses, galleries and museums, publications, specialist holidays, textile artists who teach and specialist bookshops.

Journals

There are numerous journals on individual crafts, details of which can be found in *Willings press guide*, *see* Journals & Periodicals.

Crafts
Crafts Council
Tel: 020 7278 7700 Fax: 020 7837 0858
Six issues per year

Craftsman Magazine
PSB Design and Print Consultants
Tel: 01377 255213 Fax: 01377 255730
www.craftsmanonline.co.uk/
Monthly
Information on where to buy materials and on events, and articles.

Exhibition Bulletin
Tarsus Group
Tel: 020 8846 2700 Fax: 020 8846 2801
www.e-bulletin.com/
Monthly
Provides details of exhibitions both in the UK and abroad.

Market intelligence

Mintel reports, Mintel International Group.
These provide in-depth research, looking at market factors, market

segmentation, the consumer and the future. Also available on CD-ROM. For details, visit **www.mintel.co.uk** or tel: 020 7606 4533 fax: 020 7606 5932.

Business opportunity profiles, Cobweb Information
www.cobwebinfo.com
Tel: 0191 2612853 Fax: 0191 2611910
These provide an introduction to the market, its potential customers and possible competitors. They indicate start-up costs and legal considerations. They also include further reading and useful addresses of relevant associations and organizations.

Websites

Crafts Council **www.craftscouncil.org.uk**
Craft Fairs **www.craft-fair.co.uk**
Queen Elizabeth Scholarship Trust **www.qest.org.uk**
Here you can find the directory of Queen Elizabeth Scholars who offer specialist crafts and services.

Tips and pitfalls

Don't rule out using the internet to search for specific crafts; searching for a named craft in **google.com** will give good results.

CRIME & CRIMINALS

See also Law; Statistics

Typical questions

• I want some information about the Yorkshire Ripper.
• Who were the Great Train Robbers?

Considerations

This is always a popular subject. Enquirers may be looking for crime figures in a particular area, or they may be researching, or merely interested in 'notorious' criminals.

Where to look

For crime statistics, *see* Statistics.

If you are looking for notorious crimes or criminals, some of the following publications should be useful:

Green, J. (1980) *Directory of infamy: the best of the worst. An illustrated compendium of over 600 of the all time great crooks*, Mills and Boon

Rafter, N. H. (ed.) (2000) *Encyclopedia of women and crime*, Onyx Press

Lane, B. (1993) *Chronicle of twentieth century murder*, Virgin

Nash, J. R. (1992) *World encyclopedia of twentieth century murder*, Crime Books Inc

Nash has also produced a very good dictionary of crime terminology:

Nash, J. R. (1992) *Dictionary of crime*, Crime Books Inc

Symons, M. (1994) *The book of criminal records*, Headline
Has lots of firsts, lasts, and lists of obsolete offences. Useful for enquiries about capital punishment, etc.

Electronic sources

The following websites are useful for crime protection, statistics and criminology:

Home Office **www.homeoffice.gov.uk**

Police Services of the UK **www.police.uk**

Association of Chief Police Officers **www.acpo.police.uk**

Police Foundation **www.police-foundation.org.uk**

Metropolitan Police **www.met.police.uk**

Tips and pitfalls

Local newspapers are essential for looking at local crime. Your local police force should produce reports listing crime figures in your area.

CROSSWORDS *see* DICTIONARIES

CURRENCY *see* COINS & STAMPS; MONEY

CUSTOMS, FESTIVALS & FOLKLORE

See also Etiquette & Forms of Address; Myths & Mythology

Typical questions
- Where are well-dressing ceremonies held?
- When did Father Christmas become a feature of Christmas?
- Why is shaking with the left hand thought to be evil?

Considerations
Folklore covers a wide field with connections to most aspects of life, all age groups, and all parts of the world, urban and rural. It is as much a feature of the modern technological age as of times past. It includes characters such as Father Christmas and Robin Hood, calendar customs such as April Fool's Day and St Valentine's Day, superstitions (charms, crossing fingers) supernatural beliefs (fairy rings, Devil's hoofprints) and performance customs such as morris dancing and well dressing.

Where to look
Printed sources
Customs

Hole, C. (1976) *British folk customs*, Hutchinson
A–Z with background.

Shuel, B. (1985) *The National Trust guide to traditional customs of Britain*, Webb & Bower
Background and illustrations.

Days

Debrett's guide to the Season (2000), Vine House
The 'Season' being Ascot, Chelsea Flower Show, Cowes Week, Goodwood, Glyndebourne, Henley, Wimbledon, etc.

Dunkling, L. (1988) *A dictionary of days*, Routledge
A–Z from Acadian Day and Advent to Yom Teruah and Yule Eve.

Folklore

Briggs, K. M. (1970) *A dictionary of British folk-tales*, 4 vols, Routledge

Jones, A. (1995) *A dictionary of world folklore*, Larousse

Simpson, J. and Round, S. (2000) *A dictionary of English folklore*, Oxford University Press

Zipes, J. (ed.) (2000) *The Oxford companion to fairy tales*, Oxford University Press

Opie, I. and P. (eds) (1997) *The Oxford dictionary of nursery rhymes*, 2nd edn, Oxford University Press

Vickery, R. (1997) *A dictionary of plant lore*, Oxford University Press

Superstitions

Caradeau, J.-L. and Donner, C. (1985) *Dictionary of superstitions*, Granada Popular format.

Opie, I. and Tatem, M. (eds) (1992) *A dictionary of superstitions*, Oxford University Press

Pickering, D. (1995) *Dictionary of superstitions*, Cassell

Other sources

The Folklore Society
c/o The Warburg Institute, Woburn Square, London WC1H 0AB
Tel: 020 7862 8562
www.folklore-society.com

American Folklore Society
http://afsnet.org

DATA PROTECTION *see* RIGHTS

DATES, EVENTS, CHRONOLOGIES & CALENDARS

See also Anniversaries, Customs, Festivals & Folklore; History & Archaeology

Typical questions
- Can you tell me what day of the week I was born on?
- What world events happened in 1873?
- When, exactly, did the Crimean War start?
- When does the Chinese New Year start, and why?
- What year is it in the Muslim calendar?

Where to look
Printed sources

General encyclopedias and factbooks are useful for information on calendars and specific events.

Calendars

Whitaker's Almanack, A & C Black. Annual

> This has an excellent section on time measurement and calendars, including the useful 'Calendar for any year 1780–2040', in which the day of any week of any year can be identified.

Dates

By day within a year, i.e. arranged 1 January through to 31 December:
Beal, G. (1992) *The Independent book of anniversaries*, Headline
Beeching, C. L. (1997) *A dictionary of dates*, 2nd edn, Oxford University Press
Frewin, A. (1979) *The book of days*, Collins

By event:
Butler, A. (1985) *Dent's dictionary of dates*, 7th edn, Dent

A–Z by event:
General encyclopedias will feature noteworthy events. Also the newspaper indexes such as those to the *Guardian* and *The Times*.

By year divided by event; chronologies:

The annual register: a record of world events. 1758 to the present, Keesings World
    Wide. Annual

This year-by-year record of world events provides information with
historical context, perspective and biographical information. Large
libraries may have the full set. Also available as a subscription website.

Facts on file. Weekly with cumulating indexes and annual binders

'World news digest with index.' This major news service indexes events
within each year.

The Chronicle series of heavyweight books published by Chronicle Communications such as *Chronicle of the World, Chronicle of America, Chronicle of Britain*, etc.
give newspaper-type accounts, with illustrations to events. They are very popular with children.

Very full is the four-volume series published by Helicon in 1999:

*BC–AD*Mellersh, M. E. L. *The ancient world 10,000 799*
Storey, R. L. *The medieval world 800–1491*
Williams, N. *The expanding world 1492–1762*
Williams, N. and Waller, P. *The modern world 1763–1992*, 2nd edn

There are many other similar works.

Chronological tables:
Steinberg, S. H. (1991) *Historical tables 58 BC to AD 1990*, 12th edn, Macmillan
    Columns by part of world.

Time zones: see 'Time zones' in *Whitaker's almanack*, in diaries, and many annuals.
    Websites include

www.worldtimeserver.com
www.timeanddate/worldclock/

Tips and pitfalls

In 1753 the Gregorian Calendar was adopted in the UK by the loss of 11 days, 18
February being reckoned as 1 March. This change of calendar can catch out
genealogists. In the same year the beginning of the new year also changed, from
25 March (Lady Day) to 1 January.

DECORATIONS *see* MEDALS & DECORATIONS

DEFENCE *see* ARMED FORCES

DENTISTS *see* DOCTORS & DENTISTS

DIALECT *see* DICTIONARIES

DICTIONARIES

See also Abbreviations & Acronyms; Quotations

Typical questions
- How do you spell bureaucracy?
- Which is the correct spelling: 'practice' or 'practise'?
- What other word can I use instead of 'dream'?
- What's the word for a group of lions?

Considerations
Without words we could neither talk nor write. Perhaps we could not even think. Words are the basis of communication, and hence of society and civilization. Or should it be spelled/spelt 'civilisation'?! No wonder that dictionaries are one of the oldest and largest categories of reference works.

Sometimes unfamiliar words are foreign, sometimes technical, sometimes oddly abbreviated, and sometimes used in strange ways for effect. There are so many kinds of dictionaries and uses that we can only indicate some of the main types. As with so much of reference work, know your stock, and how to use it. Many dictionaries are arranged in ways other than the obvious alphabetical (e.g. thesauruses) and most will have supplementary sequences or appendices. Yet again, the librarian is often called on to help decipher cryptic abbreviations indicating parts of speech or origin. Best to find a one-volume dictionary with good typeface to put on the enquiry counter, and get to know it well.

One frequent problem is that many people insist there is a 'correct' way to spell or use a word. Often there isn't, though books on usage and style may help. Don't waste time looking for the non-existent! Fashions change, as does language.

Where to look
Books on dictionaries

Kabdebo, T. and Armstrong, N. (1997) *Dictionary of dictionaries*, Bowker-Saur
> Gives annotations on, and details of, dictionaries on subjects ranging from abbreviations and accounting to zoology and Zulu.

Standard dictionaries

Dictionaries of a language (monolingual) range from the single volumes, such as those published by Chambers, Longmans, Collins, Oxford and numerous others, to the multi-volume *Shorter Oxford*, *Oxford English* and *Websters*.

The multi-volume *Oxford English dictionary* is 'the ultimate authority on the English language' (*The Times*). Most large libraries will have this and while it is useful for old and obscure words – it gives origins and sample uses as well – it is not a quick source to use. It is best regarded as a source of last resort, rather than a first source. It is also available as a subscription website and in a micro-print version (requiring a magnifying glass).

Collectives

A very common enquiry, often generated by crossword puzzles and quizzes, is for the collective nouns used for a group of animals, etc. Some useful titles are:

Collings, R. (1992) *A crash of rhinoceroses: a dictionary of collective nouns*, Bellew
> Publications
Sparkes, I. (ed.) (1975) *Dictionary of collective nouns and group terms*, White Lion
> Publications

Dialect and jargon

Examples are:

Green, J. (1987) *Dictionary of jargon*, Routledge
Partridge, E. (1991) *Dictionary of slang and unconventional English*, 8th edn,
> Routledge
Wright, J. (1898–1905) *English dialect dictionary*, 6 vols, H. Frowde

Foreign language dictionaries

Monolingual dictionaries are dictionaries that give meanings of words in the same language, e.g. French words defined in French. Only larger libraries are likely to have foreign (non-English) dictionaries in the foreign language. Most libraries will have bi-lingual (e.g. English–French, French–English) dictionaries for the more common languages such as French, German, Spanish, Russian, etc. Caution: some dictionaries will be a-symmetrical, translating only one way, e.g. French into English, but not English into French. Watch out for how dictionaries are arranged on library shelves: the library classification systems such as Dewey are very complex; some libraries simply arrange alphabetically by language.

Multi-lingual dictionaries

Many technical dictionaries cover several languages. Watch out for how they are arranged on library shelves. They may be located with other books on the subject (textiles, electronics, etc.) or placed together.

Names

Paxton, J. (1991) *The Penguin dictionary of proper names*, Viking
  Based on a well-known original by Geoffrey Payton. Covers personal and place names, titles, etc.

Origins (Etymologies)

Hoad, T. F. (ed.) (1993) *The concise Oxford dictionary of English etymology*, 2nd edn, Oxford University Press
Onions, C. T. (ed.) (1996) *The Oxford dictionary of English etymology*, Oxford University Press
Room, A. (1986) *Dictionary of changes in meaning*, Routledge

Phrases

Examples of dictionaries are:

Room, A. (2000) *Brewer's dictionary of phrase and fable*, 17th edn, Cassell
Longman dictionary of English idioms (1979), Longman
Delahunty, A. *et al.* (2001) *Oxford dictionary of allusions*, Oxford University Press
Cowe, P. and Mackin, R. (1975, 1983) *Oxford dictionary of current idiomatic English*, Oxford University Press.
Knowles, E. (2000) *Oxford dictionary of phrase and fable*, Oxford University Press
  Gives background to over 20,000 phrases.
Guinagh, K. (1983) *Dictionary of foreign phrases and abbreviations*, 3rd edn, H W Wilson

Le mot juste: a dictionary of classical foreign words and phrases (1980), Kogan Page

Ehrlich, E. (1987) *Nil desperandum: a dictionary of Latin tags and phrases*, Hale

Rhyming

An example is:

Fergusson, R. (ed.) (1985) *The Penguin rhyming dictionary*, Penguin

Synonyms (words of similar meaning)

Examples are:

Longman synonym dictionary (1979), Longman

Fergusson, R. (ed.) (1986) *New Nuttall dictionary of English synonyms and antonyms*, 2nd edn, Viking

Roget's thesaurus
    Numerous versions, both in the original structured style, and in later alphabetical sequences.

Subject and technical dictionaries

All subjects have special terms and vocabularies, sometimes with meanings quite different to those in common use. These may be monolingual, bilingual or multilingual. Watch out for how these are arranged in the library. They may be arranged with books on the subject, or together as a group of technical dictionaries. Many specialist words will be found in the larger language dictionaries, as well as in encyclopedias and textbook vocabularies and indexes.

Examples are: *Words and phrases legally defined*; *German–English science dictionary*; *Four-language technical dictionary of data processing, computers and office machines*.

Usage, pronunciation and grammars

Blamire, H. (1999) *The Cassell guide to common errors in English*, Cassell

Burt, A. (2000) *The A to Z of current English*, How to Books

Jones, D. (1977) *Everyman's English pronouncing dictionary*, 14th edn, Dent

Pointon, G. (ed.) (1983) *BBC pronouncing dictionary of British names*, 2nd edn, Oxford University Press

Fowler, H. W. (1998) *A dictionary of modern English usage*, 4th edn, Oxford University Press

Gowers, E. (1986) *The complete plain words*, 3rd edn, HMSO

D DICTIONARIES

Todd, L. and Hancock, I. (1990) *International English usage*, Routledge

Other special dictionaries include:

Curl, M. (1982) *The anagram dictionary*, Hale
Tuazon, R. M. and Schaffer, E. G. (1973) *New comprehensive A–Z crossword dictionary*, Grosset and Dunlap
The Oxford crossword dictionary (2000), 2nd edn, Oxford University Press

Websites
The Word Spy **www.logophilia.com/wordspy**
   Records new words and new uses for old words.

The American Dictionary of the English Language **www.bartleby.com/61**

Tips and pitfalls
Spellings vary from century to century and country to country. As do pronunciations.

Most word-processing packages have spelling checkers. Watch out for differences between American and UK usage.

DINOSAURS *see* ANIMALS & PETS

DIRECTORIES *see* ADDRESSES & POSTCODES; ASSOCIATIONS & ORGANIZATIONS; TELEPHONE DIRECTORIES

DISABILITY *see* BENEFITS; EQUAL OPPORTUNITIES; SOCIAL WELFARE

DISSERTATIONS *see* THESES & DISSERTATIONS

DOCTORS & DENTISTS

Typical questions
- I'd like to check the name of a doctor.
- Have you got a list of local dentists?
- How do I find out this doctor's area of expertise?

Considerations
As well as national directories your library will probably keep local lists of both doctors and dentists. These should be kept up to date.

Where to look
Directories
Medical directory, 2 vols, Informa Healthcare
> Lists alphabetically medical practitioners in the UK, giving professional qualifications and posts. There is also an index by town. Also available is the *Medical Directory on CD-ROM, Reference Version*, £185 + VAT. Tel: 020 7453 2441, fax: 020 7453 5567.

Dentists register, General Dental Council
> Lists alphabetically dentists in the UK giving professional qualifications and posts. There is also an index by town. This directory is also available on the website of the General Dental Council **www.gdc-uk.org**

Complaints against doctors and dentists
For doctors refer to:

General Medical Council
> 178 Great Portland St, London W1W 5JE
> Tel: 020 7580 7642 Fax: 7915 3641
> **www.gmc-uk.org**
> Look at 'Problem doctors' on the General Medical Council's website for advice and further information.

For dentists refer to:

General Dental Council
> 37 Wimpole St, London W1G 8DG

Tel: 020 7887 3800 Fax: 020 7224 3294
www.gdc-uk.org

or download the following publication from **www.gdc-uk.org**: 'What to do if you have a problem with your dentist'.

Additional website
British Dental Association
www.bda.dentistry.org.uk
Includes BDA directory.

DRAMA *see* ACTORS & ACTRESSES; LITERATURE; PLAYS; THEATRE

DREAMS & PROPHECIES *see* THE UNEXPLAINED

DRINK *see* FOOD & DRINK

DRUGS (PHARMACEUTICALS)

Typical questions
- Are there any side effects if I take Prozac?
- I want to learn more about the medicine that my doctor has prescribed me.

Considerations
Many people like to check the drugs they have been given to see what is in them and what effects they may have. It is common practice nowadays to include information leaflets with prescribed drugs. But the enquirer may want an independent point of view.

Where to look
General sources

There are several useful reference books that cover this topic. Try and make sure you have one of the following:

Cooper, B. and Gerlis, L. (1996) *Consumers' guide to prescription medicines*,
Charles Fowkes Ltd
This lists all commonly prescribed medicines and all known side-effects.

For much more in-depth information the BNF is essential:

British national formulary, British Medical Association
The BNF provides ready access to key information on the selection,
prescribing, dispensing and administration of medicines. There is a web
version at **www.BNF.org**

Annual register of pharmaceutical chemists, Royal Pharmaceutical Society
This lists all chemists alphabetically by region.

NB There is a constant interest in illegal, street drugs. Check to see what your
library has on this subject, or try the following:

Tyler, A. (1995) *Street drugs*, Coronet
Forsyth, A. J. M. (2000) *Psychoactive drugs: the street pharmacopoeia*, The
Stationery Office

Electronic sources

There are a few good guides on the internet:

RxList: the Internet Drug Index **www.rxlist.com**
WebMDHealth: Drugs and Herbs **http://my.webmd.com/cp_drugs**
The National Pharmaceutical Association **www.npa.co.uk**
Has an excellent list of links to other pharmaceutical organizations.

Tips and pitfalls

Remember not to advise the enquirer about specific medicines. Guide them only
in the direction of the relevant books or publications. If they want advice, refer
them to their doctor or chemist.

EDUCATION

See also Universities & Colleges

Typical questions

- How many women are there in higher education?
- Can you give me the address of ... education authority?
- Have you got the address of ... primary school?

Considerations

It would be difficult to list all the types of questions you could possibly be asked about such a huge subject area but suffice to say they usually fall into two categories; those relating to statistical information and those wanting contact details.

Where to look

Directories

Education authorities directory, School Government Publishing Company
> Indispensable for information and contact details of all those involved in the provision of education including government departments, local education authorities, examination organizations, secondary schools (both state and independent), teacher training bodies, higher and further education colleges, education psychological service and other organizations concerned with education.

Education yearbook, Financial Times, Prentice Hall
> Provides information and contact details of all those involved in the education provision in the UK including local education departments, central government, educational establishments and other educational organizations. There is also a section on overseas education.

The primary education directory, School Government Publishing Company
> Contains details of over 25,000 state and independent establishments providing education for children of nursery and primary ages. Also includes state sector nursery schools.

The special education directory, School Government Publishing Company
> Provides detailed listings of schools and colleges catering for special educational needs in both independent and state sectors throughout the UK.

For independent schools details:

Which school?, John Catt Educational
   A directory of 2000-plus British independent schools. Details from this directory are also available on the School Search website: **www.schoolsearch.co.uk**.

Try also :

Harries, G. E. B. (ed.) *Independent schools yearbook*, A & C Black

Journals

Times Educational Supplement
   Times Supplements
   Tel: 020 7782 3000 Fax: 020 7782 3032
   www.tes.co.uk/
   Weekly

Times Higher Education Supplement
   Times Supplements
   Tel: 020 7782 3000 Fax: 020 7782 3032
   www.thes.co.uk
   Weekly

For statistics

For brief statistics on education use the chapter in *Social Trends*, Office for National Statistics, or *Annual Abstract of Statistics*, Office for National Statistics. For more detailed statistics, use the excellent website of the

Department for Education and Skills **www.dfes.gov**.
   Many statistical publications can be downloaded freely. Go to Publications and select Statistical Publications. Arranged by subject. Highly recommended.

For research

For research publications covering all aspects of education also use the Department for Education and Skills website:

www.dfes.gov
   Go to Publications and select Research Publications.

Key Note reports, Key Note

For free executive summaries of report titles listed under education and training visit **www.keynote.co.uk**. For details of obtaining full reports, contact Key Note (tel: 020 8481 8750, fax: 020 8783 0049).

British education index

This is a subscription database of information about UK literature which supports educational research, policy and practice. It is available in various formats – print, CD-ROM and online. For details about the subscription, contact British Education Index (tel: 0113 233 5525 or **www.leeds.ac.uk/bei/**).

Organizations and websites

Advisory Centre for Education (ACE)
1c Aberdeen Studios, 22 Highbury Grove, London N5 2DQ
Advice Line: Tel: 020 7354 8321
www.ace-ed.org.uk
This provides a wide range of publications, some of which are free to download. Excellent and well worth a visit.

British Institute of Learning Disabilities **www.bild.org.uk**

Department for Education and Skills **www.dfes.gov.uk**
Also has a website for parents at **www.parents.dfes.gov.uk**.

Education Otherwise
PO Box 7420, London N9 9SG
Tel: 0870 730 0074
www.education-otherwise.org
Provides support, advice and information for families considering home-based schooling. Some local groups.

Learn Direct **www.learndirect.co.uk**

Learn Direct (Scotland) **www.learndirectscotland.com**

Learning and Skills Council **www.lsc.gov.uk**

Learning Zone **www.bbc.co.uk/education/directory**

National Grid for Learning **www.ngfl.gov.uk**

OFSTED (Office for Standards in Education) **www.ofsted.gov.uk**

Professional Council for Religious Education **www.cem.org.uk**

Sex Education Forum **www.ncb.org.uk/sexed.htm**

UNESCO (United Nations Educational, Scientific and Cultural Organization)
UK Permanent Delegation to UNESCO (Paris), 1 Rue Moillis, 75732 Paris,
France
Tel: 00 331 4568 2784 Fax: 00 331 4783 2777
www.unesco.org

ELECTION RESULTS

See also Members of Parliament

Typical questions
- I want to know the full list of candidates who stood for the Blackpool North
  constituency in 1997.
- I want to look at the election results from 2001.

Where to look
Printed sources
You can check newspapers for the election dates if you have them on microfilm
or fiche. All the results and candidates from the most recent general election are
available in *Whitaker's almanack*. For a more comprehensive round-up of British
general election results, a good source is:

Rallings, C. and Thrasher, M. (2000) *British electoral facts 1832–1999*,
Parliamentary Research Services
This gives easy access to a host of facts and figures on all general elections
since 1832, as well as European Parliament elections and over 3700 by-
elections.

Waller, R. and Criddle, B. (1996) *The almanac of British politics*, Routledge
This includes detailed accounts of every Parliamentary constituency in the
UK.

The most recent general election results are listed in the:

Times guide to the House of Commons June 2001 (2001), Times Publishing

For local elections try the following:

Local elections handbook, Local Government Chronicle. Annual

This covers every local authority ward.

You should also check local papers for local results.
For worldwide election figures, try the following source:

Gorvin, I. (ed) (1999) *Elections since 1945: a worldwide reference compendium,* Longman

Electronic sources
UKPolitics **www.ukpolitics.org.uk**
The most recent general election results, with summaries of previous elections, can be found on this website. There are over 10,000 pages about British politics and elections: biographies, past elections, manifestos, polls, constituency contacts and an excellent links section.

Elections and Electoral Systems Around the World
www.psr.keele.ac.uk/election.htm
An extensive list of general and country specific links about elections.

Tips and pitfalls
Local election results can sometimes be difficult to trace. Try and photocopy results from the local newspaper and keep them in a file for future use.

ELECTRICITY *see* UTILITIES

EMBASSIES & CONSULATES

Typical questions
• Can you give me the address of the embassy for …?

Considerations
Make sure you understand whether it is a specific country's embassy in the UK that is wanted or the UK embassy in another country. You may get asked about embassies in countries other than the UK; for these the best place to look is *Europa world year book*.

Where to look

Directories

Europa world year book, 2 vols, Europa Publications
Provides a list of diplomatic representation in each country.

London diplomatic list, Foreign and Commonwealth Office
This is an alphabetical guide to all the representatives of foreign states and Commonwealth countries in London. In addition to outlining the composition of the foreign embassies and Commonwealth High Commissions in London, it provides their addresses and the telephone numbers of each department.

Turner, B. (ed.) (2002) *Statesman's Yearbook*, Palgrave Publishers
Provides an A–Z listing of countries of the world. At the end of each country there is a list of diplomatic representatives.

Whitaker's almanack, A & C Black. Annual
Provides an A–Z countries of the world list; for each country it provides details of the UK embassy in the specific country and the country's embassy in the UK.

Yellow pages for Central London
Look under Embassies for telephone numbers. It includes consulates in its listing.

Websites

EmbassyWorld.com **www.embassyworld.com**
Excellent site.

EMPLOYMENT – LAW

Typical questions
- What are my rights as a temporary worker?
- Am I entitled to sick pay?

Considerations

Employment law is a huge area and constantly changing as new legislation comes along. It is advisable to check the dates of the sources you are using and if possible to use sources that are updated frequently such as *Croner's employment law*. Failing this, many excellent organizations dealing with employment law now have websites.

Where to look

Books

Croners Employment Law, CCH Group

> This provides information on all aspects of employment law and the rights of employees. It is updated bi-monthly.

Croners reference book for employers, CCH Group

> This provides employers with information on the various Acts and Regulations relating to employment. It is updated bi-monthly.

Try also:

Bowers, J. (2000) *Bowers on employment law*, 5th edn, Blackstone Press
Butterworths employment law guide (2001), 3rd edn, Tolleys Butterworth
Selwyn, N. (2000) *Selwyn's law of employment*, 11th edn, Tolleys Butterworth
Tolley's employment handbook, 2000–2001, Tolleys Butterworth

> This is an excellent handbook that covers every aspect of employment law.

Websites

Advisory, Conciliation and Arbitration Service (ACAS) **www.acas.org.uk**

British Employment Law **www.emplaw.co.uk**

> The employment law super portal. Excellent and probably all you need. It includes codes of practice for a range of employment situations, offers a huge number of links to useful organizations, free information from lawyers and links to employment law publishers.

DTI Employment Regulations **www.employreg.htm**

EMPLOYMENT – RIGHTS & STATISTICS

> *See also* Careers; Employment – Law; Equal Opportunities; Jobs

Typical questions

• Can you give me the number of people employed by sector?

- What is the current unemployment figure?
- I have a grievance against my employer; who can help me?

Considerations

The world of employment is full of statistics, rights and issues, law, and organizations. It is best for such a subject area as this to be familiar with a few good reference sources that are reputable and updated frequently.

Where to look

Directories

Croner's reference book for employers, CCH Group

A loose leaf publication updated monthly. This is designed to provide employers with information on the various Acts and Regulations relating to employment.

Business information factsheets, Cobweb Information
www.cobwebinfo.com

A loose-leaf publication which offers one-page factsheets on many employment issues especially for the new or small business.

Croner's pay monitor, CCH Group

Statistics

Labour market trends, The Stationery Office

This is a monthly publication, which provides news, articles and statistics for the UK's labour market.

IDS pay and labour market data, Incomes Data Services
www.incomesdata.co.uk

Excellent for statistics, surveys and employment issues.

Annual abstract of statistics, The Stationery Office

Provides labour market statistics.

Social trends, The Stationery Office. Annual

Contains data on employment.

Monthly digest of statistics, The Stationery Office

Contains data on employment.

Regional trends, The Stationery Office. Annual
> This includes regional employment figures.

Employment trends, Manpower PLC
> **www.manpower.co.uk**
> A free quarterly survey looking at employment prospects. To contact Manpower, tel: 020 7224 6688 or fax: 020 7224 5267.

Graduate market trends, Daniel Johnson
> **www.prospects.ac.uk**
> A free statistical publication. To contact tel: 0161 277 5200 Fax: 0161 277 5210.

Employment rights and issues

There are a huge number of issues surrounding employment, requiring the latest information. It is best to stick to reliable sources that are updated regularly. One such resource is the excellent government website called Tiger (Tailored Interactive Guidance on Employment Rights) **www.tiger.gov.uk**. This provides user-friendly guidance through employment law, rights and issues.

National Minimum Wage concerns and issues are covered by the DTI's National Minimum Wage website **www.dti.gov.uk/er/nmw**.

The Working Time Regulations are covered at **www.dti.gov.uk**.

Websites and organizations

Advisory, Conciliation and Arbitration Service (ACAS)
> Head Office, Brandon House, 180 Borough High St, London SE1 1LW
> Tel: 020 7210 3613 Fax: 020 72103708
> **www.acas.org.uk**

Department of Education and Skills **www.dfes.gov.uk**

DTI Employment Relations **www.dti.gov.uk/employment/index**

Department of Work and Pensions **www.dwp.gov.uk**

Employment Service **www.employmentservice.gov.uk**

Institute of Employment Rights
> 177 Abbeville Rd, London SW4 9RL
> Tel: 020 7498 6919
> **www.ier.org.uk**

Manpower **www.manpower.co.uk**
> *Quarterly employment survey* available, great for links

People Management OnLine, Chartered Institute of Personnel and Development
> **www.peoplemanagement.co.uk**
> This gives in-depth analysis of key issues for employers.

TUC **www.tuc.org.uk**
> Excellent site for research publications.

Women's Unit **www.womens-unit.gov.uk**

ENERGY

See also Utilities

Typical questions

- Do you have a contact for wind power?
- What is renewable energy?
- How much oil is produced worldwide?

Considerations

Interest in traditional energy, coal (electricity), gas and oil, has waned over the years. Enquiries are limited to contact details of energy suppliers. *See* Utilities. However, there has been a surge of interest in alternative energy as its potential and realistic use becomes more apparent. That is not to say that interest in fossil fuels has completely disappeared; this is especially untrue in the international arena.

Where to look

Directories

FT Business global coal directory, FT Business
> This directory provides details of 300 major coal producers, 300 major coal consumers and over 600 specialist coal service companies and equipment suppliers. In addition it has a who's who of the international coal industry.

International guide to the coalfields, Tradelink Publications
> **www.tradelinkpub.co.uk**

FT Business global oil and gas directory, FT Business
> This directory provides details of over 350 oil and gas producers and 700

specialist oil and gas service companies and equipment suppliers. In addition it has a who's who of the international oil and gas industry.

Offshore oil and gas directory, United Business Media
www.mfinfo.com
This directory provides information on 7000 suppliers and services within the industry. It is also available on CD-ROM.

FT Business global power directory, FT Business
This directory provides details of 300 global power distributors and 900 suppliers of equipment and services to the power industry. In addition it has a who's who of the international power industry.

World directory of renewable energy suppliers and services, James & James
This is an annual guide to the renewable energy industry and is probably the most comprehensive.

Statistics

Digest of United Kingdom energy statistics, DTI
www.dti.gov.uk/EPA/et.htm

UK energy in brief, DTI
www.dti.gov.uk/EPA/eib/index.htm
Available free.

For international energy statistics use:

Energy trends and quarterly energy prices, DTI
www.dti.gov.uk/energy

Annual energy review, European Commission
This looks at the current energy situations worldwide. A detailed analysis of all the world regions is presented, accompanied by tables and graphs to illustrate changes. It includes a CD-ROM with global energy balances and indicators for 135 countries.

Energy statistics yearbook, United Nations
This is now slightly dated but the *Monthly Bulletin of Statistics*, United Nations Statistics Division, New York, USA, provides current data.

Journals

There are numerous journals for the energy industry, details of which can be found in *Willings press guide* (*see* Journals & Periodicals).

Websites

AGORES (A Global Overview of Renewable Energy Sources) **www.agores.org**
> This is an excellent site which includes the DTI and EU institutions. It has publications, policy papers, EU reports and guides, contacts and links.

Fuel Cell Today **www.fuelcelltoday.com**
> Fuel cells, which generate electricity by combining hydrogen and oxygen, are poised to become the leading energy source of the 21st century. This is a global internet portal for companies and individuals.

Centre for Alternative Technology **www.cat.org.uk**

Coal International **www.coalinternational.co.uk**

Department of Trade and Industry (DTI) **www.dti.gov.uk/energy**
> Provides lots of free downloadable information and statistics.

Institute of Petroleum **www.petroleum.co.uk**
> This provides a list of leading oil companies.

ENGINEERING

Typical questions

- Can you tell me the manufacturer of ...?
- Can you give me the contact details of ...?
- Who makes ...?

Considerations

Often users confuse company names with trade names. In most cases it is best to check under both company and trade.

Where to look

For general information on engineering terms, definitions and fundamentals try:

Kempe's engineers yearbook, Miller Freeman Information Services
> Now in its 105th year of publication, this reference work is the authority on a whole range of engineering disciplines. It has excellent chapters on materials, manufacturing, electrical engineering, environmental engineering, energy and railway engineering. It has a detailed index.

Try also:

McGraw-Hill dictionary of engineering, McGraw-Hill.

Keller, H. and Uwe, E. (1994) *Dictionary of engineering acronyms and abbreviations*, 2nd edn, Neal-Schuman Publishers

Vernon, J. (1992) *Introduction to engineering materials*, 3rd edn, Macmillan

Dorf, R.C. (ed.) (1996) *Engineering handbook*, IEEE

Tapley, B. D. (ed.) (1990) *Eshbach's handbook of engineering fundamentals*, 4th edn, Wiley

Hicks, T. G. (1995) *Standard handbook of engineering calculation*, 3rd edn, McGraw-Hill

Directories

Engineering industry buyers guide, United Business Media Information Services
www.mfinfo.co.uk
> An excellent directory providing an alphabetical listing of companies, products and services, and brand and trade names. Most useful is the list of overseas manufacturers and their UK agents.

DIAL engineering, Reed Business Information
> Another highly recommended directory offering similar information to the above. This provides sections on companies, products and services, and trade names.

Journals

There are numerous journals for the engineering industry, details of which can be found in *Willings press guide* (*see* Journals & Periodicals). The following are probably two of the most useful:

Engineer
> Centaur Publishing
> Tel: 020 7970 4000 Fax: 020 7970 4189
> **www.e4engineering.com**

Weekly
News, comment and analysis on the engineering industry.

Abstracts in New Technologies and Engineering (ANTE)
Bowker
Tel: 01342 326972 Fax: 01342 336198
www.ANTEnet.co.uk
Provides abstracts from 350 UK and US publications – technical and trade periodicals, professional journals, magazines and selected newspapers that include engineering. It is available in print, CD-ROM and via the internet.

Market research

Key Note reports, Key Note
For free executive summaries of report titles listed under engineering and heavy industries visit **www.keynote.co.uk**. For details of obtaining full reports, contact Key Note (tel: 020 8481 8750, fax: 020 8733 0049).

Mintel industrial reports, Mintel International Group
For details visit **www.mintel.co.uk** or tel: 020 7606 4533, fax: 020 7606 5932.

Statistics

Economic trends, Office for National Statistics
A monthly publication that includes engineering and construction: output and orders.

PRODCOM quarterly industry reports, Office for National Statistics
Excellent source of UK manufacturer sales, imports and exports statistics. Available to download free of charge from **www.statistics.gov.uk/ OnlineProducts/default.asp**

Organizations and websites

Engineering Council
10 Maltravers St, London WC2R 3ER
Tel: 020 7240 7891 Fax: 020 7240 7517
www.engc.org.uk
This has an excellent website, with both priced and free publications.

131

Engineering Employers' Federation **www.eef.org.uk**
> The voice of engineering and manufacturing in the UK. Excellent for publications.

There are numerous professional bodies and organizations covering all aspects of the engineering industry. For details use the *Directory of British associations*, CBD Research Publications.

Tips and pitfalls

Engineering is the generic term for a whole host of industries involving mechanics, robotics, electronics and electricals. Ask as many questions as you can about products to try to ascertain their use and consequently work out which bit of engineering you are dealing with. Don't be afraid to check terms in an engineering dictionary.

ENVIRONMENT & GREEN ISSUES

See also Geography

Typical questions
- What is the government's environmental policy?
- Can you give me the address of some environment groups?

Considerations

When people talk about the environment they can mean a whole variety of things from the urban environment in which they live, to recycling. It is important to ascertain what the enquirer really is referring to. In this section the term environment is used to refer mainly to environmental concerns such as pollution control and quality of air, materials reclamation and recycling, ecological sustainability and energy saving, to name but a few. Many queries such as times of opening of local dumps can be answered by contacting the relevant department of your local authority. It is good practice to keep contact details and to keep them up to date.

Where to look
Directories
Environment industry yearbook, Waterlow Specialist Information Publishing

A comprehensive directory giving details of UK companies involved in the waste, water and environment industry. Includes an extensive buyers' guide covering ten primary industry areas, which is cross-referenced to the A–Z company listing.

There is a section on waste management in the *Municipal yearbook*; see Government.

World directory of environmental organizations (2001), 6th edn, International
Center for the Environment and Public Policy of the California Institute
of Public Affairs, the Sierra Club and World Conservation Union
This is a comprehensive guide to world environmental groups, projects and
issues. It includes a glossary.

Air quality guidelines for Europe, World Health Organization
These guidelines provide background information and guidance to
international, national and local authorities on a number of air pollutants.

Environmental protection yearbook, Earthscan Publications
This is a directory of pollution control equipment manufacturers, suppliers
and consultants. It includes a directory of UK organizations.

Environmental regulation and your business, Stationery Office
Looks at current legislation and regulation for the small to medium-sized
company.

Materials recycling handbook, EMAP Business Communications
This covers waste management and all aspects of recycling and
reclamation. In addition it provides a list of local authority contacts, trade
names and suppliers of specialist services.

Reduce, reuse, recycle and your business, The Stationery Office

Journals
There are numerous journals covering the environment and green issues, details
of which can be found in *Willings press guide* (see Journals & Periodicals).

Materials Recycling Weekly
EMAP McClaren
Tel: 020 8277 5540 Fax: 020 8277 5560
Weekly
Covers reclamation and recycling.

Waste Management Briefing
> Croner CCH Group
> Tel: 020 8247 3333 Fax: 020 8547 2637
> **www.croner.cch.co.uk**
> Monthly
> Covers all aspects of waste management.

Wastes Management
> IWM Business Services
> Tel: 01604 620426 Fax: 01604 604467
> **www.iwm.co.uk**
> Monthly

Market research

Key Note reports, Key Note
> For free executive summaries of report titles under Environment visit **www.keynote.co.uk**. For details of obtaining full reports, contact Key Note (tel: 020 8481 8750, fax: 020 8783 0049).

Statistics

Digest of environmental statistics, Department for Environment, Food and Rural Affairs
> Available also via **www.defra.gov.uk**.

The Environment in your pocket, DEFRA
> The latest is freely available either to download from the website or from DEFRA.

Organizations and websites

Aluminium Can Recycling Association **www.alucan.org.uk**

BBC **www.bbc.co.uk/nature/**

Department for Environment, Food and Rural Affairs **www.defra.gov.uk**
> Excellent for statistics and surveys.

Ends Environmental Consultancy Directory **www.ends.co.uk/consultants**

English Nature **www.english-nature.org.uk**
> Excellent site for research publications, maps, science and technology

papers, and a list of special nature sites.

Environment: the network for the environmental professionals
http://environment.go.net/
An excellent portal to data on the internet, research papers, articles and references.

ARKive **www.arkive.org.uk**
An initiative of The Wildscreen Trust, ARKive will be the world's electronic archive of photographs, moving images and sounds of endangered species and habitats.

Envirolink **www.envirolink.org**
A huge site including animal rights and reference information.

Friends of the Earth **www.foe.co.uk**
Subjects include food, pollution, green power, protection of wildlife and FOE campaign news.

Nature Net **www.naturenet.net**
Covers law, nature reserves, voluntary work and news.

Wild Life Trust **wildlifetrust.org.uk**

World Wide Fund For Nature **www.panda.org**

Environment Council
212 High Holborn, London WC1V 7BF
Tel: 020 7836 2626
www.the-environment-council.org.uk

European Environment Agency **www.eea.eu.int**

Envirowise: Practical Environmental Advice for Business
www.envirowise.gov.uk
An excellent site packed with information and free publications to download.

Green Party for England and Wales
1a Waterlow Rd, London N19 5NJ
Tel: 020 7272 4474
www.greenparty.org.uk

Greenpeace

Canonbury Villas, London N1 2PN
Tel: 020 7865 8100
www.greenpeace.org.uk

Industry Council for Packaging and the Environment **www.incpen.org**

Natural Environment Research Council (NERC) **www.nerc.ac.uk**

EQUAL OPPORTUNITIES

See also Employment – Law; Employment – Rights

Typical questions
- Can you provide an equal opportunities policy?
- What is meant by equal pay?

Considerations
There is a mass of information on the subject of equal opportunities. How much you want to offer the enquirer will depend on the level of the enquiry and the accessible resources that you have. Hopefully, some of the resources below will provide good free information. Some of the general resources mentioned in Employment will also cover equal opportunities. In addition, some of the newspaper indexes will be useful for articles.

Where to look
Bourne, C. (2000) *The Discrimination Acts explained*, The Stationery Office
    Excellent publication that covers the Sex Discrimination Act, Race Relations Act and Disability Discrimination Act.

Organizations
Commission for Racial Equality
    Elliot House, 10–12 Allington St
    London SW1E 5EH
    Tel: 020 7828 7022 Fax: 020 7630 7605
    www.cre.gov.uk
    This is an excellent site for news and information. It provide free publications, some of which can be downloaded from the internet.

Cabinet Office **www.cabinet-office.gov.uk**

Provides equal opportunity publications.

Disability Rights Commission
Freepost MID 02164, Stratford upon Avon, Warwickshire CV37 9BR
www.drc-gb.org/drc/

Equal Opportunities Commission (Great Britain)
Arndale House, Arndale Centre, Manchester M4 3EQ
Tel: 0161 833 9244 Fax: 0161 835 1657
www.eoc.org.uk
Excellent for publications on equal pay and the labour market.

Equal Opportunities Commission (Scotland)
St Stephens House, 79 Bath St, Glasgow G2 4JL
Tel: 0141 248 5833

Equal Opportunities Commission (Wales)
Windsor House, Windsor Lane, Cardiff CF10 3GE
Tel: 029 2034 3552

Home Office **www.homeoffice.gov.uk**

Race Relations Employment Advisory Service (RREAS)
4th Floor, 2 Duchess Place, Hagley Rd, Birmingham B16 8NS
Tel: 0121 452 5447/8/9 Fax: 0121 452 5485
E-mail: hq.rreas@dfes.gsi.gov.uk
This will provide free strategic advice on policies and practices for racial
equality in the workforce.

Women's Unit **www.womens-unit.gov.uk**

ETIQUETTE & FORMS OF ADDRESS

Typical questions

- How do I address a letter to a bishop?
- How should I greet and introduce a baroness?
- When should I use 'Yours faithfully' and when 'Yours sincerely'?
- What are the duties of a bridesmaid?

E ETIQUETTE & FORMS OF ADDRESS

Considerations

Etiquette refers to the customs or rules governing social behaviour regarded as correct: standard or conventional behaviour. While some people can get over-obsessed with correct form, it is important to be aware of the standard practice.

Where to look

General

Axtell, R. E. (ed.) (1993) *Do's and taboos around the world*, 3rd edn, J.Wiley

Bremner, M. (1992) *Enquire within upon modern etiquette and successful behaviour for today*, Hutchinson
Includes work situations.

Morgan, J. (1999) *Debrett's new guide to etiquette and modern manners*, Headline
The 'indispensable' handbook.

Forms of Address

Titles and forms of address: a guide to their correct use (1997), 20th edn, A & C Black
Covers formal invitations and addressing letters, listings of ranks, honours and official appointments, as well as the correct way of addressing people in both speech and correspondence.

Debrett's people of today, Debrett's Peerage Ltd. Annual
Although used particularly for personal details of famous people, each entry usefully concludes with the person's preferred style of address.

Montague-Smith, P. (1999) *Debrett's correct form*, 4th edn, Headline
Over 400 pages.

Letters

Kurth, R. (1999) *Debrett's guide to correspondence*, Debrett's Peerage Ltd
Covers stationery, forms of address, particular types of letter, and style.

Webster, J. (1988) *Forms of address for correspondence and conversation*, Ward Lock

Meetings

McKenzie, C. (1994) *Debrett's guide to speaking in public*, Headline

Walker, G. (1987) *Points of order for those in public life*, 4th edn, Shaw & Sons
> A pocket guide to public speaking, conducting meetings and etiquette in simple language.

Shackleton, F. (1997) *Shackleton on the law and practice of meetings*, Sweet & Maxwell
> The standard heavyweight on points of order, etc.

The season

Noel, C. (2000) *Debrett's guide to the season*, Debrett's Peerage Ltd
> Covers the main social events from Ascot and Cowes Week to Glyndebourne and Wimbledon.

Weddings

Llewellyn, J. (1997) *Debrett's wedding guide*, Headline

Funerals

Whitman, G. (1991) *The funeral guide and information book*, The Author
Baun, R. R. (ed.) (1999) *Funeral and memorial service readings, poems and tributes*, McFarland
> A useful anthology for those difficult occasions.

Websites

www.everyrule.com/etiquette.html
www.net-weddings.co.uk/Etiquette/etiquettemenu.html
www.etiquette-network.com

EUROPEAN INFORMATION

See also Companies – International

Typical questions

• What is the Single European Market?
• How do I find out about European legislation?

Considerations

There are huge amounts of information produced about Europe and from Europe.

Keeping up to date is the difficulty most library workers have. It is probably best to get familiar with a few good sources rather than to try to know them all. The internet offers an excellent tool for providing and finding European information. The websites given below should cover most enquiries.

Where to look

Directories

The European companion, The Stationery Office
   Provides biographies of the leading individuals in the European institutions.

Guide to EU information sources on the internet, Euroconfidential
   This is a one-stop source for finding EU information on the internet. All the sites listed have been checked and indexed.

Directory of EU information sources, Red Book, Euroconfidential, The Stationery Office
   The Red Book contains information on all EU institutions and lists key personnel, databases, publications, information networks and libraries specific to each institution. This is an excellent sourcebook for all European information.

Directory of Community legislation in force 01/12/2000, 2 vols, The Stationery Office
   Legislation is arranged by subject in Volume 1, while in Volume 2 there are chronological and alphabetical indexes of the acts.

Free on the EU: a guide to free sources of information about and from the European Union, European Information Association
   An excellent tool for tracking down free literature on all aspects of Europe.

Who's who in the EU?, Office for Official Publications of the European Communties, Euroconfidential, The Stationery Office
   This is a guide to the organizations and institutions of the EU.

Europe in the round CD-ROM, Vocational Technologies Ltd
   Tel: 01252 337055 Fax: 01252 336511
   This is an excellent product covering the European Union – the 15 member states plus Iceland, Norway and Switzerland – and giving information on 39 further countries. It includes statistics, maps, photographs and text

divided into sections entitled 'People and society', 'Geography and travel', 'Business and work' and 'Study and research'.

Statistics

Eurostat, the Statistical Office of the European Communities, produces statistics for the EU members. All the statistics are published by EUR-OP, which is the official publisher of the EU. For details of what's new see *EUR-OP News*. In addition, Eurostat statistics are made available through the Resource Centre for Access to Data on Europe (rcade) **www-rcade.dur.ac.uk**.

One of the main publications is:

Eurostat yearbook 2000, Statistical Office of the European Communities
Contains data for the period 1988–1998. An excellent publication for statistics on people, land and environment, national income and expenditure, enterprises and activities in Europe and the European Union.

Also published:

Europe in figures and *A social portrait of Europe*

Journals

Official Journal
If your library does not subscribe to the hard copy, you can access it via **www.eur-op.eu.int/general/en/**

Eur Op News **www.eur-op.eu.int**

Organizations

European Information Centres (EICs)

These provide information on European issues and provide help to small and medium-sized businesses. They also provide a number of networking services. These include TED (Tenders Electronic Daily) – a database of public sector contracts throughout Europe which are open to tender.

European Documentation Centres (EDCs)

These are situated in university libraries. Most hold one copy of all official publications of the European Communities. It is possible to contact your nearest EDC to clarify or assist with an enquiry or to arrange for an enquirer to use the resources for reference only.

European Public Information Centres (EPICs)

These are based in public libraries. They provide a large amount of free literature from the EU to help explain many of the differences and benefits that membership of the EU has made to the lives of people.

To find the nearest one of any of the above contact the European Commission Representation in the UK (tel: 020 7973 1992 or visit **www.cec.org.uk**).

Websites

Community Research and Development Information Service (CORDIS)
www.cordis.lu

Dialogue with Citizens and Business **www.citizens.eu.int**

DTI in Europe **www.dti.gov.uk/europe**

EC Information Society Promotion Office **www.ispo.cec.be**

Europages: the European Business Directory **www.europages.com**

European Central Bank **www.ecb.int**

European Commission Representation in the UK **www.cec.org.uk**

European Industrial Relations Observatory On-Line **www.eiro.eurofound.ie**

European Information Association **www.eia.org.uk**

European Information Network in the UK **www.europe.org.uk**

European Investment Bank **www.eib.org**

EUR-OP – the EU's publication office **www.eur-op.eu.int**

European Parliament **www.europarl.eu.int**

European Parliament UK Office **www.europarl.org.uk**

Europa **www.europa.eu.int**
An excellent starting point for basic information on the EU with links to other sites. It also has access to legal texts, publications, databases, statistics and EU grants and loans. In addition, there is a link to EUR-Lex, for EU legal texts.

*Know*Europe **www.knoweurope.net**

> *Know*Europe is a web service which provides information about the institutions, structures, countries, regions, peoples, policies and processes of the European Union and the wider Europe. For subscription information, contact Proquest Marketing Department on 01223 271225, e-mail: knoweurope@proquest.co.uk or visit www.proquest.co.uk

Tips and pitfalls

Make a point of finding out which European information units are in your area or region. Then make sure you make contact to ascertain what sources of information they have and can offer. It would be sensible to have a contact list for your library and to be sure of their referral procedure.

EVENTS *see* DATES, EVENTS, CHRONOLOGIES & CALENDARS

EXAMINATIONS

Typical questions
- Have you got the syllabus for GCSE maths?
- Have you get copies of past exam papers?
- Which local schools take the EdExcel syllabuses?

Considerations

Checking on course syllabuses and wanting to consult past examination papers are two frequent subjects of enquiry. Students, parents and teachers are the likely enquirers. Since there are many different examining boards, many different levels of examinations, often several alternative syllabuses, and schools and colleges can change the examination authorities from year to year, the librarian must tread carefully. As always, try to clarify the enquiry as much as possible. Which examination board? What year? Which syllabus, exactly? And as is often the case, critical details will be missing. You can then suggest that the enquirer needs to get more information. Often it will be appropriate that the enquirer, particularly if the enquiry relates to school examinations, should check with his or her school. (Schools will usually stock copies of both syllabuses and past papers.)

E EXAMINATIONS

Examination boards sell copies of past papers. Some libraries will stock the syllabuses of the examination boards that are in use locally, and some, probably fewer, may stock copies of past papers. Check to see what your local practice is.

Most colleges and universities set their own examinations. The same goes for professional bodies; contact these directly for latest information.

Where to look

Education authorities directory and yearbook, The School Government
Publication Co.
This has a section on examination organizations.

Also:

Education year book, Prentice Hall.

Other sources

AQA (The Assessment and Qualification Alliance)
Aldon House, 39 Heald Grove, Rusholme, Manchester, M14 4NA
www.aqa.org.uk
AQA was formed from the amalgamation of the Associated Examining Board and the Northern Examination Assessment Board.

Edexcel
Stewart House, 32 Russell Square, London WC1B 5DN
Tel: 020 7758 5661 Fax: 020 7758 5959
www.edexcel.org.uk

Joint Examining Board
30a Dyer St, Cirencester, Gloucestershire GL7 2PH
Tel: 01285 641747 Fax: 01285 650449
www.jeb.co.uk

OCR (Oxford, Cambridge and RSA Examinations)
1 Regent St, Cambridge CB2 1GG
Tel: 01223 552552 Fax: 01223 552553
www.ocr.org.uk

Scottish Qualification Authority
Ironmills Rd, Dalkeith, Midlothian EH22 1LE
Tel: 0131 663 Fax: 0131 654 2664

www.sqa.org.uk

City and Guilds of London Institute
1 Giltspur St, London EC1A 9DD
Tel: 020 7294 2468 Fax: 020 7294 2400
www.city-and-guilds.co.uk

Northern Ireland Council for the Curriculum, Examinations and Assessment
(CCEA)
29 Clarendon Road, Belfast BT1 3BG
Tel: 028 9026 1200 Fax: 028 9026 1234
www.ccea.org.uk

Tips and pitfalls

The organization of examinations and examination organizations is changing rapidly. Don't assume that what is true one year will be so the next, or that the parent knows best. Check the datedness of your sources, then check (or get the enquirer to check) with the organization setting the examinations.

EXHIBITIONS *see* CONFERENCES & EXHIBITIONS

EXPORTS & IMPORTS

Typical questions

- Can you give me a list of companies who export ... to France?
- How do I import from India?
- What percentage of ... does the UK (or another country) export?

Considerations

Firstly, let's clarify the terms exports and imports. Goods or services that are produced in one country and then sold or traded to another are known as exports. Goods or services that are brought into a country are known as imports. Enquiries relating to exports or imports are on the whole quite specialized and for many it is probably best to offer contacts to organizations that can provide specialist advice. Your local Chambers of Commerce will offer help and advice and the Department of Trade and Industry **www.dti.gov.uk** produces information on trading with numerous countries. The British Standards Institution has a very useful section on its website **www.bsi-global.com** called 'Satisfying technical requirements of world markets', which is of value to anyone thinking of exporting.

Where to look
Directories

Export handbook, Kogan Page
www.kogan-page.co.uk

H.M. Customs and Excise tariffs, The Stationery Office
Volume 1 provides general information. Volume 2 covers the schedule of duty and trade statistical descriptions, codes and rates. Volume 3 covers customs freight procedures.

Kompass British exports, Reed Business Information
Provides details of 17,000 UK companies and the products and services they export. The alphabetical products list is provided in French, German and Spanish. The printed version is available free, tel: 01342 335876.

Also available are:

British exports interactive **www.britishexports.com**
This allows access to 90,000 UK companies and can be searched in five languages – English, French, German, Spanish and Italian.

Directory of UK importers, 2 vols, Newman Books

International directory of importers, 9 vols, Coble International
This directory can either be purchased as a nine-volume set or by individual regions. The full directory would provide details of 152,000 international importers. It is also available on CD-ROM. For more, take a look at **www.importexporthelp.com**.

Croner's reference book for exporters, Croner CCH Group. Monthly
A loose-leaf reference service with monthly updates, covering the documentary and official requirements affecting the export of goods to overseas countries.

Croner's reference book for importers, Croner CCH Group. Monthly
A loose-leaf reference service with monthly updates, covering the documentary and official requirements affecting the importation of goods.

Journals

Croner's Export Digest
 Croner CCH Group
 Tel: 020 8547 3333 Fax: 020 8547 2637
 Monthly

Export Times
 Nexus Media
 Tel: 01322 660070 Fax: 01322 667633
 Ten issues per year

Importing Today
 Hemming Group
 Tel: 020 7973 6404 Fax: 020 7233 5053
 Six issues per year

International Trade Today
 Hemming Group
 Tel: 020 7973 6404 Fax: 020 7233 5053
 Ten issues per year
 Concentrates on opportunities for importers and exporters.

Statistics

International trade statistics, World Trade Organization
 These statistics are available in English, French and Spanish, in hard copy,
 CD-ROM or on the World Trade Organization website **www.wto.org**.

Websites

British Chambers of Commerce **www.britishchambers.org.uk**
 This includes 'Find your chamber'. It is excellent for information,
 economic surveys, publications, events, exports, and news and policy.

HM Customs and Excise **www.hmce.gov.uk**

Official Trade Statistics **www.trade-statistics.com**
 Import/export statistics from HM Customs and Excise

Trade Partners UK **www.tradepartners.gov.uk**
 A government network dedicated to helping British businesses build
 success overseas. It includes country and sector information.

▉E EXPORTS & IMPORTS

World Trade Organization **www.wto.org**

Excellent site for publications on world trade policy and statistics, including the *International trade statistics*, which are available free to download.

FAIRY TALES

Typical questions
- Can you help me find a few Irish fairy tales?
- Who wrote *Hansel and Gretel*?

Considerations
Most children's libraries should have a good selection of fairy tales. The main problem is finding out where an individual fairy tale might be located.

Where to look
Printed sources
The first step is to check the library catalogue to see whether or not the individual fairy tale is listed. If you cannot find it then check some of the fairy tale anthologies. They can be quite good for finding individual tales. If you are looking for foreign fairy tales, again try one of the anthologies, such as:

Ghose, S. N. and Ghose, S. N. (1996) *Folk tales and fairy stories from India*, Dover Publications

Afanasyev, A. N. (1976) *Russian fairy tales*, Random House Trade

There is quite a comprehensive index to fairy tales:
Eastman, M. H. (1926) *Index to fairy tales, myths and legends*, 2nd edn, Faxon This provides about 30,000 references in an alphabetical, as well as geographical, sequence.

Electronic sources
More and more fairy tale sites are springing up on the world wide web. One of the most useful is the:

Fairy Tales Theme Page **www.cln.org/themes/fairytales.htm**
This 'gateway' site lists many useful links for students and teachers.

Tips and pitfalls
Check with the enquirer whether they want the original fairy tale or whether an abridged version will do. Childrens' libraries contain many picture books and anthologies with abridged versions of these tales.

It might be useful to keep a checklist of some of the more popular fairy tales and to keep a note of which anthologies they can be found in.

FAMILY HISTORY & GENEALOGY

See also History & Archaeology; Local History; Parish Registers

Typical questions

- How can I trace my family tree?
- Have you got the IGI? Mormon index? St Catherine's House index?
- Where can I see old wills?

Considerations

The ever-popular activity of tracing one's ancestors produces a great deal of work for librarians, particularly those in general libraries. Many enquiries come from people who know very little about the complexities and hard work involved in tracing ancestors. In this case the role of the librarian is to indicate that the task is complex, that it will involve a lot of research, and that the first step is to 'read up' about the subject. Referral to the lending shelves is a sensible response. Other enquirers may be quite experienced in the subject and here the requests will be for specific library materials. Unless staff have experience or training in the subject it is best to refer the enquirer to the local studies or archive staff.

Staff have to beware three dangers. The first is of getting involved too deeply in the enquiry. Before help can be given, staff will need to know how far the enquirer has progressed and what he or she knows. This can take time and carries the danger of getting carried along with the enquiry beyond the call of duty. Family history is research and staff need to 'disengage' at a fairly early stage. Secondly, other people's ancestors can be incredibly boring and 'family tree-ers' amazingly garrulous. Be careful not to yawn! Have those 'rescue' strategies in place! Thirdly, newcomers think it is easy and may not take kindly to what they may regard as your unhelpful bureaucratic response. The overseas visitor who flies in on Friday night, visits the library on a busy Saturday, and expects to have 'found their folks' by closing time, is all too familiar.

'Genealogy' refers to the records of descent and ancestry whereas the term 'family history' has a wider connotation, involving the social context of a family.

Do warn enquirers that tracing family history will almost certainly involve a lot of time, visits to many different libraries and record offices, and ... expense!

Where to look:
General printed sources

Currer-Briggs, N. and Gambier, R. (1991) *Debrett's family historian: a guide to tracing your ancestry*, Debrett/Webb & Bower

Davis, B. (2001) *Irish ancestry: a beginner's guide*, 3rd edn, FFHS

Fitzhugh T. V. H. (1998) *The dictionary of genealogy*, 5th edn, A & C Black
A standard reference work for family historians, providing information on archives, the legal system, religious practice, education, topography, migration, origins of surnames, etc.

Hey, D. (1996) *The Oxford companion to local and family history*, Oxford University Press
Over 2000 entries summarizing social, urban, agricultural, legal, family and ecclesiastical history.

Gibson, J. S. W. (1988) *General Register Office and international genealogical indexes: where to find them*, FFHS

Gibson, J. S.W. (1994) *Marriage, census and other indexes for family historians*, 5th edn, FFHS

Humphrey-Smith, C. R. (1995) *The Phillimore atlas and index of parish registers*, 2nd edn, Phillimore
Coloured county maps showing parochial and other boundaries.

Boyd's marriage index
This index sometimes gets asked for. It contains entries for marriages in many parts of the country from 1538 to 1837. The original is at the Society of Genealogists, but local sections may be available locally.

Massey, R. W. (1987) *A list of parishes in Boyd's marriage index*, 6th edn, Society of Genealogists

Genealogical services directory (2001), Genealogical Services Directory
Family and local history handbook.

Wagner, A. (1983) *English genealogy*, 3rd edn, Phillimore
The origins of English families from documentary sources.

Burgess and Electoral Rolls, Voters' Lists

These annual publications list the people who were eligible to vote in local elections from 1848 onwards, and in local and national elections from 1879 onwards. Rarely are they indexed by name and the enquirer will need to know an address since names are arranged alphabetically within wards (and polling districts) until 1883, thereafter in house order within street (or part of street) within each ward and polling district.

Gibson, J. S. W. (1990) *Electoral Registers since 1832, and Burgess Rolls*, 2nd edn, FFHS.

Census data

Started in 1801, and taken every tenth year (except 1941), the Census (from 1841) gives details of every person living at a specific address. The information is confidential for 100 years.

The information in Census returns is arranged by area and street, and not by name, though local history groups and others may have compiled indexes for their own localitites.

The Census returns for 1841–1901 for England and Wales are kept at the Family Records Centre, Myddleton Place, Myddleton St, London EC1R 1UW, though they are available on microfilm for purchase by local libraries and family history societies. The 1881 Census is available to purchase on CD-ROM from the Church of Jesus Christ of Latter Day Saints, UK Distribution Centre, 399 Garrett's Green Lane, Birmingham B33 0UH. Tel: 0121 784 9555.

The 1901 Census is available via the internet.

www.census.pro.gov.uk

Civil registration

Introduced in 1837, the details on the forms that were filled in when a birth, marriage or death was registered contain important legal information. These documents are of key importance. The records are kept in London, and, for local registration, in local registry offices. Access to these is through indexes. Some local libraries and record offices have these indexes on microform (the 'St Catherine's House indexes').

Price, V. J. (1993) *Register Offices of Births, Deaths and Marriages in Great Britain and Northern Ireland*, 2nd edn, Brewin

For information on registering births, marriages and deaths today, contact your local Registrar of Births, Deaths and Marriages (listed in the phone book).

Deeds

Deeds relate to property transactions. Generally located in local archive and record offices.

Directories

Local directories were published, as telephone directories are now, which list principal inhabitants, their occupations, and frequently their address. The nature of these will vary from place to place. Kelly's is a well-known publisher of directories. Refer enquirers to the local history libraries for more details. *See also* Local History.

International Genealogical Index (The 'IGI')

An index on microfiche compiled by the Church of Jesus Christ of Latter-Day Saints ('Mormons') which covers many baptisms and some marriages up to about the 1880s. Many of the entries are taken from published or microfilmed registers. Arranged by country, then by county, surname and Christian name. Most local studies libraries will have this index. *See also* Parish Registers. Also available online at **www.familysearch.org**.

Monumental inscriptions and cemeteries.

The information on gravestones can provide useful genealogical information. *See* Parish Registers for records of gravestones in churchyards. Many local history societies have compiled records and these may be in local history libraries. Likewise inscriptions on war memorials. Refer the enquirer to local archive and local studies libraries. Municipal and other cemeteries and crematoria will keep their own indexes to graves.

Newspapers

Local newspapers are valuable for family history. They are rarely indexed though local family history societies and libraries have often compiled indexes to, for example, obituaries and personal names.

Gibson, J. S. W. (1987) *Local newspapers 1750–1920, England and Wales: a select location list*, FFHS

British Library (1975) *Catalogue of the Newspaper Library*, 8 vols, British
Museum Publications
Also available on the British Library website **www.bl.uk**.

Wills

Before 1858 the proving of wills was an ecclesiastical responsibility. Wills proved
at the Prerogative Court of Canterbury are at the Family Records Centre. Most
wills proved in the Archbishopric of York are at the Borthwick Institute of Historical Research in York.

Camp, A. J. (1974) *Wills and their whereabouts*, Society of Genealogists
Gibson, J. S. W. (1994) *Probate jurisdictions: where to look for wills*, 4th edn,
FFHS
Gibson, J. S. W. (1974) *Wills and where to find them*, FFHS

From 1858 wills were proved at the appropriate District Probate Registry, or at
the Principal Probate Registry in London, which also received copies of all wills
proved locally. Annual Indexes to post-1858 wills for England and Wales are
published. Copies of wills and letters of administration (used when no will was
left) from 1858 are held by the Probate Department, Principal Registry of the Family Division, First Avenue House, 42–49 High Holborn, London WC1V 6NP.

Electronic sources

A useful text is:

Christian, P. (2001) *The genealogist's Internet*, Public Record Office

GENUKI (Genealogical Service of the UK and Ireland) **www.genuki.org.uk**
Over 10,000 pages of information.

Cyndis List **www.CyndisList.com**
Links to over 30,000 sites in categories.

Familia **www.familia.org.uk**

Genealogy Site Finder **www.familytreemaker.com/index.html**

Timothy Owston's Pages **http://freespace.virgin.net/owston.tj/index.htm**
How to research your family history.

Genealogy Gateway **www.gengateway.com**
Over 40,000 listings.

Register of Births, Marriages and Deaths **www.ons.gov.uk**

Family Search **www.familysearch.org**
    The online version of the IGI (International Genealogical Index).

Commonwealth War Graves Commission **www.cwgc.org.uk**
    Huge database of war graves.

Public Record Office **www.pro.gov.uk**
    National archives information and useful printable leaflets.

Royal Commission on Historical Manuscripts **www.hmc.gov.uk**
    Information on manuscripts and the National Register of Archives.

Federation of Family History Societies **www.ffhs.org.uk**

Other sources

Local archive departments and registry offices will be listed in local telephone directories.

Achievements of Canterbury
    79–82 Northgate, Canterbury, Kent CT1 1BA
    Tel: 01227 462618; Fax: 01227 765617
    www.achievements.co.uk
    Provides services for genealogists.

The journals *Family Tree Magazine* (monthly) and *Genealogist's Magazine* (quarterly) carry advertisements and news which give useful information.

Family Records Centre
    Myddleton Place, Myddleton St, Islington, London EC1R 1UW
    Tel: 020 8392 5300
    www.familyrecords.gov.uk/frc.htm

See also Public Record Office.

General Register Office
    Smedley Hydro, Trafalgar Rd, Southport, Merseyside R8 2HH
    www.statistics.gov.uk/nsbase/registration/general_register.asp
    Responsible for all the registers of births, marriages and deaths.

Federation of Family History Societies
    PO Box 2425, Coventry CV5 6YX

E-mail: info@ffhs.org.uk
www.ffhs.org.uk
The umbrella organization for over 220 family history societies worldwide with 180,000 members.

The Jewish Genealogical Society of Great Britain
PO Box 13288, London N3 3WD
www.jgsgb.org.uk

Society of Genealogists
14 Charterhouse Buildings, Goswell Rd, London EC1M 7BA
Tel: 020 7251 8799 Fax: 020 7250 1800
www.sog.org.uk

Tips and pitfalls

Refer interested people to the local family history society. Here they will get informed assitance from like-minded enthusiasts and, possibly, resources not available in libraries.

FARMING

Typical questions

* How many farms are there in the UK?
* What is the present agricultural policy?
* What does diversified farming mean?

Where to look

For general terms and definitions try:

Dictionary of agriculture, 2nd edn, Peter Collin Publishing
This covers British and American terms relating to agriculture, horticulture and veterinary science.

Journals

There are numerous journals covering agriculture and farming, details of which can be found in *Willings press guide*. See Journals & Periodicals.

Farmers Weekly
Reed Business Information
Tel: 01342 326972 Fax: 01342 335612
www.fwi.co.uk
Weekly
Contains news, advice and research.

Market research

Key Note reports, Key Note
For free executive summaries of report titles listed under agriculture visit
www.keynote.co.uk. For details of obtaining full reports, contact Key Note
(tel: 020 8481 8750, fax: 020 8783 0049).

Statistics

Agriculture in the UK, 1999, Department for Environment, Food and Rural
Affairs, The Stationery Office
(or available to download at **www.defra.gov.uk**)

Farms Incomes in the UK, 1999/2000, Department for Environment, Food and
Rural Affairs, The Stationery Office
(or available to download at **www.defra.gov.uk**)

Many of the statistics mentioned under Food & Drink will be suitable to use.

Organizations and websites

British Agricultural and Garden Machinery Association **www.bagma.com**

Compassion in World Farming Trust
Charles House, 5A Charles St, Petersfield GU32 3EH
Tel: 01730 264208
www.ciwf.co.uk

Department for Environment, Food and Rural Affairs **www.defra.gov.uk**

Farming On-Line **www.farmline.com**
Lots of links.

Food and Agriculture Organization of the United Nations **www.fao.org/**

National Dairy Council **www.milk.co.uk**

National Farmers Union **www.nfu.org.uk**

Sustain – The Alliance for Better Food and Farming **www.sustainweb.org**

FASHION *see* COSTUME & FASHION

FESTIVALS *see* CUSTOMS, FESTIVALS & FOLKLORE

FILING *see* ALPHABETS & SCRIPTS

FILMS & CINEMA

See also Actors & Actresses; Awards & Prizes

Typical questions
- Who directed the film *Chocolat*?
- What year was *Chariots of fire* released?

Considerations
There are one or two 'standard' references which will be of use here. And there are some magnificent resources on the internet.

Where to look
Printed sources

Walker, J. (ed.) (2001) *Halliwell's film and video guide 2001*, HarperCollins. Annual
This is the best guide available. Over 17,000 films are included, arranged by title. Information includes year of release, country of origin, running time, synopses, principal cast lists, and credits for writer, director, producer, music, etc.

Gifford, D. (2001) *The British film catalogue*, 3rd edn, Fitzroy Dearborn
Volume 1 covers fiction film 1895–1994 and Volume 2 non-fiction film 1888–1994. A total of 28,158 films are covered.

British national film and video guide, British Library

Since 1977 this has listed all copyright films and videos cleared by the British Film Institute. Strong on non-commercial, educational films.

There is a useful guide to world cinema, which goes into more descriptive detail than Halliwell's:

Wilhelm, E. (1999) *VideoHound's world cinema*, Visible Ink Press

Journals

Screen International
    EMAP Business Communications Ltd.
    Weekly
    www.screendaily.com
    The main journal for industry news. This also includes reviews. They also produce an annual *Film and video directory* which is essential for those interested in the industry.

Sight and Sound Magazine
    British Film Institute
    Monthly
    www.bfi.org.uk/sightandsound/
    A useful source for current film reviews.

Electronic sources

If you do not have a printed source, the internet will come to your rescue. The excellent *Internet Movie Database* lists most films and includes more detailed information than Halliwell's guide. Simply type in the name of a film and hey presto! Cast lists, reviews, video availability, links. All your enquirer could want: **www.imdb.com**.

If you are interested in censorship or need to know the content of a film, try the excellent British Board of Film Classification website: **www.bbfc.co.uk**.

Tips and pitfalls

For most enquiries, it will be quicker to use the internet than search through printed guides.

FINANCE *see* ACCOUNTS, AUDITING & BOOKKEEPING

FIRMS *see* COMPANIES

FIRSTS *see* INVENTIONS & PATENTS

FLAGS

Typical questions
- What does the flag of Angola look like?
- I have seen a flag that is sky blue with a yellow cross. Do you know which country this belongs to?

Considerations
Looking for the flag of a particular country should not pose many problems. It is more difficult to find a flag from a vague description. This is where the internet can be quite helpful.

Where to look
Printed sources

Most encyclopedias will include pictures of international flags. There are also specialist flag books which will go into more detail about flags and give their histories. Try and make sure the book you use is current. New flags are appearing all the time.

Znamierowski, A. (1999) *World encyclopedia of flags*, Lorenz

Some of the older texts are still useful, even though some of the newer countries' flags will not be listed.

Barraclough, E. M. C. and Crompton, W. G. (1985) *Flags of the world*, Warne
   This book covers all international flags and their histories. There are also sections on the flags of international organizations and on yachts and merchant ships.

Talocci, M. (1989) *Guide to flags of the world*, Sidgwick and Jackson
   This is even more comprehensive and shows state arms and some county and provincial flags.

Electronic sources

Flags of the World **www.fotw.ca**

>   Contains every world flag with description and histories.

Flag Detective **www.flags.av.org/flags**

>   A great site. If you know what a flag looks like but do not know which
>   country it belongs to, you can search a database of different flag designs and
>   colours. You can select the pattern of the flag and then add the colours and
>   the site will tell you which country your flag belongs to.

FLOWERS *see* GARDENS & GARDENING, PLANTS

FOLKLORE *see* CUSTOMS, FESTIVALS & FOLKLORE

FOOD & DRINK

>   *See also* Beers & Brewing; Catering; Cookery; Farming

Typical questions

- Can you tell me a particular company's brands?
- Who manufactures …?
- I'm doing a college project on chocolate; I need to know what is the most
  popular selling chocolate confectionery.
- I need a list of food processors for … .

Considerations

The food and drink industry is vast. There are so many questions that could be
asked. You really need to clarify with the enquirer what it is they need. Food manufacturers, processors, suppliers, importers and exporters are all covered well in
the directories listed below. If you do not have specialized trade directories such
as the ones listed below, some of the more general directories such as *Kompass*,
Kelly's or *Key British enterprises* are excellent. *See* Companies for details. For statistics and market research Mintel or Keynote reports are excellent; both cover
a huge range of food products. For those not lucky enough to have such things,
try some of the websites mentioned below.

>   Supermarkets are now such a force in the food industry that the two terms have

become entwined. Students often have projects comparing two supermarkets or food retailers. The *Retail trade directory* will give you details, but do use other sources like those listed under Companies.

You may get asked about food issues, e.g. biotechnology, food safety and hygiene, and the consumer. Again some of the websites listed may be good starting points. There are a number of books that cover this area.

O'Rourke, R. (2001) *European food law*, Palladian Law Publishing
Sheridan, B. (2001) *EU biotechnology law and practice: regulating genetically modified and novel food products*, Palladian Law Publishing
O'Rourke, R. (2000) *Food safety and product liability*, Palladian Law Publishing

Further details from **www.palladianlaw.com**.

Where to look

Directories

Food trades directory of the UK and Europe, 2 vols, Hemming Information Services

Volume 1 contains details of over 9000 companies and organizations in the UK and is arranged by type of activity. Also provides sections on trade organizations, research institutes, consultants, education establishments and major food groups. There are also listings of food suppliers, i.e. manufacturers, processors, importers, exporters, agricultural producers and brokers. In addition, there is a guide to UK manufacturers of plant equipment and machinery, hygiene services and packaging materials. Also Continental agents located in the UK. Volume 2 covers details of over 6000 supplies of food products and ingredients in 29 countries of Continental Europe. Also lists details of 950 leading European companies involved in the manufacture and supply of food industry equipment and services.

Also check:

Food Trades Directory of the UK & Europe Online
www.foodtrades.co.uk

This allows limited results to non-subscribers but those subscribing to the hard copy can subscribe to the website for one year for an extra £30.

The Grocer directory of manufacturers and suppliers (2001), William Reed Publishing

This provides information on 8000 companies, 700 products and over

16,000 brand names. It covers primary producers, agents and brokers, export and import, wholesalers and distributors.

Retail directory of Europe, Hemming Information Services
Aims to provide details on all significant companies involved in retailing in Europe, some of which are from the food industry. Entries provide addresses, telephone numbers and in some cases the names of individual executives and buyers.

World food marketing directory, 2 vols, Euromonitor
Volume 1 profiles 6000 leading food companies in 60 countries. It includes a series of rankings by category, e.g. Europe: ranking of top food manufacturers. The profiles are detailed, including company brands and financial information. Volume 2 lists over 2000 sources of information on the food sector, including government, trade and online sources, and is international in scope.

For more specific food enquiries try:

Baking industry directory, British Baker
Fish industry yearbook, Oban Times
Frozen and chilled foods yearbook, DMG World Media
Who's who in the meat industry?, Yandall Publishing

Journals

Frozen and Chilled Foods
DMG World Media (UK) Ltd
Tel: 01737 768611 Fax: 01737 855470
Ten issues per year.

Grocer
William Reed Publishing
Tel: 01293 613400 Fax: 01293 610330
Weekly
Everything relating to the food industry.

Food and Drink International
Haychart
Tel: 01472 310302 Fax: 01472 310312
www.blmgroup.co.uk

Monthly

Current issues relating to the food and drink industry.

Food & Beverage Review
  Tel: 01302 738800 Fax: 01302 738811
  Six issues per year

Food & Drink News
  The Planet Group (UK) Ltd
  Tel: 01484 321000 Fax: 01484 321001
  www.planet-group.co.uk
  Monthly
  Providing up-to-date news and views on all aspects of the food and drink industry.

Food Industry News
  Beacon Publishing
  Tel: 01892 668172 Fax: 01892 603901
  Monthly
  News and information on the food and drink industry.

Food Manufacturer
  William Reed Publishing
  Tel: 01293 613400 Fax: 01293 610330
  Monthly

Statistics

The UK food and drink industry: a sector by sector economic and statistical analysis (1996), Euro PA & Associates
  Provides a view of the industry within an economic context. Chapters cover food consumption, economics of competition in food processing, cereals and oilseeds products, sugar and sweeteners, potatoes, potato products and savoury snacks, milk and dairy products, meat industry, fruit and vegetable industry, further-processed and branded products and alcoholic drinks, the future of the food and drink industry.

Food and drink statistics: a sector by sector guide to agriculture, fisheries, food and drink statistics in the UK (1998), Euro PA and Associates
  This supplements the 1996 publication.

PRODCOM annual industry reports, Office for National Statistics
> Excellent source of manufacturer sales, imports and exports statistics. Available to download free of charge from:
> **www.statistics.gov.uk/OnlineProducts/PRODCOM2000_annual.asp**

1998 National Food Survey (1999), commissioned by the Department for Environment, Food and Rural Affairs, carried out by Social Survey Division, The Stationery Office
> The latest quarterly and annual NFS statistics and a range of other statistics can be found under the heading 'Economics and statistics' at Department for Environment, Food and Rural Affairs **www.defra.gov.uk**. This is extensive in coverage and well worth a visit.

Food and drink industry UK statistics (1999), Food and Drink Federation
www.fdf.org.uk

Food and Agriculture Organization of the United Nations **www.fao.org**
> This has FAOSTAT, which is an online and multilingual database covering international statistics on food and food production, food aid, agriculture and land use and population.

Also look at:

State of food and agriculture, FAO's Annual Report.

Market research

Mintel reports, Mintel International Group
> For more details visit **www.mintel.co.uk** or tel: 020 7606 4533, fax: 020 7606 5932. These reports provide in-depth research into many different food and drink products. Also available on CD-ROM.

Key Note reports, Key Note
> For free executive summaries of report titles listed under Food & Catering and Drinks & Tobacco visit **www.keynote.co.uk**. For details of obtaining full reports, contact Key Note (tel: 020 8481 8750, fax: 020 8783 0049).

Websites

For food company and industry information:
British Egg Information Service **www.britegg.co.uk**

British Meat Education **www.meatmatters.com**

British Potato Council **www.potato.org.uk**

Canadean **www.canadean.com**
Good for industry news and links to drinks companies.

Dairy Council **www.milk.co.uk**

Egg Information Service **www.britegg.co.uk**

Federation of Bakers **www.bakersfederation.org.uk**
All about bread and the bread-making industry, both UK and European.

Flour Advisory Bureau **www.fabflour.co.uk**

Food and Drink Federation **www.fdf.org.uk**
Excellent for links.

Honey Association **www.honeybureau.org**

Just-Drinks **www.just-drinks.com**
Good for details on drinks companies and industry news.

Just-Food **www.just-food.com**
Good for details on food companies and industry news.

Meat and Livestock Commission **www.mlc.org.uk**

National Dairy Council **www.milk.co.uk**

Premierbrands **www.premierbrands.com**
Covers all the major sectors in the UK hot beverage market.

Salt Manufacturers Association **www.saltinfo.com**

Sea Fish Industry Authority **www.seafish.co.uk**

Tea Council **www.teacouncil.co.uk**
Provides an online directory of tea companies and services, statistics and news.

For food issues:
British Nutrition Foundation **www.nutrition.org.uk**

Co-operative Society **www.co-op.co.uk**
Reports on food crimes, food issues and setting up your own co-operative.

Food and Agriculture Organization of the United Nations **www.fao.org**

Packed with statistical information on agriculture, fisheries, forestry, nutrition, news, topical issues and the FAO's digital photo archive Mediabase. Excellent and well worth a visit.

Food Fitness **www.foodfitness.org.uk**

Foodfuture **www.foodfuture.org.uk**
Food biotechnology.

Foodlink **www.foodlink.org.uk**
For food safety and hygiene.

Food Standards Agency **www.foodstandards.gov.uk**

World Food Programme (United Nations) **www.wfp.org**

Tips and pitfalls
The food industry is littered with brand names, which should be kept in mind when checking for company details. Enquirers wanting to know more about particular food companies should check the internet for company sites. Many of the major food manufacturers/suppliers have excellent websites. If financial information is required Carol (Company Annual Reports On-Line) **www.carolworld.com** is well worth a visit.

FORMS OF ADDRESS *see* ETIQUETTE & FORMS OF ADDRESS

FREEDOM OF INFORMATION *see* RIGHTS

FRIENDLY SOCIETIES *see* BANKS & BANKING

FUNERALS *see* ETIQUETTE & FORMS OF ADDRESS

GALLERIES *see* MUSEUMS & GALLERIES

GAMES RULES (INCLUDING SPORTS)

Typical questions

- What are the dimensions of a standard crown bowling green?
- Have you got the rules for pool?

Where to look

Printed sources

Encyclopedias may provide an overview of some sports rules. If you need more detail, try some of the following:

Rules of the game (1990), revised edn, St Martins Press
    This 'essential' has the rules for over 150 sports. The coverage can be fairly limited, but it is certainly a good starting point.

For more in-depth coverage, try:
    Official rules of sports and games, Hamlyn

or even some of the official sports yearbooks, e.g. Lawn Tennis Association, Amateur Athletic Association.
    For card and board games, *The new complete Hoyle* (1991), Doubleday, is a good bet. This is the definitive source for the rules of all card and other indoor games.

Electronic sources

There is a great website covering card game rules at **www.pagat.com**.

Tips and pitfalls

The associations governing bodies of different sports all have websites nowadays. These sites can sometimes be useful for finding out rules.

GARDENS & GARDENING, PLANTS

Typical questions
- When are the gardens at Parham open?
- What's the best way to make compost?
- What is this flower?
- Where can I buy unusual plants?

Considerations
Details of famous or interesting gardens are one regular category of enquiry. Advice on how to do things is the other.

Where to look
General
Bagust, H. (1992) *The gardener's dictionary of horticultural terms*, Cassell

Hamilton, G. (1993) *The Gardener's World directory*, 2nd edn, BBC Books
A compendium of gardening information.

Jellicoe, G. et al. (1986) *The Oxford companion to gardens*, Oxford University Press

Royal Horticultural Society (1991) *Dictionary of gardening*, Macmillan
The four-volume 'biggie'.

Ettlinger. S. (1990) *The complete illustrated guide to everything sold in garden centres (except the plants)*, Macmillan
Mulches, nematodes, etc., etc.

Plants and flowers
Martin, W. K. (1965) *The new concise British flora*, M Joseph
The classic illustrated guide to UK flora.

Brickell, C. (ed.) (1999) *New encyclopedia of plants and flowers*, 3rd edn, Dorling Kindersley

Reader's Digest (1999) *New encyclopaedia of garden plants and flowers*, 2nd edn, Reader's Digest Associates
Two large-format encyclopedias. Photographs rather than Keble Martin's watercolour paintings.

Forey, P. (1997) *Wild flowers of the British Isles and Northern Europe*, Parkgate Books
Large-format illustrations.

Reader's Digest (1981) *Guide to trees and shrubs of Britain*, Reader's Digest Associates

Brookes, J. and Beckett, K. A. (1987) *The gardener's index of plants and flowers*, Dorling Kindersley
Plant information in tabular form.

Directories

Gardens of England and Wales open for charity, National Gardens Scheme. Annual
Gardens of quality and interest open to the public for charity. The 'Yellow Book'.

Hudson's historic houses and gardens: castles and heritage sites, Hudsons. Annual
Over 2000 properties.

Johansens historic houses, castles and gardens, Johansens

King, P. *The good garden guide*, Bloomsbury. Annual

National Trust, *The National Trust handbook*. Annual
Includes many gardens open to the public.

Buying guides

Consumers Association, *Gardening Which?*, Which? Publications. Ten per annum

Royal Horticultural Society, *RHS plant finder*, Dorling Kindersley. Bi-annual
A large listing of uncommon plants and the nurseries where they can be bought.

Other sources

Royal Botanic Gardens, Kew **www.rbgkew.org.uk**

Royal Horticultural Society
80 Vincent Square, London SW1P 2PE
www.rhs.org.uk

The National Trust **www.nationaltrust.org.uk**
More than 200 gardens and buildings of outstanding interest.

Museum of Garden History
Lambeth Palace Rd, London SE1 7LB
Tel: 020 7401 8865; Fax:020 7401 8860
E-mail: info@museumgardenhistory.org
www.museumgardenhistory.org

The Alpine Garden Society
AGS Centre, Avon Bank, Pershore, Worcestershire WR10 3JP
Tel: 01386 554790; Fax: 01386 554801
E-mail: ags@alpinegardensociety.org
www.alpinegardensociety.org

The Hardy Plant Society
Little Orchard, Great Comberton, Pershore, Worcestershire WR10 3DP
Tel: 01386 710317
www.hardyplant.org.uk

The Woodland Trust
Autumn Park, Dysart Rd, Grantham, Lincolnshire NG31 6LL
Freephone: 0800 026 9650
www.woodland-trust.org.uk
Established in 1972. Has created or saved over one thousand woods, planted over three million trees, and is the largest charity devoted to woodland conservation.

Electronic sources

Gardenworld **www.gardenworld.co.uk**
Lists over 600 garden centres and horticultural sites, plus links to other related websites. Sections on wildlife, advice, societies and specialist information.

Gardenweb **www.gardenweb.com**
Discussion-based, but good for gardening advice, plant directory, and answers to questions.

Flowerbase **http://gbni.glasshouse.nl/prg/gbni?FIRM=Flowerbase**
Enables you to look up any plant and its picture. Searches on part words.

GAS *see* UTILITIES

GAZETTEERS *see* ATLASES & GAZETTEERS

GENEALOGY *see* FAMILY HISTORY & GENEALOGY

GEOGRAPHY

See also Atlases & Gazetteers; Countries; Environment &
Green Issues; Maps; Weather

Typical questions
- What's a 'drumlin'?
- Do I live in a floodplain?

Considerations
'Geography' is one of those words that has changed its meaning over time, and
particularly from generation to generation. Do find out precisely what the
enquirer wants. Is it geography in the old-fashioned sense of places and their topography, or is it social geography, or the physical environment, or travel, or
geopolitics? Geography is one of the most distributed subjects in the Dewey
classification system.

Where to look
Printed sources

Mayhew, S. (1997) *Oxford dictionary of geography*, Oxford University Press

Clark, A. N. (1990) *Dictionary of geography*, Penguin Books

The Houghton Mifflin dictionary of geography, (1997), Houghton Mifflin
   A good standard dictionary of 'people and places'.

Porteous, A. (2000) *Dictionary of environmental science and technology*, 3rd edn,
   Wiley

Lincoln, R. J. and Boxhill, G. A. (1990) *Cambridge illustrated dictionary of
   natural history*, Cambridge University Press

Journals

Geographical [magazine], Royal Geographical Society. Monthly
Geography: an international journal, The Geographical Association. Quarterly
National Geographic, National Geographic Society. Monthly

Earthquakes

Bolt, B. A. (1999) *Earthquakes*, 4th edn, W. H. Freeman

Geology

Busbey, A. B. (ed.) (1996) *Rocks and fossils: the illustrated guide to the earth*, HarperCollins
Pinna, G. (1985) *The illustrated encyclopedia of fossils*, Facts on File
Allaby, A. and Allaby, M. (1990) *The concise Oxford dictionary of earth sciences*, Oxford University Press

Gems and minerals

Read, P .G. (1988) *Dictionary of gemology*, 2nd edn, Butterworths
Webster, R. (1998) *Gemmologist's compendium*, 7th edn, N.A.G. Press

Maps

Ordnance Survey publish geological maps of the UK. Note the two versions, 'drift' (for surface features) and 'solid' (for deep structures).

Oceans

Svarney, T. E. (2000) *The handy ocean answer book*, Visible Ink

Volcanoes

Feature stories in newspapers and magazines are popular with students doing projects. If you come across any, photocopy them and file.

Scarth, A. (1999) *Vulcan's firing: man against the volcano*, Yale University Press
Features 16 famous volcanoes.

Electronic sources

nationalgeographic.com **www.nationalgeographic.com**

Getty Thesaurus of Geographic Place Names

http://shiva.pub.getty.edu/tgn_browser
This database covers some one million names and other information about places, both modern and historical.

CIA world factbook **www.odci.gov/cia/publications/factbook/index.html**
Has profiles of every country in the world.

Your Environment **www.environment-agency.go.uk/your_env**
Information on the environment. The 'In your backyard' feature allows the users to access local environmental data by postcode.

Other sources

Geographical Association, 160 Solly St, Sheffield S1 4BF
Tel: 0114 296 0088 Fax: 0114 296 7176
E-mail: ga@geography.org.uk
www.geography.org.uk
Publications programme, including journals, conferences and educational services.

DEFRA (Department for Environment, Food and Rural Affairs)
www.defra.gov.uk
Environment Agency **www.environment-agency.gov.uk**

GEOLOGY *see* GEOGRAPHY

GHOSTS *see* THE UNEXPLAINED

GOVERNMENT

See also Acts & Regulations; Election Results; European Information; Members of Parliament; Politics

Typical questions
- I need the address of the Home Office.
- Can you tell me the members of my local government?

Considerations

It is important to realize that queries regarding government can relate to international, central or local governments. It is good practice to have details and lists of your own local government to hand. These should be kept up to date. Questions on government departments and government practice can be varied. There are, however, a number of good directories listed below which in the main will answer most general queries. In addition, in these days of open government, all the government departments and groups have excellent websites. The *Weekly Information Bulletin* provides a round-up of the week's activities in Parliament and is available on **www.parliament.uk**.

In addition, *Hansard* provides a record of what is said each day in the House of Commons and is available also on the website.

If you require European Parliament information, look at the sources and websites listed under European Information.

Where to look

Directories

For a general overview of the UK's system of government look no further than *UK 2002: The official yearbook of the United Kingdom of Great Britain and Northern Ireland*, The Stationery Office. This provides an update on the progress of devolution and the effect on the four parts of the UK.

Civil Service yearbook, The Stationery Office. Annual
> Provides details of Parliamentary officers, ministries and other public organizations and their officials.

In addition try:

KnowUK **www.knowuk.co.uk**
> This is a subscription service which provides information on the people, institutions and organizations which influence, govern and make up the UK. For details contact Proquest Marketing Department (tel: 01223 271258 or visit **www.proquest.co.uk**).

Local government

Municipal yearbook, 2 vols, Hemming Information Services
> This two-volume directory is indispensable for queries relating to government. It provides an A–Z listing of all local authorities in the UK

and covers every aspect of local government. It also provides chapters on UK central government, international and European local government. It is also available on CD-ROM.

The directory of English regional government (2001), Carlton Publishing and Printing
A new reference work, focusing on the emerging structure of England's regional government.

Local government companion (2001), The Stationery Office
This provides detailed information on local government, including the political composition of councils.

Local government gateway **www.info4local.gov.uk**
This provides a gateway for local authorities to access local government-related information that is published on the websites of central government departments and agencies.

There is also a useful portal at:

www.oultwood.com/localgov/england.htm
This is an excellent site for both local and national government links to department and council sites. It has an alphabetical listing for ease of use and links to councillors' websites.

Try also:

Brandreth, G. (consulting ed.), *Whitaker's London almanack*, The Stationery Office
Linklater, M. (consulting ed.), *Whitaker's Scottish almanack*, The Stationery Office

Central government

The Times guide to the House of Commons (2001), Times Books
The guide to the House of Lords (2001), Carlton Publishing & Printing
The directory of Westminster and Whitehall (2001), Carlton Publishing & Printing
The Whitehall companion (2001), The Stationery Office
This covers the departments of central government as well as including both the Scottish Parliament and the Welsh Assembly.

In addition you can use many of the sources mentioned under Members of Parliament.

For details about Parliamentary archives for both the House of Commons and the House of Lords contact the House of Lords Record Office (tel: 020 7219 3074, fax: 020 7219 2570 or **www.parliament.uk**).

International government

See *Europa world yearbook*, details given under European Information.

Websites

Below are listed the websites for a few government departments and bodies. The listing is certainly not comprehensive. For access to other departments, regional assemblies and other government bodies visit **www.open.gov.uk**.

Benefits Agency **www.dss.gov.uk/ba/**
British monarchy **www.royal.gov.uk**
Cabinet Office **www.cabinet-office.gov.uk**
Child Support Agency **www.csa.gov.uk**
Department for Culture, Media and Sport **www.culture.gov.uk/**
Department for Education and Skills **www.dfes.gov.uk**
Department for Environment, Food and Rural Affairs **www.defra.gov.uk/**
Department for Transport **www.dft.gov.uk**
Department for Work and Pensions **www.dwp.gov.uk**
Department of Health **www.doh.gov.uk**
Department of Trade and Industry **www.dti.gov.uk**
Foreign and Commonwealth Office **www.fco.gov.uk**
Health and Safety Executive **www.hse.gov.uk**
HM Land Registry **www.landreg.gov.uk/**
Home Office **www.homeoffice.gov.uk**
House of Commons **www.parliament.uk/commons/hsecom.htm**
House of Lords on the web **www.parliament.uk**
Ministry of Defence **www.mod.uk/**
No. 10 Downing St **www.number-10.gov.uk**
Office of the Deputy Prime Minister **www.odpm.gov.uk**
Parliamentary Education Unit **www.explore.parliament.uk**
Public Record Office (PRO) **www.pro.gov.uk**
The Stationery Office **www.ukstate.com**
Treasury **www.hm-treasury.gov.uk**

UK Houses of Parliament **www.parliament.uk**
UK Passport Agency **www.ukpa.gov.uk**

GRAMMAR *see* DICTIONARIES

GRANTS & FUNDING

Typical questions
- How do I get an educational grant?
- How do I find out about grants?

Considerations
In the main, you will probably find that you are asked about sources of educational grants. However, there are other types of grants: these include housing grants, disabled facilities grants, business grants, and grants and funding for projects, to name a few. It is worth knowing a few reliable sources for each and certainly the relevant local authority departments. The websites listed below cover a wide range of available grants and funding; however, it is not comprehensive. Grants for education are well covered by the directories listed below. It would be good practice to have contact details for your local education authority to hand. Your local Citizens Advice Bureau may also be able to provide assistance and information.

Where to look
Directories
The following are excellent reference works for grant contact details:

Directory of grant making trusts, Directory of Social Change
    Also available on CD-ROM.

The grants register: a complete guide to postgraduate funding worldwide, Macmillan Reference
    This directory provides details of grants available for students at or above postgraduate level and for professional/advanced vocational training.

Try also:

Forrester, S. and Manuel, G. (1999) *Arts funding guide*, Directory of Social

Change

This covers the National Lottery, official sources in the UK and Europe, companies and trusts.

Harland, S. and Griffiths, D. (2000) *Educational grants directory*, Directory of Social Change

Harland, S. (2000) *A guide to grants for individuals in need*, 7th edn, Directory of Social Change

There is also an excellent booklet published by the Representation of the European Commission in the United Kingdom called *Funding from the European Union*. It can be found at **www.cec.org.uk**.

Websites

Allavida (Alliances for Voluntary Initiatives and Development)
www.allavida.org
This is an international non-profit organization.

Architectural Heritage Fund **www.ahfund.org.uk**
Helps with repairs to historic buildings in the UK.

Arts and Humanities Research Board **www.ahrb.ac.uk**
Funding for university museums, galleries and postgraduate research.

Arts Council **www.artscouncil.org.uk**

Arts Council of Northern Ireland **www.artscouncil-ni.org**

Arts Council of Wales **www.ccc-acw.org.uk**

Association of Community Trusts and Foundations **www.acf.org.uk**

Awards for All **www.awardsforall.org.uk**

British Council **www.britcoun.org**

Charities Aid Foundation Grants Council **www.cafonline.org/grants-council**

Community Foundation Network **www.communityfoundations.org.uk**

Community Fund **www.community-fund.org.uk**
The independent organization set up by Parliament in 1994 to distribute money raised by the National Lottery to charities and groups.

179

Department of Culture, Media and Sport **www.culture.gov.uk**

English Regional Arts Board **www.arts.org.uk**

European Foundation Centre **www.efc.be/**

Environment Awards Net **www.environmentawards.net**

Funders Online **www.fundersonline.org/index.asp**
    This offers access to European funding and grant-making resources.

Funding Information **www.fundinginformation.org**

Grants On-line **www.co-financing.co.uk**
    This charges for access.

Digest of Health-related Research Funding and Training Opportunities
    www.rdinfo.org.uk

Heritage Lottery Fund **www.hlf.org.uk**

Higher Education Funding Councils of England, Scotland and Wales
    www.niss.ac.uk/education/hefc

J4b **www.j4b.co.uk**
    Helps businesses find out about grants and loans.

National Endowment for Science, Technology and the Arts (NESTA)
    www.nesta.org.uk

New Opportunities Fund **www.nof.org.uk**

Scottish Arts Council **www.sac.org.uk**

UK Sport **www.uksport.gov.uk**

WelcomeEurope.com **www.welcomeeurope.com/eurofunding-zine.asp**
    This provides news on European grants and loans from European
    institutions.

Tips and pitfalls

Bear in mind that grants and funding may place certain requirements on the individual or group. As a library worker you can only present the information; it would be unwise to advise an enquirer on which grants to apply for.

GREEN ISSUES *see* **ENVIRONMENT & GREEN ISSUES**

GUESTHOUSES *see* **HOTELS & GUESTHOUSES**

HEADS OF STATE *see* KINGS & QUEENS, RULERS, & HEADS OF STATE

HEALTH & HEALTHCARE

See also Doctors & Dentists; Drugs; Opticians

Typical questions
- Can you give me the address of … hospital?
- Do you know an organization for …?
- What are the symptoms of …?

Considerations

Healthcare queries can be those about particular medical conditions, health issues or finding contact details of a hospital or healthcare institute/organization. As well as using the specialized sources, it is useful to use the *Directory of British associations*, CBD Research, for enquiries relating to organizations involved in health or medical conditions and issues. For enquiries relating to prescriptive drugs and medicines *see* Drugs.

Where to look
Directories

There are some excellent medical dictionaries/encyclopedias available which will probably answer in sufficient detail the lay person's medical queries, particularly *Black's medical dictionary*, edited by Dr Gordon Macpherson, 39th edition, 2000, A & C Black. This gives 5000 definitions and descriptions of medical terms with cross-referencing to further information.

Try also:

Youngson, R. (ed.) (2001) *The Royal Society of Medicine health encyclopedia*, Royal Society of Medicine
This has 10,000 entries for medical problems, procedures and prescriptive drugs.

Lock, S., Last, J. and Dunea, G. (2001) *Oxford illustrated companion to medicine*, Oxford University Press
This covers all the major medical and nursing subjects as well as the history

of medicine and complementary therapies.

There are also a number of excellent family health encyclopedias available:

British Medical Association complete family health guide (2001), Dorling Kindersley
A medical encyclopaedia which features information on screening, drug treatments and surgery with symptom charts to aid in the interpretation of symptoms. There is also an explanation of medical genetics and what they mean for your health and 2000 medical websites on every disorder.

Apple, M. (1999) *Hamlyn encyclopedia of family health*, Hamlyn
This offers diagnosis and treatments for more than 200 ailments using orthodox and complementary medicines.

Carroll, S. (1999) *The Which? guide to men's health*, Which?

Robinson, A. (1999) *The Which? guide to women's health*, Which?

For contact details for hospitals and trusts there are a number of directories:

The Institute of Healthcare Management yearbook, The Stationery Office
This provides a comprehensive reference to both the NHS and independent healthcare. It includes details of departments, agencies and management contacts.

Binley's Directory of NHS Management, Beechwood House Publishing
This is a quarterly publication. It provides a comprehensive directory to the NHS, having 12 main sections. These include a hospitals index, primary care trust index, NHS organizations, NHS circulars, NHS press releases and much more.

Directory of hospitals and NHS trusts 1998/99, FT Healthcare
This provides information on all state and independent hospitals, NHS Trusts, NHS Executive regions and health authorities.

For details of organizations involved in complementary healthcare try:

Directory of organizations in allied and complementary health care, (2000), British Library

There is now also a move towards global healthcare communication and information. The *International directory of eHealth and telemedicine*, The Stationery Office, offers contacts for a range of services offered through this new healthcare provision.

Journals

There are numerous journals on health, medicine and the healthcare industry, details of which can be found in *Willings press guide* (*see* Journals & Periodicals). In addition, many medical/health journals are available online; details of websites can also be found in *Willings*.

Market research

Laing's Healthcare Market Review (1999), Laing and Brisson
> As well as having market reviews of certain areas of healthcare, it provides a wide range of reports on healthcare concerns and issues.

Key Note reports, Key Note
> For free executive summaries of report titles listed under healthcare and medical visit **www.keynote.co.uk**. For details of obtaining full reports, contact Key Note (tel: 020 8481 8750, fax: 020 8783 0049).

Statistics

Key data on health, Eurostat
> This covers the countries of the EU, looking at population, mortality, lifestyles, health status and healthcare.

Health statistics in the UK (2001), Office for National Statistics
> This covers a wide range of healthcare issues and systems, including mortality and determinants of health, health education and healthcare. There is some European comparison.

On the state of the public health: the annual report of the Chief Medical Officer
(1997), Department of Health
> This is excellent in coverage even though it is getting slightly out of date.

Health Survey for England, Department of Health
> This is a cumulative work that looks at the health of different groups of people each year.

Organizations

Department of Health
> Richmond House, 79 Whitehall, London SW1A 2NS
> Tel: 020 7210 3000
> **www.doh.gov.uk**

Health Development Agency
Trevelyan House, 30 Great Peter St, London SW1P 2HW
Tel: 020 7222 5300
www.had.org.uk

Health Service Commissioner
11th Floor, Millbank Tower, Millbank, London SW1P 4QP
Tel: 020 7217 4051
www.ombudsman.org.uk
Independent commissioner who will consider complaints about any aspect of NHS provision if these are not dealt with adequately by the body concerned.

Health and travel

You can check the Foreign and Commonwealth Office travel health advice website before you take your holiday **www.fco.gov.uk/knowbeforeyougo**.

Websites

You may find the following publication useful to consult if you intend to use the internet for health/medical information.

Jellinek, D. et al., (2000) *Your health and the internet*, The Stationery Office

Don't forget that you can also use the health portal of one of the major search engines such as Yahoo! **http://uk.dir.yahoo.com/Health/**

BBC Online (Health and Fitness) **www.bbc.co.uk**

British Medical Journal **www.bmj.com**

BUBL Link to Medical Sciences **http://link.bubl.ac.uk/medicine**

Department of Health **www.doh.gov.uk**

Health AtoZ **www.healthatoz.com**
A comprehensive, well-integrated health and medical resource developed by healthcare professionals.

Health Answers **www.healthanswers.com**

Health Development Agency **www.healthpromis.hea.org.uk**
Packed with information, research, policy and health promotion.

Health Information **www.patient.co.uk**

IFM Healthcare Links **www.york.ac.uk/inst/crd/ifmh/ifmlinks.html**
An excellent portal to health and medical resources; includes healthcare libraries, publications, directories, NHS sites and more; well worth a visit.

Lancet **www.thelancet.com**

OMNI (Organizing Medical Networked Information) **www.omni.ac.uk**
This is a database of 4500 medical, biomedical and health links.

Medline **www.nlm.nih.gov/databases/freemedl.html**
The biggest medical database in the world.

Medical Research Council **www.mrc.ac.uk**

Medicines Control Agency **www.open.gov.uk/mca**

NetDoctor **www.netdoctor.co.uk**
The UK's independent health website.

NHS Direct **www.nhsdirect.nhs.uk**

Royal Society of Medicine **www.rsm.ac.uk**

Surgery Door **www.surgerydoor.co.uk/**

UK Health Centre **www.healthcentre.org.uk/**
This is good for links to health topics.

World Health Organization **www.who.org**
Excellent for publications on research, statistics and international medicine or try **www.accesstoworldhealth.com** for ordering WHO publications through the Stationery Office.

HEALTH & SAFETY *see* COMPANIES – LAW

HERALDRY & COATS OF ARMS

See also Family History & Genealogy

Typical questions
- Can you tell me what my family's coat of arms is?
- This diagram is in black and white. What are the colours?
- What's the translation of this motto?
- What's a 'quartering'? And what's 'sable'?

Considerations

With heraldry we come to one of those areas of impenetrable jargon and esoteric knowledge where the gulf between the specialist and the layperson is immense and barely bridgeable. Heraldry has its own arcane form of knowledge best left to the College of Heralds and others of that ilk. The encyclopedias and guides below will help, but as in other areas of reference work, all the librarian can hope to do is point the enquirer in the correct direction and perhaps unscramble some of the jargon – such as 'or', 'argent', 'supporters' and 'couchant'. The librarian can also counter the rather naive belief that because someone in the past had a coat of arms, then someone of the same name today can use it: a belief encouraged by some of the companies that advertise genealogies and coats of arms. A knowledge of the differences between peerages, baronetages and knightages, and between Debrett's and Burke's, could usefully be learned too.

The term 'heraldry' applies to the system of personal and family graphics that were portrayed on shields, which evolved in Europe in the 12th century to meet the military and civil purposes of identification. Strict rules apply to the use of coats of arms.

Where to look

General

Brooke-Little, J. P (1975) *An heraldic alphabet*, 2nd edn, Macdonald and James
Brooke-Little, J. P. (1978) *Boutell's heraldry*, 2nd edn, F. Warne
Fox-Davies, A. C. (1985) *A complete guide to heraldry*, rev. edn, Bloomsbury Press
Friar, S. and Ferguson, J. (1999) *Basic heraldry*, A & C Black
Friar, S. (1987) *A new dictionary of heraldry*, A & C Black
Wood, A. (1996) *Heraldic art and design*, Shaw and Sons

Woodcock, T. and Robinson. J. H. (1988) *The Oxford guide to heraldry*, Oxford University Press

Zieber, E. (1895, 1909) *Orders and decorations in America*, Bailey, Bank and Biddle

Armories

(Lists of surnames against which the heraldic devices used by that family are illustrated.)

Burke, J. B. (1884) *The general armory of England, Scotland, Ireland and Wales*, Harrison

Cockrayne, G. E. (1949) *The complete peerage*, St Catherine Press

Debrett's peerage and baronetage, Debrett's Peerage Ltd. Bi-annual

Fox-Davies, A. C. (1970) *Armorial families*, David & Charles

Mosley, C. (ed.) (1999) *Burke's peerage and baronetage*, 2 vols, Fitzroy Dearborn
Gives bearings and genealogy.

Mottoes

Elvin, C. N. (1971) *A hand-book of mottoes*, revised by R. Pinches, Heraldry Today

Pine, L.G. (1983) *A dictionary of mottoes*, Routledge

National

Briggs, G. (1973) *National heraldry of the world*, Dent

Ordinaries

(These are books that illustrate heraldic devices, either graphically or using verbal descriptions, giving the families who used them.)

Fairbairn, J. (1968) *Fairbairn's book of crests of the families of Great Britain*, Genealogical Publishing Co.
Illustrations.

Papworth, J. and Morant, A.W. (1874, 1977) *Papworth's ordinary of British armorials*, Tabard Publications
Arms are listed A–Z under heraldic terms.

Paul, J. B. (1969) *An ordinary of arms contained in the public register of all arms and bearings in Scotland 1672–1901*, William Green & Sons

Other sources

The College of Arms
> Queen Victoria St, London EC4V 4BT
> Tel: 020 7248 2762 Fax: 020 7248 6448
> **www.college-of-arms.gov.uk/**
> The repository of the registered grants and confirmations of arms in the British Commonwealth.

Court of the Lord Lyon
> New Register House, Edinburgh EH1 3YT
> Tel: 0131 556 7255 Fax: 0131 557 2148

Genealogical Office
> 2 Kildare Street, Dublin 2

HISTORIC HOUSES & CASTLES

See also Museums & Galleries

Typical questions
- What are the opening hours and entrance charges for Chatsworth?
- I would like to find out about the history of Castle Howard.

Considerations

The first step is to try and find out what the enquirer actually wants! Do they want opening hours, charges, facilities, history or architecture of a specific house or castle?

Where to look

Printed sources

Tyack, D. and Brindle, S. (1994) *Blue guide to the country houses of England*, A & C Black
> This gives a county-by-county guide to nearly 400 country houses regularly open to the public. Descriptions include details about the architecture and the history of the properties and their families. There are also directions for finding the houses, and their opening hours are listed.

Alcock, S. (ed.) (1992) *Historic houses, castles and gardens open to the public,*

British Leisure Publications

This book concentrates more on the commercial aspect of houses and castles, covering opening hours, admission charges, contact details, facilities, accessibility, etc.

There will also be texts that go into much more detail about certain historic houses or castles. Check your library's catalogue for details.

Electronic sources

Some smaller libraries may not have access to the publications mentioned above. They will be able to find current information on the internet though. Some of the owners of the country houses and castles now have websites.

English Heritage list all their properties and give details such as opening hours, entry fees, descriptions, facilities, directions and even lists of events:

www.english-heritage.org.uk

The National Trust provide a similar, excellent website:

www.nationaltrust.org.uk

www.castles.org/britain
This is a list of links to the websites of most British castles, stately homes and houses.

Tips and pitfalls

As with many tourist attractions, the enquirer should always phone before visiting a place, to check that it is open when they intend to visit. Don't forget to suggest this to them!

HISTORY & ARCHAEOLOGY

See also Dates, Events, Chronologies & Calendars; Local History

Considerations

Enquiries on historical topics tend to be fairly straightforward; the terminology is known and most people have a reasonable knowledge of history, although one must be aware of differing cultural backgrounds and attitudes. Thus be careful in using words such as 'English' and 'British', 'American' and 'North American', 'Arab' and 'Muslim'.

Where to look

Printed sources

Arnold-Baker, C. (1996) *The companion to British history*, Longcross Press
A 1400-page 'treasure trove' of facts.

Gardiner, J. and Wenborn, N. (eds) (1995) *The History Today companion to British history*, Collins and Brown
4500 entries.

Kenyon, J. P., (ed.) (1994) *A dictionary of British history*, 2nd edn, Secker & Warburg
3000 articles.

The History Today who's who in British history (2000), Collins and Brown
4000 biographical entries.

Philip's world history encyclopedia (2000), G. Philip
An illustrated global history with 6500 entries.

The Victoria history of the counties of England, Boydell & Brewer, for the Institute of Historical Research
The standard history of the counties of England. Publishing in progress: visit **www.englandpast.net** for more information.

Haigh, C. (1990) *Cambridge historical encyclopedia of Great Britain and Ireland*, Cambridge University Press

Murray, T. (ed.) (2001) *Encyclopedia of archaeology*, 3 vols, ABC Clio

Orser, C. E. (ed.) (2002) *Encyclopedia of historical archaeology*, Routledge

Journals

Current Archaeology
9 Nassington Rd, London NW3 2TX
www.archaeology.co.uk
A magazine published six times a year. Reports latest excavations and discoveries.

Historical Abstracts (1955–), ABC-Clio. 3 p.a.
An abstracting journal giving details of articles and books on a wide range of historical subjects. Excludes North America. Also available on CD-ROM and on a subscription website.

America: History and Life (1964–), ABC-Clio. 3 p.a.
> An abstracting journal giving details of articles and books on US and Canadian history. Also available on CD-ROM and on a subscription website.

Electronic sources

Public Record Office **www.pro.gov.uk**
> National archives information, catalogue to resources and printable leaflets.

Oral History Society **www.essex.ac.uk/sociology/oralhis.htm**

BBC History **www.bbc.co.uk/history**

Britannia **www.britannia.com**
> Comprehensive coverage of British history.

Royal Commission on Historic Monuments
> **www.rchme.gov.uk/homepage.html**

History Resources **www.libraries.rutgers.edu/rulib/socsci/hist/amhist.html**

Register of British Historical Societies **www.uksocieties.com**
> Over 500 British-based literary and historical societies.

English History **http://englishhistory.net**

Reviews in History **www.history.ac.uk**

History On-line **www.ihrinfo.ac.uk**
> Over 30,000 records on books, journals, articles, historians, theses and seminars; service provided by the Institute of Historical Research.

Other sources

The Historical Association
> 59a Kennington Park Rd, London SE11 4JH
> Tel: 020 7735 3901
> **www.history.org.uk**
> The Historical Association is the leading UK society for the study of history. Publishes journals and has local branches from Aberdeen to Plymouth.

National Monuments Record
> Kemble Drive, Swindon SN2 2GZ
> Tel: 01793 414600

www.english-heritage.org.uk

The public archive of English Heritage. Holds more than 10 million photographs and provides information on the architecture and archaeology of England.

The Royal Commission on Historical Manuscripts

Quality House, Quality Court, Chancery Lane, London WC2A 1HP

Tel: 020 742 1198 Fax: 020 731 3550

E-mail: nra@hmc.gov.uk

www.hmc.gov.uk

Set up to meet the demand for a systematic investigation of manuscript sources. Maintains the National Register of Archives, a collection of some 40,000 lists and catalogues. These lists may be consulted in the Commission's public search rooms. The indexes for these lists may be consulted on the Commission's website. The Commission offers advice on manuscript matters.

Royal Historical Society

c/o University College London, Gower St, London WC1E 6BT

Tel/Fax: 020 7387 7532

E-mail: royalhistsoc@ucl.ac.uk

http://ihrinfo.ac.uk/rhs/

Founded to promote the study of history by means of papers and proceedings.

Institute of Historical Research, Senate House, Malet St, London WC1E 7HU

Tel: 020 786 28740 Fax: 020 786 28811

E-mail: ihr@sas.ac.uk

www.ihrinfo.ac.uk

The IHR has been the University of London's centre for advanced study in history since 1921. It provides a wide range of services for scholars worldwide.

There are many local and regional historical societies.

Tips and pitfalls

Do check *which* country's history is required!

HOTELS & GUESTHOUSES

Typical questions
* I want a list of hotels in St Tropez.
* Are there any cheap bed and breakfast places in Dolgellau?

Considerations
The short-break travel market is ever expanding and more and more people are deciding to 'tailor' their own short breaks. Most large libraries will have a decent directory of hotels and bed and breakfasts in the UK. The problems start arising when people are looking for hotels abroad.

Where to look
Printed sources
There are many hotel guides covering the UK and Ireland. For instance:

RAC inspected hotels, Great Britain and Ireland 2000, West One Publishing

If the customer is looking for hotels abroad, some of the foreign guidebooks recommend hotels and lodgings. Make sure the guide you are looking at is current, though.

For more business-orientated travel, worldwide, the following publication is useful:

Gordon, C. (ed) (1999) *World hotel directory 2000*, Pearson Education
This publication lists quality hotels throughout the world, suitable for the business traveller.

Electronic sources
If you are short of hotel guides, you can always try the internet. This is in many ways better than looking at a guidebook. Many smaller hotels, which may not get into guidebooks, can afford to set up websites. Another advantage is that you may be able to book instantly, and searching for hotels abroad could not be easier.

The best way to find hotels is simply to use a good search engine and type, for example, 'hotels Dollgellau'.

Tips and pitfalls

Most tourist information centres will have directories of UK hotels and many will provide a bed-booking service throughout the UK. Refer your enquirer to them if you are having problems.

HOUSING & BUYING A HOUSE

See also Architecture; Social Welfare

Considerations

There are many books available on buying or selling property; your library will probably have a selection in its lending department. Providing these are up to date, they will probably answer many of the queries you are likely to get. There are some detailed information sources given below. Information about properties for sale in the UK can be obtained from estate agents and local newspapers. If you require lists of estate agents, the Yellow Pages or **www.yell.com** will provide contact details. Most estate agents have websites for buying and selling houses and properties. These usually include property details and both internal and external pictures. Statistical information, such as comparing house prices by regions, can be found in a number of sources. Many of the building societies have good information on their web pages. Housing issues such as homelessness, student accommodation and the state of housing can be found either from government official statistics or through organizations. Some of the best are listed below.

Where to look
Buying or selling a house

Here is just a small selection of the type of books available on moving house. Make sure that you are using up-to-date editions and if not, make the user aware that changes may have occurred in the interim.

Walker, A. (1999) *Buying a house*, How to books
Which? way to buy, sell and move house, The Consumer's Association
Abbey, R. and Richards, M. (2001) *A practical approach to conveyancing*, 3rd
    edn, Oxford University Press

The Council of Mortgage Lenders **www.cml.org.uk**
    An excellent website, which includes some useful publications. Among
    these are: *How to buy a home in England and Wales*, *How to buy a home in*

Scotland, *Mortgage complaints*, *Buying to let* and *Handling of arrears and possessions*. It also provides information on housing finance, the housing and mortgage markets and housing policy in the UK. These include statistics. It provides data on house prices both in the UK and in Europe. Well worth a visit.

Moneyextra Homepages **www.homepages.co.uk**
Covers everything to do with moving house.

History of houses

Barratt, N. (2001) *Tracing the history of your house: a guide to sources*, PRO

Statistics

House Prices

Halifax Bank of Scotland house price index
www.hbosplc.com/view/housepriceindex/housepriceindex.asp

HM Land Registry – residential property price report **www.landreg.gov.uk**
This allows the user to key in their own house data and receive a projected future property price.

For general housing statistics and housing policy look no further than the Department of Transport, Local Government and the Regions: **www.housing. dtlr.gov.uk/research/hss**. This is excellent and provides a list of housing statistics which includes *Housing statistics annual, Housing statistics quarterly, Local housing statistics, Sales of council house statistics*. There is also a survey section which includes *Survey of English homes, English house condition survey* and *Projections of households in England 2021*.

Housing issues

For housing issues and housing policy there are a number of excellent organizations.

Chartered Institute of Housing
Octavia House, Westwood Business Park, Westwood Way, Coventry CV4 8JP
Tel: 024 7685 1700
www.cih.org
This has an excellent site for information and links.

Independent Housing Ombudsman
Norman House, 105–109 The Strand, London WC2R 0AA
Tel: 020 7836 3630
www.ihos.org.uk

Joseph Rowntree Foundation
The Homestead, 40 Water End, York YO30 6WP
Tel: 01904 629241
www.jrf.org.uk

National Housing Federation
175 Gray's Inn Rd, London WC1X 8UP
Tel: 0171 278 6571
www.housing.org.uk
Excellent for research and policy publications.

Shelter
88 Old St, London EC1V 9HU
Tel: 020 7505 2000
www.shelter.org.uk
For Wales try **www.sheltercymru.org.uk**

Websites

Chesterton **www.chesterton.co.uk/residential/index.html**
Chesterton provide a good range of research publications covering residential development and living. Many are available to freely download.

Homeless International **www.homeless-international.org**

Homes for Homeless People **www.homeline.dircon.co.uk**

National Association of Estate Agents **www.naea.co.uk**

National Homeless Alliance **www.homeless.org.uk**

ILLUSTRATIONS *see* PHOTOGRAPHS & ILLUSTRATIONS

IMMIGRATION *see* NATIONALITY & IMMIGRATION

IMPORTS *see* EXPORTS & IMPORTS

INDEXES *see* ALPHABETS & SCRIPTS

INFORMATION TECHNOLOGY

Typical questions

- What is the difference between RAM and ROM?
- Can you recommend any internet sites on art?
- I'm buying a new PC. Have you any recent guides?
- Can you explain what 'broadband' is?
- How many people in France own a PC?

Considerations

Information technology is constantly an area of great interest. As you can see from the typical questions above, this can be such a wide-ranging subject. And of course the whole area of IT is constantly changing, so it is important that you try and keep up with what is going on. Texts which are relevant one year may be obsolete the next. If you are going to keep right up to date with what is going on you should consider subscribing to a relevant journal or magazine.

Where to look

It is essential that you have a good, up-to-date dictionary of IT/computing terms. Peter Collin publish a useful set including:

Collinn, S. M. H. (1998) *Dictionary of personal computing and the internet*, 2nd edn, Peter Collin

Collinn, S. M. H. (1998) *Dictionary of computing*, 3rd edn, Peter Collin

Collinn, S. M. H. (1998) *Dictionary of information technology*, 2nd edn, Peter Collin

There are thousands of books available on computers, computing and IT. One of the most important publishers is Microsoft. They have a UK website at: **www.microsoft.com/uk/mspress/**

Magazines

What PC is a good guide for potential PC buyers. There are many other similar titles on the market. Try a few to see which suits your enquirers the best.

There are also several magazines that deal with the more technical aspects of PCs and software, e.g. *PC Pro, PC Answers*. Check *Willings press guide* for a complete listing.

Internet

There are a number of publications available which cover the internet and which recommend websites. One of the most useful has been published by Library Association Publishing:

Criddle, S. et al. (2000) *The public librarian's guide to the internet*, Library Association Publishing.
This guide gives you the basics on how to use the internet and recommends hundreds of useful web-based resources. All the recommended sites are chosen by library professionals so you know that the sites will be trustworthy.

An excellent publication for keeping up to date with new internet websites and internet technology is:

Tips and Advice Internet
Indicator Advisors & Publishers
Calgarth House, 39–41 Bank Street, Ashford, Kent TN23 1BA
Tel: 01233 653500 Fax: 01233 647100
www.indicator.co.uk/internet/
Fortnightly

Tips and pitfalls

Nobody working in libraries could have failed to notice the impact that IT is having nowadays. Nearly all libraries now provide internet access and other facilities such as word-processing. Staff now need a basic knowledge of IT in order to be able to answer simple enquiries. Taking the European Computer Driving Licence should make more staff computer literate and give them confidence to answer enquiries. However, they cannot learn everything, so having some print-based resources available is a great help. Make sure you keep these resources current though, as the IT world is changing constantly.

INSURANCE

Typical questions
- Can you give me the address of ... insurance company?
- Can you give me the address of ... assurance company?
- Have you got insurance claims statistics?

Considerations
Firstly, let's clarify assurance and insurance.

Assurance: in Britain this is the term used for insurance policies relating to death, i.e. something that will definitely happen.

Insurance is the agreement that in return for regular payments, a company will pay for loss, damage, injury or death. A common dilemma is to know the difference between insurance and assurance.

For enquirers wanting information on insurance companies the directories below will provide company details. For those who have a complaint against an insurance company then refer them to the Insurance Ombudsman Bureau. There is also the relatively new General Insurance Standards Council (GISC) which has a good informative website.

Where to look
Directories
Insurance directory: the definitive guide to UK insurance, Incisive Media
> An excellent directory providing sector-by-sector coverage of the insurance industry. It lists companies alphabetically, by subject and by geographic region. There is also a 'Who's who in insurance'.

Insurance pocket book, NTC Publications
> Provides profiles of insurance groups, and key facts and figures of industry trends.

Kluwer's insurance register, Kluwer Publishing
> **www.croner.co.uk**
> This directory provides details of 1700 (approx.) companies involved in the insurance industry. There is a useful 'Who owns whom' list.

Tolley's insurance handbook, Butterworths
> An invaluable one-stop shop of information published annually. The new edition takes into account the changes to the law resulting from the Financial Services and Markets Act 2000.

FT Business global insurance directory, FT Business
> This directory provides details of the major insurance and re-insurance companies worldwide. It includes a who's who of the insurance industry.

Journals

There are numerous journals for the insurance industry, details of which can be found in *Willings press guide* (*see* Journals & Periodicals).

Market research

The Association of British Insurers has an excellent website for free download-able research publications and statistics: **www.abi.org.uk**.

Key Note reports, Key Note.
> For free executive summaries of report titles listed under financial services (insurance companies and UK insurance market) visit **www.keynote. co.uk**. For details of obtaining full reports, contact Key Note (tel: 020 8481 8750, fax: 020 8783 0049).

Organizations

The Insurance Ombudsman Bureau
> City Gate One, 135 Park St, London SE1 9EA
> Tel: 020 7928 4488

General Insurance Standards Council (GISC)
> 9th Floor, 110 Cannon St, London EC4N 6EU
> Tel: 020 7648 7800 Fax: 020 7648 7808
> **www.gisc.co.uk**

Websites

Association of British Insurers **www.abi.org.uk**
    Provides lots of links.

INTERNET *see* INFORMATION TECHNOLOGY

INVENTIONS & PATENTS

See also Copyright

Typical questions

• Who invented television?
• When was the first motor car invented?
• How do I patent something?

Considerations

When, where, and by whom things were invented are popular sources of enquiry. They often form part of student projects, pub quizzes and crosswords. More seriously, many people invent things and want to know how to protect their invention, that is, take out a patent. In fact it is often quite difficult to establish who invented things, especially before patents were established. Much depends on how precise people are, or want to be.

Printed sources

Most encyclopedias will have information on inventions. Check shelves at Dewey 608 and 609.

Books arranged by broad topics

Giscard d'Estaing, V.-A. (1991) *The book of inventions and discoveries*, Macdonald

Brown, G. I. (1996) *The Guinness history of inventions*, Guinness Publications

Petrovski, P. (1993) *The evolution of useful things*, Knopf

Reader's Digest (1998) *The origin of everyday things*, Reader's Digest

Robertson, P. (1994) *The new Shell book of firsts*, Headline
    Includes an index by place.

Books arranged alphabetically by invention

Baker, R. (1976) *New and improved: inventors and inventions that have changed the world*, The British Library

Gives patent numbers, mostly British, for 363 inventions.

Brown, T. (1994) *Historical first patents: the first United States patents for many everyday things*, Scarecrow Press

Tibballs, G. (1994) *The Guinness book of inventions: the 20th century from aerosol to zip*, Guinness Publications

Beren, M. (1992) *How it all began: the stories behind those famous names*, Smith Settle
An illustrated guide to Airfix, Ambrosia, Anchor and other famous brands.

Books arranged chronologically by invention

Desmond, K. (1987) *The Harwin book of inventions, discoveries from pre-history to the present day*, Constable
Lacks detail but a good index by specific topic leads to the inventor and date.

Oxford illustrated encyclopedia of invention and technology (1992), Oxford University Press
Large format. A–Z by subject and name.

Van Dulken, S. (2000) *Inventing the 20th century: 100 inventions that shaped the world*, British Library
Page-length accounts of many familiar products from the biro and velcro to the ring-pull and the Dyson.

Firsts

Richardson, M. (1997) *The Penguin book of firsts*, Penguin

Patents

Van Dulken, S. (1999) *British patents of invention, 1617–1977: a guide for researchers*, The British Library

Van Dulken, S. (1998) *Introduction to patent information*, 3rd edn, The British Library

INVENTIONS & PATENTS

Electronic sources

About.Com **http://inventors.about.com/education/inventors/**
Invent Now **www.invent.org**
The Lemelson Center for the Study of Invention and Innovation
    www.si.edu/lemelson

The British Library **www.bl.uk/services/stb/etalmenu.html**
    Provides links to many other databases as well as giving information for
    inventors.

Patents Information Network **www.bl.uk/services/stb/pinmenu.html**

The Patent Office **www.patent.gov.uk**
    Gives information about how to apply for a patent.

US Patent and Trademark Depository Library **www.uspto.gov/go/ptdl**

For other countries try the list of patent offices on the British Library website
above.

Other sources

The British Library
    Patents Information, The British Library, 96 Euston Rd, London NW1
    2DB
    Tel: 020 7412 7919 Fax: 020 7412 7480
    E-mail: patents-information@bl.uk
    www.bl.uk/services/information/patents.html
    The British Library holds 44 million patent specifications from 38
    countries. It also offers general information on patents.

The Patent Office
    Concept House, Cardiff Rd, Newport, South Wales NP9 1RH
    Tel: 0645 500505
    E-mail: patent-enquiries@patents.gov.uk
    www.patent.gov.uk
    The UK Patent Office, a government department, is responsible for
    intellectual property (copyright, designs, patents and trade marks).
    Brochures may be obtained free of charge.

Supplies of brochures about patents are supplied to larger libraries.

Tips and pitfalls

Often different sources contradict each other. Check more than one source if possible. Distinguish between brand names and the process or object, e.g. Xerox is the name of a company and also the copyrighted name of a process; photocopying is a generalized name for the process.

ISBNs & ISSNs

Typical questions

* I'm publishing a book. How do I get an ISBN?
* Do I need to include ISBNs when I list books in a bibliography?

Considerations

ISBN stands for International Standard Book Number. Each ISBN is a unique number and one is allocated to every book title published. It is not part of copyright and books can be published without one. They are used by booksellers and librarians to avoid confusion over titles, joint authors and different editions. They are particularly useful since they are used in the electronic transmission of data, such as tele-ordering, shop stock control systems, and computer issue systems in libraries. The bar code used by most shops incorporates the ISBN in the full number (the EAN – European Article Number).

ISSN stands for International Standard Serial Number. Like ISBNs, the ISSN is allocated to the individual titles of journals and magazines. They are used less than ISBNs but do feature in certain library automated check-in systems.

Neither are part of the essential bibliographical record of a book for compiling bibliographies and reading lists; indeed, the same title may have more than one ISBN if there are paperback and hardback versions, or different publishers in different countries. But ISBNs are important for ordering purposes.

Where to look

Printed sources

Writers' and artists' yearbook, A & C Black. Annual
The writers' handbook, Macmillan. Annual

Both these guides have information on ISBNs and ISSNs.

Sources

For ISBNs

UK International Standard Book Numbering Agency
  Woolmead House West, Bear Lane, Farnham, Surrey GU9 7LG
  Tel: 01252 742590 Fax: 01252 742526
  E-mail: isbn@whitaker.co.uk
  www.whitaker.co.uk/isbn.htm
  The agency produce a printed guide.

For ISSNs

ISSN UK Centre
  The British Library, Boston Spa, Wetherby, West Yorkshire, LS23 7BQ
  Tel: 01937 546958/9
  Fax: 01937 546562
  E-mail: issn-uk@bl.uk

Tips and pitfalls

Take care when transcribing ISBNs. There will always be ten digits grouped in four units (the country code, the publisher number, the title number and a single check digit which may be an X). The spacing between the four units is not critical, but the number will not transmit if any figures are wrong.

The same book title may have different ISBNs if it has different formats, publishers or editions.

JOB INTERVIEWS

Typical questions
- I'm trying to find out about a company/organization that I am going to have an interview with.

Considerations
Firstly, ask the user when their interview is and how much time they have to do their research. Frequently, users are on their lunch-hour, hoping to quickly 'grab' some information like they grab a sandwich. In such cases there are probably two important things to establish: (a) if the company (or organization) is registered or unincorporated – if it's part of a group and you're struggling for information, the parent company may provide some leads; (b) the main business activity of the company – the user may tell you this but always check so you have it clear in your own mind. With these facts established you can proceed to a more thorough investigation. There is a wealth of company information available but even if your library doesn't have many business sources there are numerous websites to refer to. If the user has left enough time you can advice them to telephone the company for their annual report or check out some of the websites listed below.

As well as providing company information, you can suggest the user considers looking at the industry as a whole to have an understanding of the wider picture. This doesn't have to be in any major detail but could include the company's competitors, potential customers, product sales and ranking, who buys the product/service and maybe even a few notes on the industry's future. Now, that should impress a would-be employer.

Where to look
Directories
Please refer to the directories listed under Companies.

Market intelligence
Please refer to the market research reports listed under Market Research.

Newscuttings
European intelligence wire CD-ROM, Lexis Nexis Europe, Proquest
   This is a database of full-text news articles from the major daily newspapers.

207

It is specific to business and finance. Searches can be done either on the company name, industry sector or keyword. It is ideal for obtaining a good picture of a particular industry or company over a period of time. By the very nature of the resources included it tends to only cater for the bigger companies and their subsidiaries or associates. It is unlikely that you would find many smaller local companies included.

Local company news

This is probably something that your library has to tackle itself. It could be in the form of simply keeping newscuttings from local publications, arranged alphabetically by company.

Websites

Applegate Company Information **www.applegate.co.uk**
> Covers the following sectors: agribusiness, electronic, engineering, oil and gas, plastics and rubber, recruitment.

Business Network **www.countyweb.co.uk**

Carol (Company Annual Reports OnLine) **www.carolworld.com**
> Not only the UK but for the rest of Europe as well as the USA and Asia.

Companies – Business Profiles **www.bized.ac.uk**
> Lots of links provided.

Companies House **www.companieshouse.gov.uk**

Tips and pitfalls

Avoid comment on the merits or problems of individual companies/organizations. You simply don't know if it's a good job or a good place to work.

JOBS

See also Careers

Typical questions

- I need a list of recruitment agencies?
- Can you tell me where to look for ... jobs?

Considerations

There are numerous places where jobs are advertised. For instance, there are a number of specialized newspapers on the market that are devoted to advertising jobs in specific regions; see *Willings press guide* for title details. In addition, many of the trade and professional journals have a job section as do the national and local newspapers. Finally, there is the internet. There are literally hundreds of job sites, some better than others: it is probably useful to look at and bookmark a few which you feel would be beneficial to your library users. You may be asked about employment agencies, which can usually be found listed in the Yellow Pages.

Where to look

Graduate career directory: guide to jobs in the UK, Hobsons

Executive grapevine: the UK directory of executive recruitment consultants (2001), 21st edn, Executive Grapevine

International directory of executive recruitment consultants (2001), 10th edn, Executive Grapevine

The last two are both authoritative and comprehensive in their coverage of executive recruiters.

Apprenticeships

ApprenticeMaster Alliance
    20 Heber Rd, London NW2 6AA
    Tel: 020 8208 2853
    www.apprentice.org.uk
    Links school leavers and graduates with experts for long-term apprenticeships.

Working abroad

For an excellent guide to considerations and further information consult:

Griffith, F. (2001) *Work your way around the world 2001*, Vacation Work
    Publications

Try also:

Payaway **www.payaway.co.uk**
    This can be used to search for jobs abroad either by sector or by country. It is primarily aimed at gap-year students or travellers. It provides useful links from each country to organizations offering advice or employment.

JOBS

Newspapers

Listed below are the days for specific types of jobs.

Daily Telegraph
> Tuesday – General
> Thursday – Main Supplement
> Saturday – Senior Appointments

Financial Times
> Monday – Accountancy (junior)
> Wednesday – IT, Senior, Banking, Finance and General
> Thursday – Accountancy (senior)

Guardian
> Monday – Conservation, Environment, Housing, Media, Public
> appointments
> Tuesday – Education, International
> Wednesday – General appointments
> Thursday – Commercial, Computing, Graduate, Technical
> Friday – Housing, Public appointments
> Saturday – General appointments

Independent
> Monday – Computing
> Tuesday – Accountancy, Financial, Marketing, Media and sales
> Wednesday – City jobs
> Thursday – General, Education, Public appointments
> Friday – Legal

Times
> Monday – Education
> Tuesday – General management and legal
> Wednesday – La crème de la crème, Accountancy, Finance,
> Media, Sales
> Thursday – General, Executive supplement

Journals

Opportunities – Public Sector Recruitment and Career Development Weekly
> Link House, West St, Poole, Dorset BH15 1LL
> Tel: 020 8667 1667

www.opportunities.co.uk

Overseas Jobs Express
20 New Rd, Brighton, East Sussex BN1 1UF
Tel: 01273 699777
www.overseasjobexpress.com

Websites

Accountancy, banking, computing, education, healthcare and secretarial
www.reed.co.uk

Applegate **www.applegate.co.uk**
Select 'recruitment directory' from menu.

Employment Service Direct **www.employmentservice.gov.uk**
The executive agency of the Department for Work and Pensions; it can be contacted on 0845 6060234 and all calls are charged at local rates; the website is excellent, offering a search facility to find your local job centre; it also includes information for employers.

Experienced professionals **www.hotjobs.com**

Graduate jobs **www. prospects.csu.ac.uk**

Guardian site **www.jobsunlimited.co.uk**

Jobcentre Plus **www.jobcentreplus.gov.uk**
Enables the user to search for jobs as well as providing links to New Deal, benefits and other external related links.

Job Index **www.job-index.co.uk**
Provides a database of recruitment organizations.

Tips and pitfalls

This really is an area where you could find yourself offering too much to the enquirer. It is best to have a few trusty resources, which you feel offer good coverage. There isn't one particular source of information that could be used for all: jobs just aren't like that. In reality, most enquirers will want the latest job adverts, which will mean looking at newspapers or journals. If your region does a specific job advertisement publication, it would be sensible to subscribe to it. It will certainly be well used.

211

JOURNALS & PERIODICALS

See also Articles in Journals; Newspapers; Publishing

Typical questions

- Have you got the *Farmers Weekly*?
- Where can I get a journal you don't have?
- What periodicals are published on model making?

Considerations

A great amount of information, news and comment is in journals so it is little wonder that libraries get a great number of questions about them. No library can have them all and many of the enquiries received will be about getting issues the library does not have. For this type of enquiry you will need to be aware of your library's procedures for obtaining them, or for referring people to other libraries that do stock them.

There is no clear demarcation between journals, periodicals, magazines and other categories such as serials, newsletters and proceedings. Generally we are referring here to publications produced at regular intervals such as weekly, monthly or quarterly.

Where to look

Lists of journals and periodicals

BRAD (British Rate and Data), Emap Communications. Monthly

Willings press guide, Hollis. Annual
>	A–Z within countries. Gives prices, addresses and brief content descriptions to over 50,000 periodicals, magazines and broadcast media.

British Library, *Current serials received*. Annual
>	**www.bl.uk/serials**
>	Over 60,000 titles in the stock of the British Library.

Writers' and artists' yearbook, A & C Black. Annual
>	Lists popular British and Irish journals and magazines.

The serials directory: an international reference book, EBSCO. Annual
>	Over 150,000 entries.

Indexes to articles
see Articles in Journals

For older journals

British union catalogue of periodicals (1955–58), 4 vols, Butterworths
> A record of periodicals of the world, from the 17th century to the present day. Despite the date, the work is still useful for identifying titles and locations.

British Library Catalogue **http://blpc.bl.uk**
> Use the advanced mode to access periodicals.

There are a number of co-operative journal databases, but these are generally available only on subscription, e.g. LAMDA, the journal collections of ten academic libraries.

Electronic sources

The publication of journals in electronic formats (either alongside print versions, or just as e-journals) and the existence of services providing CD-ROMs and web-site access to a range of indexes means that this is a confusing and volatile area. Your library may offer some of these services. Do check. Use a search engine such as Google to find information on individual titles.

Tips and pitfalls

Beware journals that have changed their titles, have amalgamated with others, have titles identical with others, or have simply ceased.

KINGS & QUEENS, RULERS & HEADS OF STATE

Typical questions
- When was Victoria queen of England?
- Does Belgium have a king?

Where to look
Encyclopedias and almanacks (e.g. *Whitakers*) should all list British monarchs from the past, as well as current world heads of state. If you want to go into more detail, try:

Cannon, J. and Griffiths, R. (1988) *Oxford illustrated history of the British monarchy*, Oxford University Press
This covers the history of the period from c.400 to the present day and lists all the monarchs.

For rulers worldwide, Guinness have produced a useful book:

Carpenter, C. (1978) *Guinness book of kings, rulers and statesmen throughout the world, from 300 BC to the present day*, Guinness Publications

There are also many biographies available on both the current royal family and kings and queens of the past. Check your shelves for availability.

Electronic sources
There is a useful website listing all heads of state and rulers from around the world, both past and present:

www.info-regenten.de/regent/regent-e

For the history of the UK monarchy, try the official site:

www.royal.gov.uk

LANGUAGES & TRANSLATING

See also Dictionaries

Typical questions
- How can I get this article translated?
- What language do they speak in Syria?
- Why are the Russian and Greek alphabets alike?

Where to look
Printed sources

Allen, C. G. (1975) *A manual of European languages for librarians*, Bowker
    A researcher's manual with details of alphabets, grammar and orthography.

Burchfield, R. W. (1992) *The English language*, Oxford University Press

Campbell, G. (2000) *Compendium of the world's languages*, 2 vols, Routledge
    Over 300 A–Z entries on languages and dialects.

Collinge, N. E. (1992) *An encyclopaedia of language*, Routledge.
    Detailed chapters.

Crystal, D. (1997) *The Cambridge encyclopedia of language*, 2nd edn, Cambridge University Press
    Large format, illustrated, and relatively non-technical.

Crystal, D. (1992) *An encyclopedic dictionary of language and languages*, Blackwell
    A general brief-article encyclopedia.

Dalby, A. (1998) *Dictionary of languages: the definitive guide to more than 400 languages*, Bloomsbury
    Feature article on every language.

See Yellow Pages and Thomson directories for local translators and translating services.

Electronic sources

AltaVista's Babel Fish allows you to type in up to 150 words, or even a website address, and claims to translate it into eight languages:

http://babel.altavista.com

Other sources

Many libraries and information units compile lists of local translators. Check to see if any local lists are produced.

Local colleges and universities may have staff knowledgeable in different languages.

Institute of Translation and Interpreting
Exchange House, 494 Midsummer Boulevard, Central Milton Keynes MK9 2EA
Tel: 01908 255905 Fax 01908 255700
E-mail: info@iti.org.uk
www.iti.org.uk/pages/index.cgi

Institute of Linguists
Saxon House, 48 Southwark St, London SE1 1UN
Tel: 020 7940 3100 Fax: 020 7940 3101
E-mail: info@iol.org.uk
www.iol.org.uk/

Association of Language Excellence Centres
The Garden Studios, 11–15 Betterton St, London WC2H 9BP
Tel/fax: 0704 401 2532
E-mail: members@lxcentres.com
www.lxcentres.com/

Tips and pitfalls

For short translations, try colleagues, and even your regular users! However, make sure they are competent.

LAW

See also Acts & Regulations

Typical questions

- What is the law on …?
- What does 2AER stand for?
- What's the most I can get for this offence?
- Do I still need a licence for my dog?
- Where can I find the case Jardine v. Jardine?

Considerations

A request for information about law is a request most of us fear. Apart from the complexity of law as a subject, there is always the fear of 'What if I get it wrong and give incorrect information?' We are right to fear this, though as long as we are not knowingly providing incorrect information, this worst 'they' can get us for is probably incompetence. In addition, most staff will be covered by the employer's indemnity policy. But we still have to be careful. Always preface your answer to a legal enquiry by quoting the source you are using. Always advise the enquirer to seek legal advice from a qualified lawyer. And never, even light-heartedly, voice an opinion. You may know you are ignorant, but the enquirer may believe librarians know everything!

The good news is that most legal enquiries do not require knowledge of the law, just a knowledge of your library. Many, if not most, enquiries, particularly those from students and *very* smartly dressed strangers (barristers) will be for specific books, particular cases, or named Acts and Regulations. Precise details are probably known and the only difficulty may be helping the enquirer to interpet cryptic references and navigate confusing indexes. Staff should request some training to cope with these.

Requests for 'the law' on a particular subject can be troublesome, particularly if the enquirer seems unfamiliar with using printed sources. In such cases, and often these result from a summons, a prosecution or a solicitor's letter, it is hard not to get drawn into the detail of the enquiry. Sad and hard-luck cases are legion – 'I can't afford a solicitor, the CAB won't help, you are my final hope.' At times one has to be hard and heartless.

Other points

- Check whose law is wanted, that is, whether English law, Scottish law, or European.
- Be aware of the types of book needed: practitioner/textbook or non-technical books such as the *Which?* guides. The practitioner books are often known by personal names, Kemp & Kemp (on damages), Chitty (on contract) and Tristram & Cote (on probate).
- Unusual words can confuse, e.g. tort. Do use law dictionaries.
- The dates of sources can be crucial.

Where to look
Printed sources
General

Flye, J. and Morgan, S. (2000) *Legal adviser: your legal questions answered*, Law Pack

Richards, K. (1998) *401 legal problems solved*, Which? Books
A question and answer handbook with useful directory section.

Shepperton, T. (2001) *Legal advice handbook*, Law Pack

Consumers Association (2000) *150 letters that get results*, Which? Books
Includes sample letters on legal problems.

Moys, E. M. (ed.) (1987) *Manual of law librarianship*, 2nd edn, Gower

Dane, J. and Thomas, P. A. (1987) *How to use a law library*, 3rd edn, Sweet & Maxwell

Rutherford, L. and Bone, S. (eds) (1993) *Osborn's concise law dictionary*, 8th edn Sweet & Maxwell
An A–Z of legal terms.

Walker, D.M. (1980) *The Oxford companion to law*, Clarendon Press

Stone's justices' manual, Butterworths. Annual
Stone's, commonly known as 'The Blue Book', is a three-volume compendium of English law. It is to be found in most reference libraries and is compiled for lay magistrates.

Bailey, S. H. and Gunn, M. J. (1996) *Smith and Bailey on the modern English legal system*, Sweet & Maxwell

Civil court service, Jordans. Annual with supplements
Also available as a subscription website and on CD-ROM. Known as 'The Green Book', this sets out the civil procedure rules, practice directory, protocol and court guide.

Encyclopaedia of forms and precedents, Butterworths. Continuously updated
Also available as a subscription website and on CD-ROM. Contains over 10,000 practical forms and precedents covering all aspects on non-contentious law.

Law Society, *The Law Society's directory of solicitors and barristers*, Law Society.

Annual
Also on CD-ROM.

Current law yearbooks, Sweet & Maxwell
These give recent changes to the law.

Halsbury's laws of England, Butterworths. Continuous revision with loose-leaf
up-dating services, annual volumes and revised subject volumes
This multi-volumed subject encyclopedia of English law is the best-known
standard source and often the best first source to consult. Note that the
index references are to numbered paragraphs, not pages! *Halsbury's laws*
should not be confused with *Halsbury's statutes*, which is an encyclopedia of
Acts of Parliament.

Family court practice, Family Law. Annual.
This is the standard guide to practice and procedure in family courts.

Stroud's judicial dictionary of words and phrases (2000), 6th edn, Sweet &
Maxwell
A comprehensive dictionary of law. Also available on CD-ROM.

Hussain, J. (1999) *Islamic law and society: an introduction*, Federation Press

Manson-Smith, D. (1998) *The legal system of Scotland*, Scottish Consumer
Council

Murdoch, H. (1993) *A dictionary of Irish law*, 2nd edn, Topaz

Abbreviations

Most problems relate to the citation of law reports. Legal reference sources usually provide a key to abbreviations. Particularly useful are:

Raistrick, D. (1993) *Index to legal citations and abbreviations*, 2nd edn, Bowker-
Saur
Halsbury's laws of England (2001), vol. 1, 9th edn, Sweet & Maxwell
Osborn's concise law dictionary, Butterworths

Law reports

Law reports are a special class of literature with their own structure, style of citation, rationale and publishing patterns. Law reports are the detailed record of court
cases in which important or significant points of law occur. Such reports record

the facts, issues, decisions and, more importantly, the legal principles upon which the judgement was made. Such reports will influence subsequent decisions and are therefore often cited and required. Generally such cases appear in the High Courts or Courts of Appeal. Note that the many high-profile cases reported in the press have no 'report' in the sense used here.

All England law reports, Butterworths. Weekly with annual cumulations
Weekly law reports, Incorporated Council of Law Reporting for England.
   Weekly

The above are rival publications which carry details of the judgements and a report of the arguments of counsel.

The law reports, Incorporated Council of Law Reporting for England. Annual
   volumes
   These are the 'official' reports of cases and are checked by the judges. They are preferred by the courts. Over the years there have been several series. Currently there are four: Appeal Cases (AC), Chancery Division (Ch), Queen's Bench Division (QB), and Family Division (Fam).

The digest, Butterworths. Updated replacement volumes
   A multi-volume encyclopedia of law reports giving a subject approach. Useful for covering legal jurisdiction beyond England, but not beyond the Commonwealth, and older cases.

There are many different series of law reports. Examples are the *European human rights reports, Industrial cases reports* and *VAT tribunal reports*. Only the larger and specialist law libraries are likely to have these.

Case citators

To find out if, and where, a court case is reported, the following can be used:
Current law case citator (1972–), Sweet & Maxwell. Revised cumulated volume
   annually

The digest, noted above, has separate volumes indexing the cases the publication features.

   All England reports, noted above, lists all the cases it features, in its consolidated tables and indexes.

Law reports indexes
   These index not only the law reports themselves, but also cases published

in the *AER*, *Criminal appeal reports*, *Lloyds law reports*, *Local government reports*, *Road traffic reports*, and *Tax cases*.

Halsbury's laws of England, noted above, has detailed indexes to cases cited in each of its volumes (though the subject area needs to be known).

Textbooks on law usually index cases cited.

Electronic sources

Many of the above sources are available in electronic form. Law publishers such as Butterworths (e.g. All England Direct) and Sweet & Maxwell offer many of their voluminous texts on databases, often combining many such sources. Details will be found on the publishers' websites.

Solicitors – online.com **www.solicitors-online.com**

> This is a directory of law firms in England and Wales with access by name of solicitor and firm, and by subject. Has information on choosing and using a lawyer. It is based on the Law Society's records.

Court Service website **www.courtservice.gov.uk**

> The Court Service is an agency of the Lord Chancellor's Department which is responsible for the running of the Court Service. Gives details about the courts and subjects such as wills and probate and jury service.

Other sources

The Law Society
> 113 Chancery Lane, London WC2A 1PL
> Tel: 020 7242 1222
> E-mail: info.services@lawsociety.org.uk
> **www.lawsociety.org.uk**
> The professional body for solicitors in England and Wales. Provides services and support for solicitors; sets standards, and works to improve access to the law

The Incorporated Council of Law Reporting for England and Wales
> Megarery House, 119 Chancery Lane, London WC2A 1PP
> Tel: 020 6471 Fax: 020 7831 5247
> E-mail: postmaster@iclr.co.uk
> **www.lawreports.co.uk**

Tips and pitfalls

Be aware of where the local specialist law collections are, but note that access to these collections may be restricted. Sometimes special arrangements can be negotiated for library staff to gain access on an enquirer's behalf, or specific cases can be supplied as photocopies.

Get to know how law books are arranged in the library; there are many different versions of most classifications – even a specialist law classification (Moys). Books on the law of a certain subject may be shelved with other books on the subject, e.g. child law in a social welfare section rather than with other law books.

Be prepared, when referring someone to a solicitor, for the response 'But I am a solicitor!'

LEGAL DEPOSIT *see* COPYRIGHT

LEISURE & RECREATION

See also Games Rules; Libraries; Museums & Galleries; Sports

Typical questions

- How much do people spend on leisure activities?
- Where's the nearest swimming pool?
- I'm doing a tourism course. What useful sources do you have?

Considerations

This subject can probably be split into two types of questions. Firstly there are those needing either lists of various leisure facilities or local contacts for leisure activities. Much of the local information you should have readily available. In the majority of cases your local authority will have its own website detailing local amenities and events. The second is more in-depth, usually regarding tourism or leisure spending statistics. For this you will require statistical publications and/or market research reports, both of which can be expensive. If your library does not subscribe to such things then you could make use of the various sites on the internet. Some general publications also contain leisure and recreation statistics, such as *Annual abstract of statistics*, *Social trends*, and *Regional trends*.

Where to look

Directories

Municipal yearbook, 2 vols, Hemming Information Services
> Useful for details and contacts of departments within local authorities.

Travel trade gazette, United Business
> This publication covers 16,000 companies involved in the travel and holiday industry.

Journals

There are numerous journals for the leisure industry, details of which can be found in *Willings press guide* (*see* Journals & Periodicals).

Leisure and Hospitality Business
> Centaur Communications
> Tel: 020 7970 4000 Fax: 020 7970 4392
> **www.leisureweek.co.uk**
> 25 issues per year

Market intelligence

Mintel leisure reports, Mintel International Group
> Provides in-depth research into the leisure and recreation industry. Looks at market factors, market segmentation, the consumer and the future. Also available on CD-ROM. For details visit **www.mintel.co.uk** or tel: 020 7606 4533, fax: 020 7606 5932.

Key Note reports, Key Note
> For free executive summaries of report titles listed under travel and tourism visit **www.keynote.co.uk**. For details of obtaining full reports, contact Key Note (tel: 020 8481 8750, fax: 020 87830049).

Statistics

> British Tourist Authority, *Digest of tourist statistics*, British Tourist Authority and Tourism Intelligence Quarterly
> **www.visitbritain.com**.
> For links to tourist boards and other tourism-related sites, register on the tourism industry professional site.

Yearbook of tourism statistics, 2 vols, World Tourism Organization
  www.world-tourism.org

Tourism Market Trends (2000), The Stationery Office
  There are five titles in this series: Africa, East Asia and the Pacific, Europe,
  Middle East, and South Asia.

Organizations and websites

There are hundreds of organizations dealing with the huge range of sports and
leisure activities available. There is a very good selection of contacts in *Key
organizations 2002*, Carel Press. In addition, using one of the search engines such
as **google.com** will also give good results.

Association of British Travel Agents **www.abtanet.com**

Association of Leading Visitor Attractions **www.alva.org.uk**

Business in Sport and Leisure
  17a Chartfield Ave, Putney, London SW15 6DX
  Tel: 020 8780 2377
  www.bisi.org

Visit Britain **www.visitbritain.com**

Institute of Leisure and Amenity Management
  ILAM House, Lower Basildon, Reading, Berks RG8 9NE
  Tel: 01491 874800
  www.ilam.co.uk

LeisureHunt **www.leisurehunt.com**

Re:Source The Council for Museums, Archive and Libraries
  www.resource.gov.uk

Star UK **www.staruk.org.uk**

LETTERS *see* ETIQUETTE & FORMS OF ADDRESS; WRITERS & WRITING

LIBRARIES

Typical questions
- What is the address and telephone number of Leeds Central Library?
- Can I see the library catalogue on the internet?

Considerations
Most questions about libraries tend to centre around addresses and opening hours, and whether or not they have a certain book or periodical in stock.

Where to look
Printed sources
Libraries in the United Kingdom and the Republic of Ireland, Facet Publishing. Annual

This essential directory lists all public, school and academic library services in the country, as well as selected government, national and special libraries. There is also a useful list of departments of librarianship or information science and key library agencies.

For library and careers news, the journal of the profession is *Library and Information Update*. This is published by the CILIP: the Chartered Institute of Library and Information Professionals. You can contact them at:

CILIP
7 Ridgmount St, London WC1E 7AE
Tel: 020 7255 0500 Fax: 020 7255 0501
Text phone: 020 7255 0505
E-mail: info@cilip.org.uk
www.cilip.org.uk/
CILIP was formed in April 2002 by the merger of the Institute of Information Scientists and The Library Association.

Electronic sources
Most UK library authorities will have their own websites showing locations and opening hours of libraries. Some may even give access to their catalogues. Try the local authority's website and there should be links from there. Or there is a list on the following website:

dspace.dial.pipex.com/town/square/ac940/weblibs.html

The internet is the ideal platform for increasing access to your library's catalogue. Many libraries now have their catalogues on the world wide web.

The British Library online catalogue and website is at

www.bl.uk

For university, college and public library catalogues on the internet, try:

www.niss.ac.uk/lis/obi/obi.html

For national libraries worldwide:

www.library.uq.edu.au/natlibs/

Tips and pitfalls

Always suggest that the user phones the library concerned before visiting, as opening hours can change and branch libraries can even close completely.

LITERATURE

See also Bibliographies, References & Citation; Books; Poems & Poetry; Writers & Writing

Typical questions

- What books did J. B. Priestley write?
- I'd like to know more about the Shakespeare authorship controversy.
- What other books were written at the time Emily Brontë wrote *Wuthering Heights*?
- Who wrote *Beowulf*?
- What Indian classics are available in English?

Considerations

Little needs to be said about literature enquiries since most library staff will be pretty well aware of the subject and reference books on literature are numerous. As always, do seek clarification: misunderstandings, misconceptions and, importantly, mis-spellings, can all result in wasted time.

Printed sources

General

Entries on literary topics and authors can be found in a wide variety of resources, including general encyclopedias. Do advise readers to check the index as well as the main A–Z sequences.

Encyclopedias

Encyclopedia of American literature (1999), Gale

Cassell's encyclopaedia of world literature (1973), 3 vols, Cassell

McGraw-Hill encyclopedia of world drama (1983), 2nd edn, McGraw-Hill

Drabble, M. (ed.) (2000) *Oxford companion to English literature: a thousand years of English literature*, 6th edn, Oxford University Press
Just one of the many Oxford University Press companions; other examples are *Oxford companion to French literature* and *Oxford companion to German literature*.

Stapleton, M. (1983) *The Cambridge guide to English literature*, Cambridge University Press.
An A–Z encyclopedia.

Benet, W. R. (1998) *The reader's encyclopedia*, 4th edn, edited by B. Murphey, A & C Black.
A one-volume encyclopedia on world literature. Some 10,000 biographies of poets, playwrights, novelists and essayists, plot summaries, sketches of principal characters, myths, legends and folklore, biographies of artists, musicians and historical personages, as well as recipients of major literary awards.

Guides

Hawkins-Dady, M. (ed.) (1996) *Readers' guide to literature in English*, Fitzroy Dearborn

Smallwood, P. J. (1985) *A concise chronology of English literature*, Croom Helm
Displays parallel chronological sequences of literary and world events.

Marcuse, M. J. (1990) *A reference guide to English studies*, University of California Press

L LITERATURE

A remarkably comprehensive annotated guide in 780 large-format pages.

Guides to content

Many enquirers, usually quiz and crossword enthusiasts, want to know details of characters or places in a particular novel. Two useful sources are:

Magill, F. (ed.) (1949, 1952, 1960) *Masterpieces of world literature in digest form*, 3 vols, Harper

Haydn, H. and Fuller, E. (1949) *Thesaurus of book digests*, Arco

Biographical

International authors and writers who's who, Melrose. Bi-annual

Seymour-Smith, M. (1990) *Who's who in twentieth century literature*, Weidenfeld

British Council (1979) *British writers*, 8 vols, Scribners

St James Press produce the following annual titles:

Contemporary poets
Contemporary dramatists
Contemporary novelists

Histories

Cambridge history of English literature, 15 vols, Cambridge University Press

Bibliographies

Cambridge bibliography of English literature (1974–7), 2nd edn, 3rd edn in progress, Cambridge University Press

Bibliography of American literature (1955–1991), Yale University Press

Annual bibliography of English language and literature (1922–), Modern Humanities Research Association
Online and CD-ROM versions. Includes periodical articles as well as books.

See also the British Library and Library of Congress catalogues (*see* Libraries).

Selected lists

Bradbury, M. (2001) *The modern British novel 1878–2001*, 2nd edn, Penguin Books
Discursive text with extensive listing of authors and titles.

Smith, F. S. (1963) *An English library: a bookman's guide*, 4th edn Andre Deutsch
An annotated guide to the best books.

Raphael, F. and McLeish, K. (1981) *The list of books: a recommended library of over 3,000 works*, Mitchell Beazley
Wider subject coverage but less annotation than Smith above.

Seymour-Smith, M. (1998) *The 100 most influential books ever written: the history of thought from ancient times to today*, Citadel Press

Rogers, J. (ed.) (2001) *Good fiction guide*, Oxford University Press
34 subject essays and 1,000 writers in A–Z order.

Theory

Gale study guides to great literature: literary topics, e.g. magic realism (1999), Gale
Hawthorne, J. (1998) *A glossary of contemporary literary theory*, Arnold
Cuddon, J. A. (1999) *The Penguin dictionary of literary terms and literary theory*, 4th edn, Penguin

Reviews

Times Literary Supplement
London Review of Books

Most broadsheet newspapers and periodicals review books.

Children

Lansberg, M. (1988) *The world of children's books*, Simon & Schuster
Includes over 400 recommended titles.

This, and others, are updated by the annual *100 best books*, published by Booktrust.

Electronic sources

Bibliomania **www.bibliomania.com**
Hundreds of searchable full-text works of classic and popular fiction, short stories, drama, poetry, research and religious texts. Includes *Brewer's dictionary of phrase and fable*, *Webster's dictionary*, *Roget's thesaurus* and *Biographical dictionary of English literature*. Includes literary criticism. A huge resource.

A similar project is Bartleby **www.bartleby.com**

BUBL Language and Literature **http://bubl.ac.link/lan.html**
A catalogue of selected internet resources.

Register of UK Societies **www.uksocieties.com**
Directory of over 500 British-based literary and historical societies.

Literary resources **www.andromeda.rutgers.edu/-jlynch/Lit**

IPL Online Literary Criticism Collection **www.ipl.org/ref/litcrit**

Online texts
The Online Books Page **http://onlinebooks.library.upenn.edu/**
Project Gutenberg **http://promo.net/pg/list.html**
Internet Classics **http://classics.mit.edu**

Other sources
In addition to web-based literature resources, there are a number of reprint and microfiche services available, such as ProQuest's 'The Nineteenth Century' collection of over 13,000 texts available on microfiche. The online catalogue is free at: **http://c19.proquest.co.uk**

LOCAL GOVERNMENT *see* GOVERNMENT

LOCAL HISTORY

See also Family History & Genealogy; History & Archaeology; Parish Registers

Typical questions
• I want to research my locality. Where do I start?
• Where can I see tithe awards?
• Who lived in my house before me?

Considerations
Local history is the subject of a large number of enquiries. Typically, they will require a detailed knowledge of what is available in the nearest local studies

library, the local history sections of larger libraries, and local archives and record offices. Do know where these are, though before referring enquirers to them, do ascertain that referral is necessary, and do warn enquirers that seeking local information can be a lengthy process.

While a number of general principles apply, for which some of the handbooks listed below may be useful, each locality is different, has a different history, and therefore has material unique to itself. What may be the case in one place may not apply in another.

Where to look
Printed sources

Campbell-Kease, J. (1989) *A companion to local history research*, A & C Black
320 pages of reference for the local historian.

Hey, D. (ed.) (1996) *The Oxford companion to local and family history*, Oxford University Press
Over 2000 entries.

Stuart, D. (2001) *Latin for local and family historians*, Phillimore

Martin, C. T. (1976) *The record interpreter*, 2nd edn, Phillimore
Provides a glossary of abbreviations and archaic terms, together with Latin forms of British names.

Local History Magazine. Six issues per year
www.local-history.co.uk/home.html
Useful advertisements and news items.

The Local Historian. Quarterly
www.balh.co.uk/
Journal of the British Association for Local History

Specialist Sources

Local history enquiries will often entail consulting the rich (and confusing) variety of local printed and non-book material. These include the following. Do consult with, or refer enquirers to your nearest local history library or archives office.

Trade directories

From the late 18th century until today, directories form a valuable source of

local information. The amount of information varies from directory to directory, but most will contain a general account of the district, details of local government, a list of streets and their residents, an alphabetical list of residents, and a classified trades section. The Post Office directories appearing from the 1880s are particularly useful. After World War 2 the Barrett directories, then the Thomson directories, continued the tradition. Check with your local studies library for details of what is available.

Telephone directories
Old copies of these may be kept.

Local newspapers
These are invaluable for local history, but rarely are they indexed. Researchers will need to spend a long time searching unless they can find dates from other sources. Many will be on microfilm. Check your local studies library for details of what is available. (*The Times* and other national papers may be available and may contain news of local events. *The Times* is on microfilm back to 1785 and is indexed.)

Other printed sources
Other printed sources include: local journals and magazines, newscuttings, illustrations and photographs, Census enumerators' returns, local authority documents, parish and nonconformist registers (*see* Parish Registers), monumental inscriptions, pamphlets and leaflets.

Series such as the Harleian Society, The Thoresby Society and the Surtees Society, which reprint documentary material, are often asked for by scholars.

Electronic sources
Most places will have a large variety of local websites.

Up My Street **www.upmystreet.com**
    Contemporary information by postcode.

Public Record Office **www.pro.gov.uk**
    National archives information and useful printable leaflets.

Historical Manuscripts Commission **www.hmc.gov.uk**

Local History Magazine **www.local-history.co.uk**

Borthwick Institute **www.york.ac.uk/inst/bihr/**
　　A centre for the north of England.

Oral History Society **www.essex.ac.uk/homepage.html**

Other sources

National index of parish registers: a guide to Anglican, Roman Catholic and Non-
　　Conformist registers together with information on bishop's transcripts, modern
　　copies and marriage licences, Society of Genealogists

Local record searchers

A number of people offer their services to search records for a charge. Their
knowledge of the location of local resources, experience of using these resources,
and understanding of local history make it convenient to use their services, especially for people living away from the area. Local history libraries will often have
a list of local searchers. Further record searchers may be found in the advertisement pages of journals such as *Local History Magazine*, *Family Tree Magazine*,
Genealogists Magazine and local or regional magazines such as *The Dalesman*.

Association of Genealogists and Researchers in Archives
　　29 Badgers Close, Horsham, West Sussex, RH12 5RU
　　www.agra.org.uk
　　This provides training courses in record searching and gives accreditation
　　to successful candidates.

British Association for Local History (BALH)
　　PO Box 1576, Salisbury, Wiltshire SP2 8SY
　　Fax: 01722 413242
　　E-mail:info@balh.co.uk

Local history groups will often have knowledgeable members. It may be appropriate to refer enquirers to one of these.
　　Local history libraries or departments and local archives and record offices will
have a variety of special collections, catalogues and indexes. Refer enquirers to these.

Tips and pitfalls

Many of the resources useful for local history will be fragile and restrictions
may be made about their use. Warn enquirers that many will also be on microfilm and microfiche.

MAGAZINES *see* JOURNALS & PERIODICALS

MANUFACTURING

Typical questions
- What is the UK's manufacturing output?
- What is the state of manufacturing worldwide?

Considerations
When enquirers are asking about manufacturing make sure they understand what it is. *Kompass*, *Dun & Bradstreet's key British enterprises* and *Kelly's* all provide lists of manufacturers for all types of products. You will find details of these directories in Companies. In addition, look at specific subject headings for specific sources.

Where to look
Directories

As well as the above try:

Kelly's OnLine **www.kellysearch.com**
> This covers the manufacturing industry. The enquirer can search by company name, product/services, postcode and trade name.

Statistics

Manufacturing worldwide: industry analysis statistics (1999), Gale Group
> This provides data on 500 manufactured products and commodities. It also gives details of 4000-plus companies in 119 countries.

PRODCOM annual and quarterly industry reports are an excellent source of manufacturer sales figures. These are available to download from **www.statistics. gov.uk/onlineproducts/PRODCOM2000_annual.asp** or **www.statistics. gov.uk/OnlineProducts/default.asp.**

Economic trends, The Stationery Office
> Look for world trade in goods.

Producer prices indices: the economy, The Stationery Office
> This is available at **www.statistics.gov.uk.**

Market research

It is not always easy to obtain market research on the manufacturing industry. However:

Barclays Corporate Banking **www.corporate.barclays.com**
    offers a number of reports on the manufacturing sectors.

Use also:

Mintel industrial reports, Mintel International Group
    For details visit **www.mintel.co.uk** or tel: 020 7606 5932.

Websites

Confederation of British Industry
    Centre Point, 103 New Oxford St, London WC1A 1DU
    Tel: 0207395 8247
    www.cbi.org.uk

Engineering Employers' Federation **www.eef.org.uk**
    The voice of the engineering and manufacturing in the UK. Excellent for publications.

Heavy Industry News **www.heavyindustry.com**

Institute of Manufacturing
    Warwick Corner, 42 Warwick Rd, Kenilworth, Warwickshire CV8 1HE

MANUSCRIPTS *see* ALPHABETS & SCRIPTS; ARCHIVES

MAPS

See also Atlases & Gazetteers; Geography

Typical questions

- I want an Ordnance Survey map of the Yorkshire Dales.
- Have you any old maps of Bulgaria?
- Have you a Victorian map of Bradford?

MAPS

Considerations

It is not necessary to list all the different types of maps and atlases available. Most encyclopedias will contain basic maps, and as for Ordnance Survey maps, simply go and check to see what you have on the shelves. Problems are more likely to be encountered in smaller branch libraries where stock may be limited.

Where to look

Old maps

Most local studies departments of libraries will stock old maps of their areas. Check your local studies department to see what is available.

Useful address

Ordnance Survey, Romsey Rd, Southampton SO16 4GU
> Tel: 08456 05 05 05.
> Fax: 023 8079 2615
> **www.ordsvy.gov.uk/**

Electronic sources

You can download maps at some of the following sites.

> **www.mappy.com**
> **www.old-maps.co.uk**
> **www.multimap.co.uk**

There is an excellent collection of country and historical maps at the following:

> **www.lib.utexas.edu/maps/index.html**

Tips and pitfalls

Beware of copyright on maps, especially OS ones. As a simple rule, you are allowed to take four A4 copies of a single extract from an OS map, and these must be for private use only. OS will send you a notice if you ask them.

Local tourist offices will often have free maps of the area to give away.

MARKET RESEARCH

See also European Information; Statistics

Typical questions
* I'm doing some market research on...
* What is the potential future trend for...?
* How do children spend their pocket money?
* How popular is TV?

Considerations

Market research is either primary or secondary, or put another way, field or desk. Field research is actually going out and collecting the raw data and desk is using printed sources of data already available. For people interested in doing field research for themselves, look no further than *Business information factsheets* for one-page easy guides. Those carrying out desk research for either a business plan or a college project can use reports prepared by specialist market research companies or some of the vast range of statistics available. However, for those with limited access to printed sources there are lots of excellent websites to use. There is an extensive list given here which should offer a range of free reports and surveys.

Where to look
Directories

For market research companies use:

International directory of market research organizations, a joint venture between
> The Market Research Society and Norton Sterling Associates, IMRI Ltd
> **www.IMRIresearch.com**
> The website is useful for market research links.

Business and industrial marketing research companies and consultants 2000 buyer's guide, Market Research Society
> **www.mrweb.co.uk/big/**
> This site is also useful for information on desk research.

Market intelligence

Mintel reports, Mintel International Group
> These market reports provide in-depth research. They look at market

factors, market segmentation, the consumer and the future. Also available on CD-ROM. For details visit **www.mintel.co.uk** or tel: 020 7606 4533, fax: 020 7606 5932.

Key Note reports, Key Note

For free executive summaries of report titles visit **www.keynote.co.uk**. For details of obtaining full reports, contact Key Note (tel: 020 8481 8750, fax: 020 8783 0049).

Other market research companies include:

Euromonitor
Tel: 020 7251 8024
www.euromonitor.com

Frost and Sullivan
Tel: 020 7730 3438
www.frost.com

Jordans
Tel: 0117 923 0600
www.jordanpublishing.co.uk

and there are others.

Free reports

Barclays **www.corporate.barclays.com**

Barclays produces a whole range of industry reports. These can be downloaded from the website. In addition, there are also economic reports.

HSBC – Business Economics Unit
Tel: 020 7260 7213
This produces an excellent market report series called 'Taking the pulse'.

LloydsTSB Commercial **www.lloydstsbcommercial.com**

Websites

Bird Online **www.bird-online.co.uk/keynote**
Provides free executive reports from Key Note.

Cabinet Office (People's Panel) **www.cabinet-office.gov.uk**

CyberAtlas **http://cyberatlas.internet.com**
    Surveys and statistics.

Datamonitor **www.datamonitor.com**

Fletcher Research **www.fletch.co.uk**

Free Pint **www.freepint.co.uk/portal/market/**
    Excellent for market research summaries from Datamonitor.

Government National Statistics **www.statistics.gov.uk**

International Market Research Mall **www.imrmall.com**

Key Note **www.keynote.co.uk**
    For free executive summaries

Major Market Profile **www.majormarketprofiles.com**
    For free summaries of international market reports

Market Research on the Web **www.irn-research.com/database.htmla**
    European gateway from IRN (Information Research Network), containing
    news and links to sites of interest to researchers. An excellent starting point
    for research.

Mori **www.mori.co.uk/**
    Excellent site for reports.

Nestlé **www.nestlefamilymonitor.co.uk/** or **www.nestle.co.uk**
    Excellent for family monitors reports.

Research Index **www.researchindex.co.uk/data/home.htm**
    This database indexes news stories on industries and companies.

Tips and pitfalls

Market research sometimes requires persistence and patience. Sometimes you can
find things quickly, other times the subject area may need more time. It is important that your enquirer appreciates this. You may need to use more than one report
or set of statistics to build up a picture and it is sometimes hard to get this across
to enquirers. However, if you can produce something fairly quickly which provides
some basic information that the user can be working on, such as *Annual abstract of
statistics*, you can then feed other sources through to build up a good picture. By which
time the user has settled down into 'doing research' and not hoping for a quick answer.

MEDALS & DECORATIONS

See also Antiques; Coins & Stamps; Etiquette & Forms of Address; Uniforms

Typical questions

- I found this medal when sorting through some junk. What is it?
- Have you a list of winners of the Victoria Cross?
- What are these medals worth?

Considerations

Distinguish between enquiries which have a family connection, such as where a medal was awarded to an ancestor, and collectors of militaria and memorabilia. They need different treatment.

Among the current generation, knowledge of campaign and war medals is generally absent, and, indeed, answering questions on the subject perhaps distasteful. However, the librarian must bear in mind that decorations were worn with pride and often represented great courage and sacrifice. One must be aware of the attitudes and context of the time when the medals and decorations were awarded, and for what they were awarded.

Medals and other commemorative objects extend into other areas of public service, and beyond into the field of 'collectables'.

Where to look

General

Buckland, C. *The medal yearbook*, Pen and Sword. Annual
    Guide for medal collectors, giving prices and availability.

Clarke, J. D. (2001) *Gallantry medals and decorations of the world*, Pen and Sword
    270 decorations for 43 countries. Includes ribbons.

Holmes, R. (ed.) (2001) *The Oxford companion to military history*, Leo Cooper

The London Gazette, HMSO. Weekly
    The official government publication where awards are announced and citations given. These details will get reported in national and relevant local newspapers.

Biographical sources

Honoured by the Queen: recipients of honours (1995), Belgrave Press
   Lists some 200,000 people honoured 1952–94.

Commemoratives and non-service

Eimer, C. (1989) *An introduction to commemorative medals*, Seaby

Setchfield, F.R. (1986) *The official badge collector's guide*, Longman
   Hobby badges rather than medals. The 'official' designation is surely
   'tongue-in-cheek'!

Gordon, L.L. (1979) *British battles and medals*, 5th edn, Spink
   Covers 18th to 20th centuries.

Arlsby, C. (1989) *Allied combat medals of World War II. Volume 1: the British, the
   Commonwealth and Western European nations*, P Stephens Ltd

Description and identification

Abbott, P .E. and Tamblin, T. A. (1971) *British gallantry awards*, Guinness
   Superlatives

Dorling, H. T. (1983) *Ribbons and medals*, 20th edn, Osprey

Gaylor, J. (1996) *Military badge collecting*. Leo Cooper

Hieronymussen, P. (1975) *Orders, medals and decorations of Britain and Europe*,
   2nd edn, Blandford Press

Mericka, V. (1976) *Book of orders and decorations*, Hamlyn
   Gives background.

Ripley, H. (1976) *Buttons of the British army 1855–1970: an illustrated reference
   guide for collectors*, Arms and Armour Press
   Updated price guides issued from time to time.

Joslin, E. C. et al. (1988) *British battles and medals: a full list from 1588*, Spink

Wilkinson, F. (1992) *Badges of the British army, 1820 to the present: an illustrated
   guide for collectors*, Arms and Armour Press

Etiquette

Tinson, A.R. (1999) *'Medals will be worn.' Wearing medals past and present*,

1844–1999, Token Publishing

Prices and valuations

Arden, Y. (1976) *Military medals and decorations: a price guide for collectors*, David & Charles

Litherland, A. R. and Simpkin, B. T. (1990) *Spink's standard catalogue of British and associated orders, decorations and medals, with valuations*, Spink

Victoria Cross

Harvey, D. (2001) *Monuments to courage*, 2 vols, distributed by Pat M. da Costa, 124 Oatlands Drive, Weybridge Drive, Surrey KT13 9HL
Fully illustrated guide to each of the 1350 VCs.

The register of the Victoria Cross (1988), 2nd edn, Beshara Press
Gives brief details and photographs of recipients.

Electronic sources

Military Books **www.militarybooks.co.uk**
A consortium of book dealers.

Pen and Sword **www.pen-and-sword.co.uk**
Specialist publisher website, includes Leo Cooper books.

Other sources

Orders and Medals Research Society
PO Box 248, Snettisham, Kings Lynn PE31 7TA
www.omrs.org.uk

Spink and Son Medal Service
69 Southampton Row, London WC1B 4ET
E-mail: info@spinkandson.com
www.spink-online.com
Commercial dealer.

Tips and pitfalls

The usual librarianly caveat about giving advice and opinion applies, particularly to the enquiries: 'What's this worth?' and 'What's this?'

MEDICINE *see* DRUGS; HEALTH & HEALTHCARE

MEETINGS *see* CONFERENCES & EXHIBITIONS; ETIQUETTE & FORMS OF ADDRESS

MEMBERS OF PARLIAMENT

See also Election Results; Government

Typical questions

- Who is my local MP?
- Can you give me the address of my local MP?
- What is the name of the Minister of Transport?
- Who is my MEP?

Where to look

Directories

Dod's parliamentary companion 2001, Vacher Dod Publishing

This provides an alphabetical listing of all MPs, giving for each their age, education, marital status and details of their parliamentary career. It includes contact details both in the constituency he/she represents and at the House of Commons. In addition it lists alphabetically all the constituencies in the UK in order to locate the MP for that area. Also gives an alphabetical listing of the members of the House of Lords.

The political companion (2001), The Stationery Office

This contains biographies of MPs, MEPs, Lords and members of the Greater London Authority, Scottish Parliament and Executive, Northern Ireland Assembly and the Welsh Assembly.

Who's who in the EU (2000/1), Office of Official Publications of the European Communities

This provides contact details of elected members of the European Parliament.

The Times (2001) *Guide to the House of Commons*, Times Books

Gives brief details of MPs by constituency, with alphabetical surname index and related parliamentary information.

M MEMBERS OF PARLIAMENT

Contacting an MP

MPs will deal with enquiries/issues from their constituents. If the enquirer does not know the constituency in which they live, the internet service Constituency Locator is a must:

www.locata.co.uk/commons

Enquirers can write to their MP's office at the:

House of Commons
London, SW1A 0AA.

For ex- or deceased MPs try:

Stenton. M and Lees. S (1981) *Who's who of British Members of Parliament 1832–1979*, 4 vols, Harvester Press

In addition you could try *Who was who* or *Who's who*.

Websites

Europarl **www.europarl.eu.int**
Another excellent site for everything to do with the European Parliament including MEPs.

Political Links **www.politicallinks.co.uk**
Published by Vacher Dod Publishing. This is an excellent site. You won't need anything else to answer questions on parliament and politicians.

You can also try **www.upmystreet.com** for local MPs.

MINORITIES *see* RIGHTS

MONARCHY *see* KINGS & QUEENS, RULERS & HEADS OF STATE

MONEY

See also Coins & Stamps; Employment (for wages/salaries); Prices

Typical questions
- What is the exchange rate for Italy?
- What currency is used in Kuwait?
- What was £1 worth 20 years ago?

Where to look

Directories

If you are looking for details on monetary units and denominations for any country in the world look no further than the website of

Bankers Almanac **www.bankersalmanac.com**
> Go into 'Information bank', click 'Currencies of the world', and select either 'View countries' or 'View currencies'. It gives the monetary unit for both notes and coins.

For information on the Euro, look no further than
> Euro Information: the Official Treasury Euro Resources **www.euro.gov.uk**
> This is an excellent, informative site. It provides pictures of the notes and coins. It also has lots of publications which can be downloaded.

Statistics

Economic Trends, Office for National Statistics
> A monthly publication, by the Office for National Statistics in collaboration with the statistics divisions of the government departments and the Bank of England, which brings together all the main economic indicators.

Financial Times
> Daily
> World currencies listed on Monday.

Old Money: Current Value
> **www.ex.ac.uk/~RDavies/arian/current/howmuch.html**

Journals

The Economist
>The Economist Newspaper
>Tel: 020 7830 7000 Fax: 020 7839 2968/9
>**www.economist.com**
>Weekly
>Gives currency and exchange rates.

Moneyfacts
>Moneyfacts Group
>Tel: 01603 476476 Fax: 01603 476201
>**www.moneyfacts.co.uk**
>Monthly
>A guide to the UK savings and mortgage rates.

Money Management
>FT Business
>Tel: 020 7896 2525 Fax: 020 7896 2099
>Monthly

Websites

Currency Converter **www.currencysite.com**

Current Exchange Rates **www.oanda.com**
>Allows you to convert from any currency to any currency.

MOTOR INDUSTRY *see* CARS & THE MOTOR INDUSTRY

MOTTOES *see* DICTIONARIES; HERALDRY & COATS OF ARMS

MUSEUMS & GALLERIES

>*See also* Art

Typical questions
- What are the opening hours and charges of the Tate Modern?
- Which exhibitions are on at the Lowry Centre in Salford at the moment?

Considerations
Most main libraries should have a directory of museums, showing opening hours, charges, etc. For up-to-date information regarding current exhibitions, though, the internet is ideal.

Where to look
Printed sources

Museums yearbook, Museums Association. Annual
> Contains a directory of museums, listing museums alphabetically by town. Information includes admission charges, opening hours and facilities. There is also a listing of members of the Museums Association and a directory of related organizations, e.g. suppliers.

Electronic sources

There is a huge listing of UK museums by area at:

www.24hourmuseum.org.uk

You can also search this site for specific collections.
> For world museums try the following site:

http://Vlmp.museophile.com/world.html#museums

For news, contacts and links from the Museums Association, try their website:

www.museumsassociation.org

Tips and pitfalls
If your enquirer is looking for details of a particular museum and its current exhibitions, simply use a search engine on the internet and type in the name of the museum.

MUSIC

Typical questions
- How much are these records worth?
- How can I buy an old record?
- When was Bill Haley's 'Rock around the clock' a hit?
- How many Number Ones did Elvis Presley have?
- What's the story behind *Die Fledermaus*?

Considerations
The literature of music is huge. The subject is huge. The topics featured below are just those that can cause difficulties. Most general enquiries about composers and music history can be answered from the many, many general dictionaries and encyclopedias.

Occasionally, a knowledge of music notation will be required. Know which members of staff have this knowledge. It is also useful to know the musical tastes of staff.

Downloading performances via the internet is not considered here, nor indeed the supply of different musical media, print, audio or video, for loan or in-house listening or viewing.

Where to look
General

The new Grove dictionary of music and musicians (2001), 2nd edn, Grove Music
  This is the standard 'biggie' 29-volume classic resource.

Arnold, D. (ed.) (1983) *The new Oxford companion to music*, 2vols, Oxford University Press

Harrap's illustrated dictionary of music and musicians (1990), Harrap

Jacobs, A. (1996) *Dictionary of music*, 6th edn, Penguin

Kennedy, M. (1994) *The Oxford guide to music*, 2nd edn, Oxford University Press

New Oxford history of music, (1974), 11 vols, Oxford University Press

Randel, D. M. (1986) *The new Harvard dictionary of music*, Belknap Press

248

Sadie, S. (ed.) (1985) *The Cambridge music guide*, Cambridge University Press
Chapter-length essays with detailed index.

Baker's biographical dictionary of musicians (2001), 9th edn, Gale
A six-volume heavyweight containing over 41,000 addresses.

European music directory, K. G. Saur. Annual

Contemporary musicians

Cummings, D. M. (ed.) *International who's who in music and musician's directory*,
vol. 1: *Classical and light classical fields*, International Biographical Centre.
Bi-annual

Festivals

Adams, R. (1986) *A book of British music festivals*, R. Royce

Price guides

Hamlyn, N. (1997) *The Penguin price guide for records and CD collectors*, Penguin
Over 14,000 valuations.

Pelletier, P. (ed.) (1991) *The essential British price guide to collecting 45/78 rpm
singles 1950–1960*, Record Information Services

Record Collector (2000) *Rare record collector*, Record Collector
Over 100,000 entries.

Publishing

Music publishers international ISMN directory (2000), 3rd edn, K G Saur

Recordings

Penguin guide to compact discs (1999), Penguin
Classical good CD guide, Gramophone Publications. Annual

Songs and lyrics

Amin, K. and Cochrane, J. (1986) *The great British songbook*, Faber

Lax, R. and Smith, F. (1989) *The great song thesaurus*, 2nd edn, Oxford
University Press

The rock song index: essential information on the 7,500 most important songs of rock

and roll (1997), Schirner Reference

Kennedy, P. (ed.) (1975) *Folksongs of Britain and Ireland*, Oak Publications
A classic heavyweight collection of folksongs.

Reed, W. L. and Bristow, M. J. (eds) (1985) *National anthems of the world*, 6th edn, Blandford Press

Popular American songs (2001), 10 vols, Gale

Electronic

Song File **www.songfile.com**
Lyrics to pop music.

Music Search **www.musicsearch.com**
A search engine for music.

Lyrics **www.lyrics.com**
Words to pop songs.

Themes

Barlour, H. and Morgenstern, S. (eds) (1970) *A dictionary of musical themes*, Benn
Classical music; requires knowledge of music notation.

Gelfand, S. (1994) *Television theme recordings: an illustrated discography 1951–1994*, Popular Culture Ink
Gives details of the original music.

Titles

Room, A. (ed.) (2000) *A dictionary of music titles: the origin of the names and titles of 3,500 musical compositions*, McFarland

Types of music

Blues

Russell, T. (1998) *The Blues*, Gale
Blues **www.bluesworld.com**

Classical

Staines, J. and Buckley, J. (eds.) (1998) *The Rough guide to classical music*,

Rough Guides

Classicalmusic **www.classicalmusic.co.uk**
Articles, news, guides and concert listings.

Country

Stambler, I. and Landon, G. (2000) *Country music – the encyclopedia*, Griffin

Jazz

Kernfeld, B., (ed.) (2001) *The new Grove dictionary of jazz*, 3 vols, 2nd edn, Grove Music

Kirchner, B., (ed.) (2000) *Oxford companion to jazz*, 2nd edn, Oxford University Press

Jazz Online **www.jazzonln.com**

Jazze.com **www.jazze.com**

Jazz Corner **www.jazzcorner.com**

Light

Ganzel, K. (ed.) (2001) *Encyclopedia of musical theatre*, 2nd edn, Gale

Opera

Harewood, Earl of, and Peattie, A. (eds) (1997) *The new Kobbé's opera book*, 11th edn, Ebury Press

International dictionary of opera (1993), 2 vols, St James Press

Operadata **www.operadata.co.uk**
Listings and background.

See also **www.opera.co.uk**

Popular music

Clarke, D. (ed.) (1989) *The Penguin encyclopedia of popular music*, Viking

Grammond, P. (1991) *The Oxford companion to popular music*, Oxford University Press

Hardy, P. and Laing, D. (1990) *The Faber companion to 20th century popular music*, Faber

Larkin, C. (ed.) (1997) *The Virgin encyclopedia of popular music*, Virgin

Roberts, D. et al. (2000) *British hit singles*, 14th edn, Guinness

Larkin, C. (1998) *The Virgin encyclopedia of dance music*, Virgin

Clickmusic **www.clickmusic.co.uk**
> Gives details of bands, gigs and groups.

Ultimate Band List **www.ubl.com**
> Huge database of groups and singles.

VirginMega **www.virginmega.com**
> One of many useful retailer sites with large listings.

Pop charts

Roberts, D. et al. (2000) *British hit singles*, 14th edn Guinness Publications
Bronson, F. (1997) *The Billboard book of number one hits*, (1955–), 4th edn, Billboard Publications
Gambaccini, P. (ed.) (1992) *Top 40 charts*, Guinness Publications
Rice, T. (ed.) (1986) *Guinness British hit albums*, Guinness Publications
Whitburn, J. (2000) *The Billboard book of USA top 40 hits*, 7th edn, Billboard Publications

Rock

The Rough guide to rock, (1999), 2nd edn, Rough Guides
Stambler, I. (1980) *The encyclopedia of pop, rock and soul*, Macmillan

MYTHS & MYTHOLOGY

See also Fairy Tales

Typical questions
- Who was the Roman god of love?
- I want to know more about the Norse god Odin.

Considerations
This subject area is relatively straightforward and should not cause too many problems. The more obscure mythologies are the most difficult to find information about.

Where to look
Printed sources

There are many sources to turn to here. There are the basic encyclopedias which will cover the more common myths, and more specialized ones concentrating solely on the subject. An excellent new addition to this field is:

Coulter, C. R. and Turner, P. (2000) *Encyclopedia of ancient deities*, Fitzroy
  Dearborn

You can also try some of the other standard references if you do not have the above:

Willis, R. (2000) *Dictionary of world myth*, Duncan Baird
Larousse encyclopedia of mythology (1996), Bounty Books

Most enquiries will be about the more common mythologies, such as Greek, Roman, etc. and most libraries should have individual texts on these mythologies.

Electronic sources

There is an excellent resource at:
Encyclopedia Mythica **http://pantheon.org**

NAMES

See also Atlases & Gazetteers

Typical questions

- Have you got a book about the meanings of Christian names?
- I am trying to find out where the name of the town Skipton originates from.

Considerations

You can generally split this area into three subjects: the meaning of place names, the meaning of surnames and the meaning of first names. Enquirers may be researching a place, doing their family tree or even choosing a name for their baby.

Where to look

Printed sources

There are no general encyclopedias that will cover these subjects. You will need to look at more specialist dictionaries.

People's names

For first names there are several useful texts available.

Cresswell, J. (1990) *Bloomsbury dictionary of first names*, Bloomsbury
Dunkling, L. and Gosling, W. (1983) *Everyman's dictionary of first names*, Everyman Reference.

For surnames, two of the best books available are:

Hanks, P. and Hodges, F. (1988) *A dictionary of surnames*, Oxford University Press
Reaney, P. H. (1991) *A dictionary of English surnames*, 3rd edn by R. M. Wilson, Routledge

There are also many books available about names around the world and their meanings. For example there are books on Welsh, Scottish, Irish, Muslim, Jewish and African names.

Place names

Try the following titles for British place names:

Ekwall, E. (1960) *The concise dictionary of English place names*, Oxford
University Press

Room, A. (1988) *Dictionary of place-names in the British Isles*, Bloomsbury

For world place names, the following is a good bet. It covers over 1000 of the world's more familiar place names:

Room, A. (1987) *Place-names of the world*, Angus and Robertson

Electronic sources

An excellent site for first names is:

Behind the Name: the etymology and history of first names
www.behindthename.com

For last names try:
www.vitalog.net

NATIONALITY & IMMIGRATION

See also Law

Typical questions

- How do I get a passport?
- On what grounds can aliens qualify to be British?
- Is 'English' a nationality?

Considerations

This subject is one to treat carefully. While, rightly, library staff must be wary of getting too involved in personal cases, enquiries may just be student projects. There may also be language difficulties, and not just foreign languages. The differences within English can be a problem: thus describing someone as an 'immigrant', or an 'alien', or even 'English' rather than 'British', can cause unintended offence.

Be ready with other sources of referral such as local social services departments, Citizen Advice Bureaux, law centres, Home Office and local solicitors' phone numbers. Many solicitors and agencies specialize in nationality matters.

Where to look

Printed sources

Chatwin. M. (ed.) (1999) *Immigration, nationality and refugee law handbook: a user's guide*, Joint Council for the Welfare of Immigrants

Halsbury's laws of England, vol. 18(2), Butterworths
under Foreign Relations – Law – Nationality

Jones, R. (1994) *How to emigrate: your complete guide to a successful future overseas*, How To Books

Macdonald, I. A. and Blake, N. J. (1995) *Immigration law and practice in the United Kingdom*, 4th edn, Butterworths
900-page legal textbook.

Parliament *Immigration and Asylum Act 1999*, The Stationery Office

Phelan, M. (2001) *Immigration law handbook*, 2nd edn, Blackstone Press

Migration and social security handbook (2001), 3rd edn, CPAG

Shah, P. A. (2000) *Refugees, race, and the legal concept of asylum in Britain*, Cavendish Press

Refugee Council Information service (current) *An information survival kit for public and voluntary sector employees working with refugees and asylum seekers* Loose-leaf format available on subscription.

Electronic sources

Home Office, Immigration and Nationality Directorate
www.ind.homeoffice.gov.uk
Useful current information.

Other sources

Office of the Immigration Services Commissioner (OISC)
6th Floor, Fleetbank House, 2–6 Salisbury Square, London EC4Y 8JX
Tel: 020 7211 1500 Fax: 020 7211 1553
www.oisc.org.uk

Immigration Law Practitioners' Association
Lindsey House, 40/42 Charterhouse St, London EC1M 6JN

Tel: 020 7251 8383 Fax: 020 7251 8384
E-mail: info@ilpa.org.uk
www.ilpa.org.uk
The website has a directory of practitioners.

Refugee Council
3 Bondway, London SW8 1SJ
Tel: 020 7820 3000
www.refugeecouncil.org.uk

Passports and visas

The UK Passport Service, an agency of the Home Office, provides a website to assist new applicants and existing passport holders who are British nationals:

www.ukpa.gov.uk

The Foreign and Commonwealth Office provides a website giving information about visas and obtaining a UK passport while overseas:

www.fco.gov.uk

Tips and pitfalls

Check *which* nationality is of concern before rowing up the wrong creek!

NATURAL HISTORY *see* ANIMALS & PETS; BIRDS; ENVIRONMENT & GREEN ISSUES; GARDENS & GARDENING; GEOGRAPHY

NAVY *see* ARMED FORCES

NEWSPAPERS

See also Journals & Periodicals

Typical questions
- Have you got last week's *Times*?
- Where can I get a copy of a Polish paper?

N NEWSPAPERS

- What newspapers cover Tamworth, and where can I get them?
- Where can I get an issue of a paper from when my father was born?

Considerations

Newspapers are one of the most important of information resources and getting hold of newspapers a frequent requirement. Sometimes what is wanted is the account of an event in the past; sometimes the enquirer has been given a particular reference. Few libraries keep newspapers for more than a few months unless they are local. In the latter case the local studies library is the place to refer people to. Few newspaper offices keep their own papers for long and tend to refer people to the local library. Advising people how they can get hold of papers the library does not have is a common task.

Printed sources

Directories

Willings press guide, Hollis Directories Ltd. Annual
    Newspaper and magazine listings.

BRAD (British Rate and Data), Emap Communication. Monthly
    Newspaper and advertising media directory.

Locations

Finding back numbers of newspapers is a common need and hard to resolve. The British Library has the largest collection:

www.bl.uk/collections/newspaper/newscat.html

Indexes

The lack of indexes to newspapers is one of the most common problems. Two UK newspapers that do have printed indexes are:

The Times (1785–), Primary Source Microfilm (Gale)
The Guardian (1986–), UMI/IPI
    Both are available in hard copy and on microfilm.

Electronic sources

There are several subscription CD-ROM and web-based services that provide the text of newspapers. For example Proquest provides CD-ROM and web versions of many UK national papers.

Most newspapers now provide a selection of their papers on their websites, at least for a time:

Express **www.express.co.uk**
Guardian **www.guardian.co.uk**
Daily Telegraph **www.telegraph.co.uk**
Mirror **www.mirror.co.uk**
Times/Sun **www.thetimes.co.uk**
Sunday Times **www.Sunday-times.co.uk**
Financial Times **www.ft.com**
Independent **www.independent.co.uk**
Star **www.megastar.co.uk**

Overseas newspaper websites

See AJR Newslink for newspapers in the UK and around the world:

http://ajr-newslink-org/news.html

A major collection of newspapers is that at the British Library Newspaper Library. See **www.bl.uk/collections/newspaper/sources.html**.

Other sources

A number of commercial services provide presentation copies of old papers. One is:

W H Smith Historic Newspapers
PO Box 3, Newton Stewart, Wigtownshire DG8 6TQ
Tel: 01988 402222

The British Library Newsplan project has sponsored a number of local directories. Contact your local studies library or the Newsplan website:

www.bl.uk/collections/nplan.html

Tips and pitfalls

Some newspapers have more than one edition so that even if someone has the correct date and page number, the item may not be in the issue the library has.

NURSERY RHYMES

See also Fairy Tales

Typical questions

- What are the words to 'Hey Diddle Diddle'?
- I want a book of children's nursery rhymes.

Considerations

Nursery rhymes are part of our literary heritage and most libraries should have books containing the classics.

Where to look

The most complete study ever made of nursery rhymes is:

Opie, I and Opie, P. (1951) *Oxford dictionary of nursery rhymes*, Oxford University Press
This book lists rhymes, their variations and their origins.

You may get enquiries about children's skipping rhymes or rhyming games. See if you have a copy of the following old text. It is excellent for finding such old rhymes.

Opie, I and Opie, P. (1959) *The lore and language of schoolchildren*, Oxford University Press

Tips and pitfalls

Most children's libraries should have anthologies of nursery rhymes, many with pictures.

NUTRITION *see* HEALTH & HEALTHCARE

OLYMPIC GAMES

See also Records; Sports

Typical questions
- Who won the men's 100m in the 1988 games?
- Where were the Olympics held in 1980?
- Who holds the Olympic record for the decathlon?

Where to look
Printed sources

A 'must have' book in this field is:

Greenberg, S. (2000) *Whitaker's Olympic almanack*, HMSO
> This little gem contains coverage of every summer and winter Olympics, with descriptions of venues, sports, competitors and records.

The same author also wrote:
> Greenberg, S. (1991) *Guinness Olympic factbook*, Guinness

Electronic sources

The 'Olympic Museum' aims to have all results on its site in the future:

www.museum.olympic.org/scripts/the_games/the_games_e.asp

OPERAS *see* MUSIC

OPTICIANS

Typical questions
- Can you give me the telephone number of ... optician?
- How do I find out if ... optician is registered?

Where to look
Directories

For an alphabetical list of opticians use the

 **OPTICIANS**

Opticians' register, General Optical Council
   www.optical.org.

Websites

Association of Contact Lens Manufacturers **www.acim.org.uk**
   Excellent links to other eyecare sites.

Eyecare Information Service **www.eyecare-information-service.org.uk**

General Optical Council **www.optical.org**

ORGANIZATIONS *see* ASSOCIATIONS & ORGANIZATIONS; CHARITABLE ORGANIZATIONS

PAINTINGS *see* ART; MUSEUMS & GALLERIES

PARISH REGISTERS

See also Family History & Genealogy; Local History

Typical questions

- How can I find details of my grandfather's birth?
- Where can I find the baptismal registers for St Michael's Church?

Considerations

Parish registers in the UK officially started in 1538, but in many places not until 1598 or later. They show baptism *not* birth, marriage, and burial *not* death. The amount of detail varied considerably until the introduction of printed registers for marriages in 1754, and for baptisms and burials in 1813.

Where to look

Present-day registers are generally kept at the relevant parish church, but most older ones have been deposited in local record offices.

Some registers have been printed by regional societies such as the Yorkshire Parish Register Society. Check if this is the case in your area, since, if so, the task of tracing entries is considerably eased. The existence of indexes is also important. In many cases the registers may have been transcribed and/or microfilmed.

Printed sources

Some parish registers have been printed. Check with your local record office or local history library.

Webb, C. C. (1987) *A guide to parish records in the Borthwick Institute of Historical Research*, Borthwick Institute

Society of Genealogists (1987) *A catalogue of parish register copies in the Society of Genealogists' collection*, 8th edn, Society of Genealogists

Society of Genealogists (1974) *A catalogue of parish register copies other than in the Society of Genealogists' collection*, 2nd edn, Society of Genealogists

Humphrey-Smith, C. (1995) *The Phillimore atlas and index of parish registers*, 2nd edn, Phillimore
  Gives the boundaries of individual parishes.

National index of parish registers (1968–), Society of Genealogists. In progress
  This multi-volume index is a useful location source.

Many local and regional and national societies have published parish records. Examples are the Canterbury and York Society and the Catholic Record Society.

Bishops' transcripts

From 1598 copies of registers had to be sent annually to the Diocesan Registry.

Gibson, J. S. W. (1997) *Bishops' transcripts and marriage licences, bonds and allegations: a guide to their location and indexes*, 4th edn, FFHS

Marriage bonds and allegations

These were required when people married by licence rather than banns. The licence would have been kept by the couple who were to marry, but the allegation, a statement made by the intending bride and groom, and the bond, assurances by bondsmen (usually friends or relatives), were kept at the Diocesan Registry.

Those for the Diocese of York for the years 1660 to 1950 are at the Borthwick Institute. Some lists have been published.

See the Gibson book above.

Non-parochial registers

Many non-parochial registers, such as those created by Non-Conformists and non-Christian communities, are now at the Family Records Centre.

The International Genealogical Index (IGI)

In their quest to retrospectively baptize the past generations of Christians, the Church of Latter-Day Saints ('Mormons') have microfilmed and digitized a large percentage of existing parish records (and other genealogical records). Most large libraries have the IGI, usually on microfiche, and this is a convenient first check for personal details. Genealogists are advised to check back with the original records since the IGI information is minimal.

Other sources

The Parish Register Society was founded in 1896 to print the parish registers of England and Wales. It was dissolved in 1934, its work being continued by the Society of Genealogists.

Society of Genealogists
   14 Charterhouse Buildings, Goswell Rd, London EC1M 7BA
   Tel: 020 7250 8799 Fax: 020 7250 1800
   E-mail: library@sog.org.uk
   www.sog.org.uk

Tips and pitfalls

Many parish registers are incomplete with parts missing; compliance with requirements was sometimes lax and survival over the centuries fitful. This has proved the value of having the bishops' transcript copies, though the transcriptions were often poorly done.

Genealogy, and the esoterica of parish registers, are areas of enquiry to be transferred to specialist local historians, record searchers and archivists. The general librarian's role is mainly to clarify the enquiry so that useful information about sources can be given and relevant referrals made.

PARLIAMENT *see* ELECTION RESULTS; GOVERNMENT; MEMBERS OF PARLIAMENT

PASSPORTS & VISAS *see* NATIONALITY & IMMIGRATION

PATENTS *see* INVENTIONS & PATENTS

PERIODICALS *see* JOURNALS & PERIODICALS

PETS *see* ANIMALS & PETS

PHARMACEUTICALS *see* DRUGS

PHOTOCOPYING *see* COPYRIGHT

PHOTOGRAPHS & ILLUSTRATIONS

Typical questions

- Where can I locate a picture of women workers in shawls?
- Can you give me advice on looking after old photographs?
- Can I use an old photograph in a book I'm writing?
- What sort of film is best to use for taking pictures indoors?

Considerations

The internet has made available millions of images. Many art galleries, for example, now make their collections digitally available and many commercial suppliers use the internet as a shop window.

Copyright queries can be troublesome. Bear in mind that the ownership of a picture or photograph is not the same thing as having the right to give permission to copy. Art galleries and museums will usually charge a fee to use an image of one of their pictures. Warn enquirers to be particularly careful if they plan to publish. Copyright usually lasts for 70 years from the photographer or illustrator's death.

Where to look
Buying guides

Which Camera **www.whichcamera.co.uk**
Camera Review **www.camerareview.com**

Collections of images

Corbis **www.corbis.com**
   A large online picture library.

Freefoto **www.freefoto.com**
   A large database of images, free for non-commercial use.

Lycos Images **www.lycos.com/picturethis/**
A database of 80,00 freely available images plus access to over 18 million on the web.

Mirror Pix **www.mirrorpix.com**
Pictures from the Mirror Group newspapers' photo archive.

Photos To Go **www.photostogo.com**
Over 200,000 images.

Time Inc. Photo Collection **www.thepicturecollection.com**
Images from a company famous for its photo journalism.

Among the many art galleries that have databases of their collection are the National Gallery (**www.nationalgallery.org.uk**), the New York Metropolitan Museum of Art (**www.metmuseum.org/collection**), the National Portrait Gallery (**www.npg.org.uk**) and the Tate Gallery (**www.tate.org.uk**).

Picture agencies

The British Association of Picture Libraries and Agencies has a directory of picture libraries in the UK:

www.bapla.org.uk

Technical aspects

Ang, T. (2001) *Dictionary of photography and digital imaging: the essential reference book for the modern photographer*, Argentum

Hedgecoe, J. (1997) *The new photographer's handbook: the definitive reference manual of photographic techniques, procedures and equipment*, 2nd edn, Ebury Press

Zakia, R. and Stroebel, L. (1993) *The Focal encyclopedia of photography*, 3rd edn, Focal Press

Betterphoto **www.betterphoto.com**

Other sources

British Journal of Photography **www.bjphoto.co.uk**
An online magazine which includes an archive of articles, visits to galleries, information on careers and equipment suppliers.

PLAYS

The Royal Photographic Society (RPS)
    The Octagon, Milson St, Bath BA1 1DN
    Tel: 01225 462841 Fax: 01225 448688
    www.rps.org
    The leading society for the advancement of photography. Has some 10,000 members in 59 countries. Gives details of latest news and exhibitions with a good range of links to other websites.

Tips and pitfalls
Local photographic societies are often most useful. Local studies departments of libraries often hold photographic collections for their area.

PHRASES *see* DICTIONARIES; PROVERBS

PICTURES *see* ART; PHOTOGRAPHS & ILLUSTRATIONS

PLACES *see* ATLASES & GAZETTEERS; COUNTRIES; NAMES

PLANNING *see* ARCHITECTURE; CONSTRUCTION

PLANTS *see* GARDENS & GARDENING, PLANTS

PLAYS

See also Literature; Theatre

Typical questions
- Who wrote *An inspector calls*?
- Where can I got a copy of *An inspector calls*?
- Is *An inspector calls* being performed anywhere in this area?
- Can I get multiple copies of a play so we can have a group reading?

- What plays can you suggest for seven characters?

Considerations

On the question of getting a 'play set', i.e. enough copies of a play so that every character can have a copy, check your library's facility to borrow sets from a regional centre. Most regional library systems have play collections. They may also have a catalogue of what is available

In order to perform a play in public, permission must be obtained if the play is in copyright. Even if the play is long out of copyright, the actual text being used may be in copyright. Also bear in mind that public performances may need to be licensed. If performance is contemplated, suggest the enquirer contacts a local dramatic society for advice.

Where to look

Printed sources

General

Matlaw, M. (1972) *Modern world drama: an encyclopedia*, Secker & Warburg
  '80 countries, 688 playrights. 1058 plays and drama terms.'

Bibliographical information

British national bibliography and the British Library catalogue are useful in identifying published plays. See Bibliographies, Reference & Citation.

Biographical Information

McGraw-Hill encyclopedia of world drama (1972), 4 vols, McGraw-Hill
Berney, K. (1993) *Contemporary dramatists*, 5th edn, St James Press

Performance

Parkin, K. (1962) *Ideal voice and speech training*, S French

Indexes and play selection

Connor, B. M. (1988) *Ottemiller's index to plays in collections: an author and title index to plays appearing in collections published between 1900 and 1986*, 7th edn, Scarecrow Press
The guide to selecting plays for performance, Samuel French Ltd. Annual
  The standard guide (annotated) to plays. French's make available plays for

amateur performances in the UK. Includes information about rights and copyright.

Shipley, J. T. (1956) *Guide to great plays*, Public Affairs Press (USA)
Outlines and performance histories.

Shank, T. J. (ed.) (1963) *A digest of 500 plays; plot outlines and production notes*,
Collier-Macmillan

Other sources

Amateur Theatre Network **www.amdram.co.uk**

National Drama Festivals Association
Hon. Sec. Tony Broscomb, Bramleys, Main St, Shudy Camp,
Cambridgeshire CB1 6RA
Tel: 01799 584920 Fax: 01799 584921

Performing Right Society (PRS)
29–33 Berners Street, London W1T 3AB
Tel: 020 7580 5544 Fax: 020 7306 4050
www.prs.co.uk

Samuel French Ltd
52 Fitzroy St, London W1P 6JR
Tel: 020 7387 9373 Fax: 020 7387 2161
E-mail: theatre@Samuelfrench-London.co.uk
www.samuelfrench-london.co.uk

Local drama groups and societies are useful in all sorts of ways.

Tips and pitfalls

Your local or regional library bureaux may have their own catalogue of play sets.
If so, it would be clever to advise a potential borrower to select from what *is* available rather than what is not.

POEMS & POETRY

See also Literature; Quotations

Typical questions

- Have you the poem 'There's a yellow one-eyed god to the north of Khatmandu'?
- I'm trying to remember a poem I learnt at school, but I've forgotten its title. Can you help?
- Have you a poem suitable for a leaving 'do'?

Considerations

Where the author is known, finding a particular poem is relatively straightforward. The library may have a volume of the poet's works, or some of them. If that fails, try the many anthologies and collections of poetry that are published. Most of them will have indexes of poets, first lines and sometimes subjects.

Poems are generally listed in indexes by title and by first lines. Where neither of these is known (or is misremembered – the poem in the first question above is, in fact, 'There's a one-eyed yellow idol to the north of Khatmandu'), then the librarian has to use dictionaries of quotations or try the approach by subject.

Where to look

Anthologies

Palgrave, F. T. (1994) *Palgrave's golden treasury of the best songs and lyrical poems in the English language*, 6th edn, updated by Press, J., Oxford University Press

Palgrave's *Treasury* is perhaps the best known of all poetry anthologies.

Ricks, C. (1999) *The Oxford book of English verse*, Oxford University Press
Contains 850 favourite poems.

The English poetry full-text database (1995), Chadwyck-Healey
A CD-ROM database of some 165,00 poems by 1250 poets.

Poets Corner **www.poets-corner.org**
A massive database of out-of-copyright poems with author, title and subject indexes, plus other poetry-related information.

Biographical sources

Bold, A. (1985) *Longman dictionary of poets: the lives and works of 1,000 poets in the English language*, Longman
> Brief outlines.

International who's who in poetry and poets' encyclopedia, Melrose Press. Bi-annual

Indexes to titles and first lines

Granger, E. (1996) *The Columbia Granger's index to poetry in collected and selected works*, Columbia University Press
> The current version of *Granger's index*, one the most famous of all reference books. Fiche and CD-ROM versions available.

Other sources

The Poetry Society
> 22 Betterton St, London WC2H 9BX
> Tel: 020 7420 4818 Fax: 020 7240 4818
> E-mail: info@poetrysoc.com
> **www.poetrysoc.com**
> They publish *Poetry News* and *Poetry Review* and offer many other membership benefits. They also answer information enquiries.

Poetry Library **www.poetrylibrary.org.uk/poetry/index.html**
> Has a 'Lost Quotations' message board.

Tips and pitfalls

Some poems are regulars, always being asked for. It is worth keeping a handy index of details to save staff time in the future. Even having copies of the most popular poems themselves to hand out or photocopy is a tip that will save time.

Many queries can be resolved using a good search engine such as **google.com** to find sources. Half-remembered poems can result in endless searches, and may be the (rare!) occasion to say, 'I give up!'

Recourse to fellow staff can sometimes bring answers!

POLITICS

See also Biographies; Countries; Election Results;
Government; History & Archaeology; Members of Parliament;
United Nations

Typical questions
• Have you details on all the Middle Eastern terrorist groups?
• Have you got a copy of the 1992 Conservative election manifesto?

Where to look
General

Miller, D. (ed.) (1987) *The Blackwell encyclopaedia of political thought*, Blackwell
    Reference
McLean, I. (1996) *Concise dictionary of politics*, Oxford University Press

Biographies

Economist (1991) *Dictionary of political biography*, Economist Books
    Brief biographies. 'The essential guide to who really counts in the world of
    international politics.'

Ransley, J. (ed.) (1991) *Chambers dictionary of political biography*, Chambers

Robbins, K. (ed.) (1990) *The Blackwell dictionary of British political life in the
    twentieth century*, Blackwell Reference

Roth, A. (1994–97) *Parliamentary profiles*, 4 vols, Parliamentary Profiles Press
    Detailed tongue-in-cheek profiles of all the UK MPs. A little dated but still
    useful.

Who's who in European politics (1990), Bowker-Saur
    700 pages.

Compilations

Butler, D. and Butler, G. (1994) *British political facts, 1900–1994*, Macmillan
Cook, C. and Paxton, J. (1981) *European political facts, 1789–1848*, Macmillan
Cook, C. and Paxton, J. (1978) *European political facts, 1848–1918*, Macmillan
Cook, C. and Paxton, J. (1992) *European political facts, 1918–1990*, Macmillan

P POLITICS

Events and yearbooks

Annual register of world events: a review of the year (1758–), Keesings Worldwide
  Good for national and international events.

Britain: an official handbook, The Stationery Office. Annual

Drost, H. (1995) *What's what and who's who in Europe*, Cassell
  Information on people, places, organizations, events and terms.

Europa yearbook, Europa Publications
  Gives statistics and information for each country.

International yearbook and statesmen's who's who (1953–), Bowker

Newspapers are a prime source for political events (*see* Newspapers).

Statesman's yearbook: the essential political and economic guide to all the countries of the world, Macmillan. Annual

Whitaker's almanack, A & C Black. Annual
Contains a great deal of information of world conditions, events during the year.

Yearbook of world affairs, Institute of World Affairs. Annual

Parties and movements

Barberis, P. et al. (2000) *Encyclopedia of British and Irish political organizations: parties, groups and movements of the twentieth century*, Pinter

Craig, W. F. S. (ed.) (1988) *British general election manifestos 1959–1987*, 3rd edn, Dartmouth Publications

Day, A. J. (ed.) (2000) *Directory of European Union political parties*, J. Harper Publishing

Hewitt, C. and Cheetham, T. (2000) *Encyclopedia of modern separatist movements*, ABC-Clio

Mercer, P. (1994) *Directory of British political organizations*, Longman

Revolutionary and dissident movements: an international guide (1991), 3rd edn, Longman

Sharitz, J. M. et al. (1991) *Almanac of modern terrorism*, Facts On File

Other sources

Virtually all political parties have their own websites, e.g.

Labour Party **www.labour.org.uk**
Liberal Democrats **www.libdems.org.uk**
Conservatives **www.conservatives.com**
Scottish National Party **www.snp.org**

For a complete list of political parties' websites try:

http://bubl.ac.uk/uk/parties.htm

Fabian Society
11 Dartmouth St, London SW1H 9BN
Tel:020 7227 4900 Fax: 020 7976 7153
E-mail: info@fabian-society.org.uk
www.fabian-society.org.uk

POP MUSIC *see* MUSIC

POPULATION

Typical questions
- What is the population of ...?
- What percentage of the UK population is married?
- Can you provide a breakdown of the ethnic population for ...?

Considerations
There can be a whole range of queries regarding population; there are after all several different levels to consider – world, continent, country, regional and district. In addition, groups of people with certain characteristics are also small populations. Therefore questions about ethnic groups, number of married people that live in a certain area, numbers of people employed in various sectors, are all questions about populations of a type. Your library will probably keep local population and characteristic statistics based on Census details. See details below. It may be that your local council, based on their own data, produces an economic profile that includes local population data. Population statistics are widely available in many publications; a list of the most authorative is given below. For quick reference you can use *Whitaker's*.

There are now numerous websites providing population statistics; a few are listed below.

275

 **POPULATION**

Where to look
UK statistical publications

The Stationery Office provides a number of excellent publications which all include population data:

Annual abstract of statistics, The Stationery Office
A comprehensive collection of statistics covering the UK, including population.

Population trends, The Stationery Office
This provides the latest quarterly information on births, marriages, divorces, migration (internal and international), population estimates and projections.

Social trends, The Stationery Office
A compendium of social statistics from a wide range of government departments and other organizations, presenting a broad picture of the British. Includes population data.

Monthly digest of statistics, The Stationery Office
There is a chapter on population and vital statistics.

Regional trends, The Stationery Office
A compendium publication with the most comprehensive official statistics about regions of the UK. It has a section on population and households.

Census

The 1991 Census is rather out of date these days and until the 2001 results are available you may have to rely on publications using the 1991 data. However, an alternative is the National Statistics Neighbourhood Statistics website **www.statistics.gov.uk/neighbourhood** which is excellent. This collates local statistics from local authorities and public bodies. By 2003 it will start to include the 2001 Census.

International statistics

Demographic yearbook, United Nations
This is an international source of statistics on 200 countries. It includes data on distribution and trends in population.

Encyclopaedia of global population and demographics, Fitzroy Dearborn

Europa world year book, 2 vols, Europa Publications
> A statistical survey is given for each country. This includes population statistics by country, regions and principal towns.

Eurostat yearbook: the statistical guide to Europe, European Commission
> Provides comparative data between countries of population, looking at age and sex for past, present and future.

Monthly bulletin of statistics, United Nations Statistics Division
> Provides monthly population statistics for most of the countries and territories of the world.

Regions statistical yearbook, European Commission
> Provides data on EU population.

Statistical yearbook, United Nations
> Part 2 of this yearbook provides population statistics for all countries or areas of the world for which data was available. It is also available on CD-ROM. For more details take a look at **www.un.org**.

Trends in Europe and North America 2001, United Nations Economic
> Commission for Europe
> Includes population size, mortality rates and life expectancy statistics.

Websites

Government Official Statistics **www.statistics.gov.uk**

Your Nation **www.your-nation.com**
> Excellent site for country-specific information. Enables the user to rank and compare countries. Well worth a visit.

Population Information Network (POPIN) **www.un.org/popin**

POSTCODES *see* ADDRESSES & POSTCODES

PRICES

See also Employment – Rights & Statistics; Money

Typical questions

- What is the latest figure for the Retail Price Index?
- What are the latest Consumer Price Indices?
- Can I have a breakdown of the purchasing power of the pound since 1990?

Where to look

Statistics

Consumer Price Indices MM23 Business Monitor, The Stationery Office.
Monthly
A monthly publication which provides all you need to know about the cost of living from monthly changes to historical indexes. It provides a full picture of inflation and consumer prices in the UK.

Annual abstract of statistics, The Stationery Office
This has an excellent chapter on prices. It covers the Producer Price Index, Retail Price Index, Tax and Price Index and the purchasing power of the pound.

Economic Trends, The Stationery Office. Monthly
Provides a prices table.

Monthly Digest of Statistics, The Stationery Office
Provides a section on prices and wages

International prices

Main Economic Indicators, Organization for Economic Co-operation and Development (OECD). Monthly
Provides economic indicators for the 30 OECD members and 11 non-member countries.

Share prices

Hoover's Online (UK) **www.hoovers.co.uk**
This links to various stock exchanges for share prices.

London Stock Exchange **www.prices.londonstockexchange.com**

Stockpoint **http://investor.stockpoint.com**

Journals

Investors Chronicle
> FT Business
> Tel: 020 7896 2000
> Weekly
> Provides a section called 'Statistics', which includes UK and international economic indicators

Financial Times
> Financial Times
> Tel: 020 7873 3000 Fax: 020 7873 3922
> Daily
> Look in Companies and Markets section

Websites

Prices and Earnings Around the Globe
> **www.ubs.com/e/index/about/research/economicresearch.html**

PRIZES *see* AWARDS & PRIZES

PRONUNCIATION *see* DICTIONARIES

PROPHECIES *see* THE UNEXPLAINED

PROOFREADING

> *See also* Publishing; Writers & Writing

Typical questions

- Have you a list of the marks used to proofread a text?
- What does 'Stet' mean on this typescript?
- How do I get my book proofread?

PROOFREADING

Considerations

The general points of preparing texts for publication are covered in the section 'Writers & Writing'; this section is about the specific task of checking texts destined for publication or presentation. Writers may be asked to check their own scripts, or deal with those proofread by someone else. Standard conventions apply, although each publisher will still have their own preferences. Always check with the publisher if they have a preferred style.

Where to look

Most books on writing will contain a section of proofreading marks. These include *The writers' and artists' yearbook*, *The writer's handbook*, and *Whitaker's almanack*.

Butcher, J. (1992) *Copy-editing: the Cambridge handbook for editors, authors, publishers*, 3rd edn, Cambridge University Press
The classic handbook.

The British Standard is:

BS 5261- 2: 1976 (1995) *Specification for typographic requirements, marks for copy preparation and proof corrections, proofing procedure*, British Standards Institution

Other sources

Society of Authors
84 Drayton Gardens, London SW10 9SB
www.societyofauthors.org

Local writers' circles and writing groups will have knowledgeable members who may give advice and help.

Tips and pitfalls

The important thing in proofreading a text is that the printer understands what corrections to make. Better to write out in full what you want rather than use symbols you don't understand.

PROVERBS

See also Quotations

Typical questions
• Where does the phrase 'Handsome is as handsome does' come from?
• What's the meaning of 'To pay through the nose'?

Considerations
There are many books of proverbs about. Most good reference libraries should have one or two decent dictionaries of proverbs.

Where to look
Printed sources

Here are some examples of texts available:

Stevenson, B. (1987) *Macmillan book of proverbs, maxims and famous phrases*, Macmillan
Simpson, J. (1998) *Concise Oxford dictionary of proverbs*, Oxford University Press

Tips and pitfalls
Make sure that the phrase is actually a proverb, and not a famous quotation. If you are not sure, it may be worth checking a dictionary of quotations too.

PSEUDONYMS

See also Biographies; Literature

Typical questions
• What's the real name of Elton John?
• What other names does P. D. James write under?

Considerations
Many famous people use pseudonyms – false names – without us knowing. Often that is how they wish it to be. The need to find out the 'real' name is generally that of the quiz and puzzle addict, or to settle a bet! Old-fashioned cataloguers and bibliographers may want to know too.

Where to look

Indexes

Atkinson, F. (1982) *Dictionary of literary pseudonyms: a selection of popular modern writers in English*, 3rd edn, Clive Bingley
Some 4,000 authors listed under both their real names, giving the pseudonym they used, and under the pseudonym, giving their real name.

Carty, T. J. (1995) *A dictionary of literary pseudonyms in the English language*, Mansell

Halkett, S. and Laing, J. (1926–62) *Dictionary of anonymous and pseudonymous English literature*, Oliver and Boyd
The nine-volume standard.

Houghton, W. E. (1966–88) *Wellesley index to Victorian periodicals 1824–1900: tables of contents and identification of contributors*, 4 vols, University of Toronto Press
Nineteenth century journalism/literature.

Sharp, H. S. (1975) *Handbook of pseudonyms and personal nicknames*, 2 vols, Scarecrow Press

Library catalogues

The catalogues of national and university libraries are particularly good for identifying pseudonyms. *See* Libraries.
See also dictionaries and encyclopaedias in the subject area concerned.

Electronic sources

Bookbrowser **www.bookbrowser.com/Pseudonyms**
Works from pseudonym to real name and vice versa. Contemporary people.

PUBLIC LENDING RIGHT *see* COPYRIGHT

PUBLISHING

See also Journals & Periodicals, Writers & Writing

Typical questions
- Can you give me a list of publishers of children's books?
- I've written a book, how do I go about getting it published?
- Who is the publisher of … journal?

Where to look
Directories
Book publishers

The Booksellers Association directory: UK and Irish book publishers, Booksellers Association
> Covers all the major book publishers in detail. In addition it covers smaller publishers, digital media publishers, remainder dealers, map producers, distributors and wholesalers. There is a subject index at the back listing the specializations of all the publishers included in the directory.

Directory of publishing United Kingdom, Commonwealth and Overseas, Cassell and the Publishers Association
> Contains details of 1500-plus publishers from 21 countries and 120-plus authors' agents. In addition it includes details of distributors and wholesalers both in the UK and overseas.

Whitaker's red book directory of publishers, J Whitaker & Sons
> Provides a selected list of 3300-plus publishers in the UK and Ireland. The criterion for inclusion is publishers with high output or well known and widely sold books. For the full list of 41,000 publishers consult *Whitaker's books in print* or *Whitaker's Bookbank CD-ROM*. For more information contact 01252 742541 or e-mail sales@whitaker.co.uk

Journal publishers

Willings press guide, 2 vols, Hollis Publishing
> **www.willingspressguide.com**
> Excellent two-volume publication providing details of thousands of newspapers, magazines, periodicals and broadcasting in the UK (Volume 1) and the rest of the world (Volume 2). Lists over 50,000 contacts. Also

available in CD-ROM and web formats. Tel: 0870 736 0015 or fax: 0870 736 0011 for more details.

BRAD: the monthly guide to advertising media, Emap Communications
BRAD is a classified directory of media in the UK and the Republic of Ireland that carries advertising. It is divided into eight market sectors including national newspapers, regional newspapers, consumer press and the business press. Each sector has a classification index.

Benn's media, 3 vols, United Business Media
www.ubminfo.co.uk
Volume 1 provides publishing details of the UK media including newspaper and periodicals. Volume 2 covers the same for Europe. Volume 3 has the same again for the rest of the world.

Statistics

Fishwick, F. *Book trade yearbook*, Publishers Association
www.publishers.org.uk

PRODCOM annual industry reports, Office for National Statistics
Excellent source of manufacturer sales, imports and exports statistics. Available to download free of charge from **www.statistics.gov.uk/ OnlineProducts/PRODCOM2000_annual.asp**.

Getting published

Writers' & artists' yearbook, A & C Black
An excellent source of information for all budding authors, whether it's writing books, poetry or newspaper articles.

The Publishers Association website provides sections on getting published and careers in publishing: **www.publishers.org.uk**.

Websites

Booksellers Association of the UK and Ireland **www.booksellers.org.uk**
Useful for book industry links both international and UK.

Publishers Association **www.publishers.org.uk**
Excellent website for publishing issues, market information and statistics.

QUOTATIONS

See also Literature; Poems & Poetry; Proverbs

Typical questions

- Who said 'Let them eat cake'?
- Can you suggest some humorous quotes I can use for a talk I am giving?
- What's the correct wording of 'All that glitters is not gold'?

Considerations

Finding the source of quotations is a frequent task for library staff. There are numerous compilations of quotations. It is a subject beloved of crossword and quiz compilers. Writers and after-dinner speakers are also a regular category of enquirer. Bear in mind that there is sometimes genuine uncertainty of the first recorded use of a 'quote' and it is worth checking more than one source if there is time, or the enquirer has time!

Collections of quotations are arranged in many ways, by subject, by first word, and by the person quoted. Although most books will have indexes for the approach not chosen in the main sequence, it is useful to know which books in your stock are best for which purpose. There are numerous books on quotations; often you will have to look through all of them on the library shelves in search of the elusive quote. This is one of those categories of enquiries, especially for the phone enquirer doing a crossword, where one has to put a time limit on how long to spend searching. Perhaps a check in three sources is enough for the quiz addict.

There are also books of quotations on particular subjects. These will generally be located with other books on that subject, e.g. medical quotes, biblical quotes.

Where to look

Printed sources

Bartlett, J. (1993) *Familiar quotations*, 16th edn, Little, Brown and Co

Cohen, J. M. and Cohen, M. J. (1998) *The new dictionary of quotations*, Penguin

Fadiman, C. and Bernand, A. (2000) *Bartlett's book of anecdotes*, 2nd edn, Little, Brown

Jeffares, A. N. and Gray, M. (1995) *Dictionary of quotations*, HarperCollins

Knowles, E. (2000) *The Oxford dictionary of quotations*, 5th edn, Oxford

University Press

20,000 quotes from 2500 people.

Sherrin, N. (ed.) (2000) *The Oxford dictionary of humorous quotations*, Oxford University Press

A personal selection of 5000 quotations

Electronic sources

Bartletts **www.bartleby.com/100/**

Website based on the 1929 edition of Bartlett's dictionary. c.11,000 quotes.

Quoted **www.geocities.com/~spanoudi/quote.html**

About 25,000 entries.

Tips and pitfalls

A check round colleagues is often useful. Bear in mind that the Bible, Milton and Shakespeare between them account for a large percentage of quotes. Which of your colleagues has had a classical, humanist or liberal education?

RECORDINGS *see* MUSIC

RECORDS (ACHIEVEMENT)

See also Olympic Games

Typical questions

- What is the longest suspension bridge in the world?
- Who was the tallest ever living human being?
- What is the fastest animal on four legs in the world?

Where to look

Printed sources

There is one obvious place to look for facts like this:

Guinness book of records, Guinness Publications. Annual
> The format of the book seems to change year by year, but you should be able to find answers in here. It is indexed and this should make your job easier, as the format can be quite difficult to navigate.

Another useful publication is;

Ash, R. (2001) *The top ten of everything*, Dorling Kindersley
> This annual includes records, facts and trivia. For example, it will give you Britain's best-selling comics, the world's longest running musical, the top ten soft drinks. It is a wealth of information and facts. Try and have a look at the book and you will be amazed at its contents.

Electronic sources

Guinness have a useful website if you do not have access to the printed version of their book of records:

www.guinnessworldrecords.com

RECREATION *see* LEISURE & RECREATION; SPORTS

 RELIGION

REFERENCES *see* BIBLIOGRAPHIES, REFERENCES & CITATION

REGULATIONS *see* ACTS & REGULATIONS

RELIGION

See also Myths & Mythology; Parish Registers; Saints; The Unexplained

Typical questions
- Have you got the 'authorized' Bible?
- When is the festival of Diwali?

Considerations
Religion, like sex and politics, can be a dangerous subject. Be very careful not to pass a personal opinion. While most enquirers are likely to be open and straightforward, there are enough who will be neither to warrant care.

No attempt is made here to categorize enquiries by religion, denomination or sect. Each religion has its own literature, reference books and local organizations.

General encyclopedias are usually very good on religions and religious topics.

Where to look
Printed sources

Hinnells, J.R. (ed.) (1997) *A new handbook of living religions*, Blackwell
One of the best in a large number of possibilities.

Harris, I. et al. (1992) *Contemporary religions: a world guide*, Longmans
Virtually a dictionary.

Holm, J. (1991) *Key guide to information sources on world religions*, Mansell
An annotated bibliography.

Weller, P. (1993) *Religions in the UK: a multi-faith directory*, University of Derby
Over 600 pages.

MacGregor, G. (1990) *The Everyman directory of religion and philosophy*, Dent

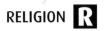

The world's religions: a Lion handbook (1994), 2nd edn
  Basic, colourful, factual.

Festivals

Brown, A. (ed.) (1986) *Festivals in world religions*, Longman
SHAP calendar of religious festivals, Shap Working Party. Annual

Sacred books

The Bible, the Koran, the Torah, and other writings which form the basis of Christianity, Islam, Judaism, etc. are to be found in many different versions. Details of these will be found in the general sources above. In addition to the different versions (which will appeal to different branches of followers), there may be commentaries, dictionaries and concordances to these on the library shelves.

Organizations

World Council of Churches
  PO Box 2100, 150 Route de Ferney, 1211 Geneva 2, Switzerland
  www.wcc-coe.org

Newspapers

Different religious organizations have their own newspapers and journals which will focus on news from the standpoint of that organization. Examples are: *The Catholic Herald, Methodist Recorder, Jewish Chronicle, Crescent International*.

Tips and pitfalls

Most religions and denominations have websites and yearbooks. Local telephone directories have good coverage of places of worship.

This is not a subject that library staff should get too involved with, unless they, or a colleague, feels confident of their knowledge, and can dispense it without bias. In religion, like politics, an enquiry for information can quickly develop into an argument. Even when the librarian is sure the enquirer is wrong, and they often are, there are times when it is wise to be quiet.

One feature that staff should be aware of is how parts of the Bible are cited. Generally this consists of three elements: Name of 'book' or part of the Bible, followed by the chapter number, followed by the number or numbers of the verse. This arrangement dates from the Vulgate version. Thus 'Proverbs 3: 6–11' would refer to verses six to eleven of the third chapter of the Book of Proverbs.

OT and NT refer to the Old Testament and New Testament respectively.

REPAIR MANUALS

Typical questions

- Have you got the car manual for a Ford Escort?
- Have you got a circuit diagram for a Sony ... video recorder?
- I'm trying to repair our washing machine. Have you got a repair guide?
- What's the difference between an Enfield and a Croydon tap?

Considerations

Generally, enquiries about repairs fall into two categories: the DIY (Do It Your-self) and the technical data enquiry. The first category is best answered by the loan of a book (with the request not to get it wet or oily!). Reference departments may carry some of the large-format popular DIY guides, but the enquirer is best advised to take them to the photocopier.

It is the expensive technical data manual that will be most requested of the information librarian, and here there are difficulties. Either the librarian will not have a clue about the subject (let alone how to use the book), or no books will exist! Manufacturers of equipment rarely publish their manuals or specifications since they would far rather you bought more of their products instead. Against this, however, many of the enquirers will know exactly what they want and are technically literate.

Where to look

Car and motorcycle manuals

The manuals published by the Haynes Publishing Group for each car/bike model serve most needs: **www.haynes.co.uk**.

Directories of repair specialists

Yellow Pages **www.yell.co.uk**
Thomson Directories **www.thomweb.co.uk**
Bigfoot for US **www.bigfoot.com**

General DIY

Holloway, D. (2000) *The Which? book of plumbing and central heating*, Which?

Books

Lawrence, M. C. (2000) *The Which? book of wiring and lighting*, 4th edn, Which? Books

Lawrence, M. C. (1999) *Which? way to fix it*, 4th edn, Which? Books

The Federation of Master Builders **www.fmb.org.uk/consumers**
Covers most aspects of home maintenance. Has a directory of reputable builders in the UK.

Improveline **www.improveline.com**
Information about home improvement with a directory of repair specialists.

Many retail suppliers have hints on their websites, e.g. **www.comet.co.uk**.

Hometips **www.hometips.com**
DIY tips and advice, US orientated.

The Plumber **www.theplumber.com/hillsplb.html**
Online help. US orientated.

Willings press guide (*see* Journals) lists several DIY magazines.

Television and video

Trundle, E. (1988) *Newnes guide to TV and video technology*, Newnes

Television servicing, U-View Publishers. Annual
Circuit wiring diagrams.

Video servicing, U-View Publishers. Annual
Circuit wiring diagrams.

RETAILING & CONSUMER SPENDING

See also CONSUMER INFORMATION

Typical questions
- Have you got a list of supermarkets?
- Have you got a list of factory outlets?
- I've got to do a project on the retail industry.
- How much do people spend on …?

R RETAILING & CONSUMER SPENDING

Considerations

There is both the retailer and the consumer to consider when looking at the retail industry. Is the enquirer interested in consumer patterns or are they themselves the consumer? What type of retail outlet is the user interested in? The retail industry covers a wide range of outlets, including supermarkets, department stores, mail order/home shopping, chemists, factory and discount stores, and market traders.

When more in-depth comment on the retail industry is required, market research reports are an excellent source of statistics and analysis.

Users may also want to complain about goods they have bought. It is best to refer to the Trading Standards, National Consumer Council or the Office of Fair Trading. For more details of the above and consumer law *see* Consumer Information.

Where to look

Directories

World retail directory and sourcebook, Euromonitor

> This provides information on 2600-plus leading retailers in over 90 countries.

Retail directory of Europe, Hemming Information Services

Retail directory of the UK, Hemming Information Services

> This directory provides details of the most significant retailing companies both in the UK and the Republic of Ireland. In addition to company details it also provides, if available, the names of individual buyers and managers. The book has two sections – companies listed by type of retail operation and surveys of the important shopping areas in over 450 towns.

Shopping centre and retail directory, William Reed Directories

> This provides alphabetical listings of 1200 shopping centres in the UK and the Republic of Ireland, multiple retailers and commercial property agents, owners and developers.

Market yearbook, World's Fair

> This publication provides market details (type of market, market days, charges and contacts) arranged geographically.

Please refer also to the directories mentioned under Companies.

Journals

There are numerous journals that cover retail and retailers, details of which can be found in *Willings press guide* (see Journals & Periodicals).

European Retail Analyst
> Bracora Ltd
> Tel: 01242 680519 Fax: 01242 680793
> **www.conciseb2b.com/euroretail**
> Monthly
> Market intelligence on retail sector in Europe.

UK Retail Report
> Retail Intelligence
> Tel: 020 7696 9006 Fax: 020 7696 9004
> Ten issues per year

Statistics

Retail pocket book, NTC Publications

Consumer trends, The Stationery Office. Quarterly
> This provides data on household expenditure.

Economic trends, The Stationery Office. Monthly
> Includes the Retail Price Index and GDP.

Monthly digest of statistics, The Stationery Office
> Includes national accounts, retailing statistics and both the Retail Price Index and the Consumer Price Index.

World retail data and statistics, Euromonitor
> This directory provides retailing statistics from 50 countries in addition to socio-economic trends and consumer expenditure patterns.

World consumer income and expenditure patterns, Euromonitor
> This provides an overview of how the consumer spends their earnings. It includes data from 52 countries and looks at expenditure on household goods, food and drink, clothing and footwear, healthcare and toiletries, sports goods, books and toys, to name but a few.

Market research

Mintel retail reports, Mintel International Group

Provides in-depth research into the retail industry. Looks at market factors, market segmentation, the consumer and the future. Also available on CD-ROM. For details visit **www.mintel.co.uk** (tel: 020 7606 5932, fax: 020 7606 5932).

Retail business market surveys, Euromonitor
Provides in-depth research and statistics into a wide range of products. Looks at consumer spending, output, prices and prospects.

Key Note reports, Key Note
For free executive summaries of report titles listed under retailing visit **www.keynote.co.uk**. For details of obtaining full reports, contact Key Note (tel: 020 8481 8750; fax: 020 8783 0049).

Supermarkets, a report on the supply of groceries from multiple stores in the UK (2000) Cm 4842, Competition Commission **www.competition-commission.org.uk**

Websites

British Chambers of Commerce **www.britishchambers.org.uk**

British Retail Consortium **www.brc.org.uk**
Excellent for retail policies and issues, surveys and statistics. It has loads of publications available to download.

RIGHTS

See also Equal Opportunities; Law; Social Welfare

Typical questions
- I'm in dispute with a neighbour. What are my rights?
- What rights do children have?
- What have you got on the Human Rights Act?

Considerations

'Rights' are a topic of great concern. They present a problem for the librarian as the subject did not exist in its modern form when the Dewey classification was established. The 323s (political rights) is one place to find books on rights, another is in law, and a third is in ethics (179). 'Rights' as an abstract concept (ethics) needs to be distinguished from the 'rights' of a particular group (politics), animals included. Legal rights is another category. An element of preliminary interrogation is often needed to get the librarian on the right wavelength. Be aware, also, that this is an area of both legal necessity and passionate concern.

Where to look
Printed sources

Allen, R. (2000) *Employment law and the Human Rights Act 1998*, Blackstone Press

Brownlie, I. (1992) *Basic documents on human rights*, 3rd edn, Clarenden Press International and regional agreements.

Cooper, I. (1983) *Which? way to complain*, Consumer Association

Fenwick, H. (1998) *Civil liberties*, 2nd edn, Cavendish Publishing A 650-page compendium.

Foreign and Commonwealth Office and Department for International Development *Human rights*, The Stationery Office. Annual Useful annual survey.

Leckie, D. and Pickersgill, D. (1999) *The 1998 Human Rights Act explained*, The Stationery Office A brief introduction.

Parliament *Human Rights Act 1998*, HMSO

Wadham, J. and Crossma, G., (eds) (2000) *Your rights: the Liberty guide to human rights*, 7th edn Pluto Press Includes selected texts and directory information. UK law.

Halsbury's laws of England, Butterworths This multi-volume legal encyclopedias may be useful here.

Wadham. T. and Mountfield H. (1999) *Blackstone's guide to the Human Rights Act 1998*, Blackstone Press

Humana, C. (1992) *World human rights guide*, 3rd edn, Oxford University Press Tabled guide to countries of the world.

United Nations human rights yearbook, UN. Annual

R RIGHTS

Children

Alston, P. *et al.* (eds.) (1992) *Children, rights and the law*, Oxford University Press

Data protection

Parliament, *Data Protection Act 1998*, HMSO
    Covers information on electronic and manual records.

Carey, P. (2000) *Data protection in the UK*, Blackstone Press

The Office of the Data Protection Commissioner
    Wycliff House, Water Lane, Wilmslow SK9 5AF
    Tel: 01625 545740
    www.dataprotection.gov.uk
    This office issues numerous information leaflets.

Leigh-Pollitt, P. and Mullock, J. (2001) *Data Protection Act explained*, The Stationery Office (Point of Law series)

www.lcd.gov.uk/foi/datprot.htm

Data Protection Public Register **www.dpr.gov.uk**

Freedom of information

Parliament, *Freedom of Information Act 2000*, HMSO

Wadham. J. et al. (2001) *Blackstone's guide to the Freedom of Information Act 2000*, Blackstone Press
    Provides text of Act, commentary, and chapters on open government and FOI in other countries.

The Freedom Association
    PO Box 2820, Bridgnorth, Shropshire WV16 6YR
    Tel: 01746 861267
    www.tfa.net

General

National Association of Citizens' Advice Bureaux **www.nacab.org.uk**
    CABs provide information on civil rights among many other social topics.
    See telephone directories for local offices.

Health

MIND (2001) *Legal rights and mental health: the Mind manual*, 14th edn, Mind

Homes

Child Poverty Action Group (1998) *Rights guide for home owners*, 12th edn, CPAG

Minorities

Commission for Racial Equality
Elliot House. 10–12 Allington St, London SW1E 5EH
Tel: 020 7828 7022
www.cre.gov.uk
The CRE have several regional offices.

Liberty (National Council for Civil Liberties)
21 Tabard St, London SE1 4LA
Tel: 020 7403 3888
www.liberty-human-rights.org.uk
An independent human rights organization.

Minority Rights Group
379 Brixton Rd, London SW9 7DE
Tel: 020 7978 9498
www.minorityrights.org

Prisoners

Amnesty International
1 Easton St, London WC1X 0DW
www.amnesty.org
Worldwide campaigning movement with particular concern for prisoners of conscience.

Tips and pitfalls

As with all legal enquiries, let the texts speak for themselves.

ROADS *see* TRANSPORT

ROYAL AIR FORCE *see* **ARMED FORCES**

ROYAL NAVY *see* **ARMED FORCES**

ROYALTY *see* **KINGS & QUEENS, RULERS & HEADS OF STATE**

RULERS *see* **KINGS & QUEENS, RULERS & HEADS OF STATE**

SAINTS

See also Religion

Typical questions
- Who is the patron saint of librarians?
- I want to know more about St Hilda.

Considerations
General encyclopedias will cover the more common saints but try and make sure you have a specific dictionary or encyclopedia too.

Where to look
Printed sources

Farmer, D. H. (1992) *The Oxford dictionary of saints*, Oxford University Press
This dictionary contains concise accounts of the lives, cults and artistic associations of around 1250 saints from Great Britain and Europe. Make sure you have a copy!

Electronic sources

Catholic Online: Saints and Angels **http://saints.catholic.org/index.shtml**
An excellent resource. Most saints are covered. Lives, patronages and feast days are all shown.

SCHOOLS *see* EDUCATION

SCRIPTS *see* ALPHABETS & SCRIPTS

SHOPS & SHOPPING *see* RETAILING & CONSUMER SPENDING

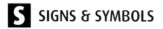

SIGNS & SYMBOLS

See also Alphabets & Scripts

Typical questions

- What's the sign for a low bridge?
- What does the symbol on this packaging mean?
- What does '?' in chess notation stand for?

Considerations

Signs and symbols are used almost everywhere, on labels giving washing instructions, on the machines that do the washing, on keyboards and on documents. And this is before looking at the symbolism used in art and in cultural history. Information about many symbols, in art or on road traffic signs, for example, will be covered in books on the subject or in general encyclopedias in the case of cultural symbols such as the cross or swastika. A number of specialist works do exist which display symbols whose meaning may be unknown. Obviously, arrangement is problematical!

Where to look

Printed sources

Foley, J. (1993) *The Guinness encyclopedia of signs and symbols*, Guinness Publications
Modern symbols such as trade marks.

Lungman, G. (1991) *Dictionary of symbols*, ABC-Clio
Strong on classical symbols.

For domestic symbols, such as washing temperatures and cleaning symbols, books on household work are useful, such as:

Phillips, B. (1989) *The Daily Mail book of household hints and tips*, Dorling Kindersley

Electronic sources

Symbols **www.symbols.com**
2500 Western signs in 54 groups from 'ideograms carved in mammoth teeth by Cro Magnon man, to hobo signs and subway graffiti'. Interactive facility whereby you can describe the symbol you want.

SOCIAL WELFARE

See also Benefits; Charitable Organizations; Nationality &
Immigration; Rights

Typical questions
- What are the rules about when people can go into care?
- How can a disabled person get help?

Considerations
A distinction needs to be drawn between those enquirers who are seeking help, and students doing projects.

Librarians on information desks frequently encounter people who are in genuine need or in distress. Some guidelines and useful addresses which can be produced quickly are needed, such as the local Salvation Army (and how to get there). Sometimes the police may have to be contacted – have their local number to hand. Such encounters can be upsetting, but help given tactfully can be rewarding.

Where to look
General

Guide to the social services: social policy and legislation explained, Waterlow.
Annual
Includes directory information.

Thomas, H. and Pierson, J. (1995) *Dictionary of social work*, Collins
Educational

Tonge, K. (2002) *Social security and state benefits: a practical guide*, Tolley

Vernon, S. (ed.) (1998) *Social work and the law*, Butterworths

Jacobs, M. (ed.) (1998) *The care guide: a handbook for the caring professions and other agencies*, Cassell

Davies, M. (ed.) (1997) *The Blackwell companion for social work*, Blackwell

UK Communities Online **www.communities.org.uk**
Covers issues of sustainability, social inclusion and economic regeneration in the context of using the potential of information technology for community networking.

For government documents try: **www.the-stationery-office.com**

Children

Hershman, D. and McFarlane, A. (2001) *Children Act handbook 2001*, Family Law
Contains amended and annotated texts and the 1989 Children Act and other relevant documents.

Contact A Family **www.cafamily.org.uk**
For families who care for children with disabilities and special needs.

Child Line UK **www.childline.org.uk**
Tel: 0800 1111 (Freephone)
A 24-hour helpline for children and young people in trouble or danger.

Community care

Mandelstam, M. (1998) *An A–Z of community care law*, Jessica Kingsley Publishers

Disability

Darnborough, A. and Kinrade, D. (1998) *Directory for disabled people*, 7th edn, Prentice Hall

Disability Net **www.disability.co.uk**
Good links to UK government and non-government agencies. Includes job agencies. UK focus.

Paterson, J. *Disability rights handbook*, Disability Alliance. Annual
A guide to benefits and services for all disabled people, their families, carers and advisers.

RNID for Deaf and Hard of Hearing People **www.rnid.org.uk**
Royal National Institute of the Blind **www.rnib.org.uk**

Elderly

Darnborough, A. and Kinrade, D. (1992) *Directory for older people*, 2nd edn, Woodhead Faulkner
Shukla, R. B. and Brooks, D. (1996) *A guide to the care of the elderly*, HMSO

Ashton, G. R. (1998) *Elderly people and the law*, Butterworths

Age Concern **www.ace.org.uk**
Advice and information relating to the welfare of older people.

Missing people

Rogers, C. D. (1986) *Tracing missing persons: an introduction to agencies, methods and sources in England and Wales*, Manchester University Press

Red Cross International Tracing and Message Service
Tel: 020 7235 5454
www.redcross.org.uk

Salvation Army. See telephone directory for your local branch.

Housing

Care homes for older people: national minimum standards (2001), The Stationery Office

Suicide

The Samaritans **www.samaritans.org.uk**
Gives reports and information produced by The Samaritans. Provides a confidential e-mail service.

Volunteering

Pybus, V. (ed.) (1997) *The international directory of voluntary work*, 6th edn, Vacation Work

The National Centre for Volunteering
Regents Wharf, 8 All Saints St, London N1 9RL
Tel: 020 7520 8900
www.volunteering.org.uk

Other sources

Do refer people to the local authority Social Services offices and the Citizens' Advice Bureau.

Tips and pitfalls

Stay objective.

SONGS *see* MUSIC

SPEAKING *see* ETIQUETTE & FORMS OF ADDRESS

SPELLING *see* DICTIONARIES

SPORTS

See also Games Rules, Olympic Games

Typical questions
- Who won the FA Cup in 1953?
- Who was in the team that played in the World Cup final for England in 1966?
- Who won the men's championship at Wimbledon in 1982?
- Where do Essex play their home cricket matches?

Considerations

The range of queries you may receive about sports is vast. There are so many different kinds of sports, and so many different types of questions that could be asked. This is such a popular subject area. Enquirers may be looking for sports' histories, winners of competitions, rules, teams, records, even colours of shirts.

Where to look
Printed sources

There is not space in this book to cover every individual sport. The general sports encyclopedias only are covered. You can also find basic information in a general encyclopedia.

Cuddon, J. A. (1980) *The Macmillan dictionary of sports and games*, Macmillan
    Has around 6000 entries for sports, events, awards and terms.

Arlott, J. (ed.) (1975) *The Oxford companion to sports and games*, Oxford University Press
    Describes around 200 sports and games with historical notes.

There are also many 'yearbooks' for specific sports. These can be of great use when looking up previous seasons' results, records, teams, etc. Some examples are:

Rothmans football yearbook
Rothmans rugby league yearbook
Wisden cricketer's almanack

Electronic sources

There are thousands of good sports websites. Again, each individual sport will have its own good websites. As a starting point, try some of the following:

http://sports.yahoo.com
http://directory.google.com/Top/Sports/

For up-to-date sports news and scores try:

www.bbc.co.uk/sport
www.sportinglife.com

Tips and pitfalls

Check your library shelves to see what reference books you have on sport. Try and familiarize yourself with them and their contents. This will make life so much easier when dealing with enquiries.

STAMPS *see* COINS & STAMPS

STATISTICS

See also European Information; Market Research; Population

Typical questions
- Have you got any statistics for pet ownership?
- Where do I locate statistics on health?

Considerations

Statistics can be either official, i.e. from government, or unofficial, e.g. from trade associations, companies, independent market research companies and banks. Vast amounts of statistics are produced and it is difficult to know about them all. Undoubtedly, the best way to find out about government-produced statistics is to use the excellent government statistics website **www.statistics.gov.uk**. This allows you to search by keyword or specific title. Many of the titles can be downloaded freely or it will give you purchase details. Unofficial statistics are produced by such a wide variety of organizations that it would be impossible to provide a list here. However, the *World directory of non-official statistical sources* (2000), Euromonitor, may help. This is an excellent tool to locate reports, statistics and surveys produced by companies, banks and trade associations. In addition, a lot of the suggestions under Market Research and European Information will equally be useful for tracking down statistics.

Where to look

International

World statistics pocketbook, United Nations

Provides international statistics on 209 countries, covering basic economic, social and environmental data. The data is drawn from 20 international statistical sources. Also look at the United Nations Statistical Division website **www.un.org/Depts/unsd/**.

Statistical abstract of the United States, US Bureau of Census

National

Annual abstract of statistics, Office for National Statistics

A comprehensive collection of statistics covering the UK. Contains data on population, manufacturing, social services, finance, education, transport and defence.

Social trends, Office for National Statistics

A compendium of social statistics from a wide range of government departments and other organizations presenting a broad picture of the British. Contains data on population, households and families, education, employment, income and wealth, expenditure, health, social protection, crime and justice, housing, environment, transport and leisure. Data are in the form of tables, charts and interpretative commentary. In addition some editions contain special reports on specific topics.

Monthly Digest of Statistics, Office for National Statistics

Compendia of the latest social and economic statistics. Contains data on the population, employment, social services, production and output, transport,

national income and expenditure, law enforcement, agriculture, food, drink, tobacco, energy, chemicals, metals, engineering and vehicles, textiles, construction, retailing, external trade, overseas and home finance, prices and wages, leisure and weather.

Regional

Regional trends, Office for National Statistics
A compendium publication with the most comprehensive official statistics about regions of the UK. Contains profiles of each of the 11 standard regions, data on the regions across the European Union, social or economic topic areas which allow comparisons to be made. Also includes key data for the sub-regions and key statistics for the local authority districts.

Financial

Economic Trends, Office for National Statistics
A monthly publication, by the Office for National Statistics in collaboration with the statistics divisions of government departments and the Bank of England, which brings together all the main economic indicators.

Financial Statistics, Office for National Statistics
A monthly publication which contains data on public sector finance, central government revenue and expenditure, money supply and credit, banks and building societies, interest and exchange rates, financial accounts, companies and capital issues, balance sheets and balance of payments.

Historical

Mitchell, B.R. (1988) *British historical statistics*, Cambridge University Press
This provides statistics of the UK since 1700.

Mitchell, B. R. (1981) *European historical statistics 1750–1975*, 2nd rev. edn, Macmillan Press

Mitchell, B.R. (1998) *International historical statistics*, 4th edn, 3 vols., Stockton Press

Journals

Horizons, Office for National Statistics. Monthly
    Free and very useful.

Websites

Government Official Statistics **www.statistics.gov.uk**

World Trade Organization **www.wto.org**
    Includes the International Trade Statistics that are free to download.

Tips and pitfalls

Despite popular belief, statistics are not available for every situation, topic or issue that hits the headlines. It may be necessary to approach some enquiries from a wider perspective or various different angles but the one thing to remember is you cannot provide statistics that simply don't exist. Finding statistics does require a creative mind, in the sense that a bit of lateral thinking is often rewarded. Market research reports and surveys are great sources of statistics as are reports from associations and organizations. It is not out of the question either to ask for a few statistics over the telephone from relevant groups. Furthermore, don't be afraid to suggest, especially to students, that they could collect their own data specific to their project.

STATUTORY INSTRUMENTS *see* ACTS & REGULATIONS

SUICIDE *see* SOCIAL WELFARE

SUPERNATURAL *see* THE UNEXPLAINED

SUPERSTITIONS *see* CUSTOMS, FESTIVALS & FOLKLORE

SYMBOLS *see* SIGNS & SYMBOLS

TAX

Considerations

Tax information is for the tax specialist. There are a number of general publications which can clarify basic enquiries. If these are not sufficient for the query you are dealing with refer the enquirer to a local tax consultant or one of the contacts below. Some of the most commonly asked about forms of tax are income tax, VAT, corporation tax, inheritance tax, capital gains tax and council tax. There is an excellent section on government revenue in *UK Yearbook 2002*, The Stationery Office. It explains the collection of taxes and taxation policy and defines the main forms of taxes, dividing them into taxes on income, taxes on capital, and taxes on expenditure. It also mentions local government revenue.

Where to look

Directories

Any of the following are good for tax rates and facts. It is essential that you are using the current edition:

Homer, A. and Burrows, R. *Tolley's tax guide*, Tolley Publishing
Williams, S. *Lloyds TSB tax guide*, Profile Books
Genders, D. *Daily Telegraph tax guide*. Pan
Foreman, A. *Allied Dunbar tax handbook*, Financial Times Prentice Hall

For more analysis and developments try:

Simon's Weekly Tax Intelligence, Butterworths Tolley

International Tax Review
Euromoney Institutional Investor
Tel: 020 7779 8551 Fax: 020 7779 8582
www.internationaltaxreview.com
Ten issues per year

Butterworths orange tax handbook, Butterworths Tolley
This contains up-to-date legislation relating to National Insurance contributions, stamp duty and VAT.

Butterworths yellow tax handbook, Butterworths Tolley
This contains up-to-date legislation relating to income tax, statutes,

corporation tax and capital gains tax.

Dolton, A. and Saunders, G. (2001) *Tolley's tax cases*, Tolley Publishing

Council tax

Queries regarding council tax are best dealt with by the council tax department of your local authority. You will find the telephone number in your local telephone book or use **www.yell.com** or **www.upmystreet.com** to locate. There is a significant amount of information on the internet which may answer some enquiries. Go to the Local Government Finance Index **www.local.dtlr.gov.uk/index.htm**, select Council tax from the A–Z listing. Choose Council Tax Index.

For Northern Ireland, where rates are still paid, queries will be dealt with by the Rate Collection Agency: contact details and offices are given in the local telephone book under the Government of Northern Ireland.

Journals

Tax Bulletin, Inland Revenue. Six issues per year

Statistics

Inland Revenue statistics, Inland Revenue Analytical Services Division, Office for National Statistics

Complaints about the Inland Revenue

There is a brief and informative section at **www.digita.com/**.

Websites

Digita Tax Centre **www.digita.com/**

HM Customs and Excise **www.hmce.gov.uk**

Inland Revenue **www.inlandrevenue.gov.uk**

Road Tax Calculator **www.theaa.com/allaboutcars/index.html**

National Insurance Contributions **www.inlandrevenue.gov.uk/nic/**

Tax Associations **www.taxsites.com**
American but useful for international tax associations

Tax Calculator **www.digita.com/**

Tax Zone **www.accountingweb.co.uk/tax/index.html**

Treasury **www.hm-treasury.gov.uk**
   Produces a 'Tax ready reckoner and tax reliefs' booklet.

TELEPHONE DIRECTORIES

Typical questions
- Can you give me the phone number of the Royal Albert Hall?
- What is the code for Birmingham?
- Which area does this code relate to?

Considerations
Firstly, the codes for all UK areas and international telephone codes can be found at the back of all telephone books. So even if you only have your local telephone book you can answer dialling code queries. Telephone books are marvellous publications providing you have certain pieces of information. If your library is lucky enough to have a full set of UK phone books then you will need to refer to the Phone Book Index to find the number of the volume you need for the town or city requested. The White Pages and the Yellow Pages do not always share the same volume number. The Yellow Pages in many cases cover a number of towns or cities; using the *National planner*, you can look up the town and be referred to the correct volume. The White Pages are divided into two sections: the first section is an alphabetical list of businesses/organizations, the second section is an alphabetical list of individuals. The Yellow Pages is a classified directory that businesses and others pay to be included in. This is something to bear in mind. It is arranged alphabetically by subject. There is an index at the back that will suggest other terms to use if you are having trouble finding what you are looking for.

Where to look
UK telephone directories
For a known business/service or name use the relevant White Pages. To find contacts for a particular industry, service or public service use the Yellow Pages. Dialling codes can be found in all White Pages or BT's *Phone book companion*. This is available to purchase from BT (0800 833 400) and contains all the UK codes listed numerically by code and alphabetically by name. It also includes an international code list and decoder too.

T TELEPHONE DIRECTORIES

For help locating the right telephone book use: *National planner*, Marketing Services Group, Yellow Pages

Phone book index. Order through BT Phone Book Manager, Room 302A, Telephone House, Smithfield Rd, Shrewsbury SY1 1BA.

The following are also helpful:

BT phone books on CD-ROM
   For information and subscription costs, tel: 0800 919 199.

Telephone helpline directory, Telephone Helplines Association
   This directory contains details of 1000 national, regional and local telephone helplines throughout the UK.

International directories

For availability contact BT's International Directories Unit, tel: 0800 731 8114.

Websites

British Telecom **www.bt.com/phonenetuk**

OFTEL (Office of Telecommunications) **www.oftel.gov.uk**

Telephone Directories of the World **www.teldir.com**
   An excellent site, with 400 links to Yellow Pages, White Pages, business directories, e-mail addresses and fax listings from over 170 countries all around the world.

Total Telecom A–Z of Telecoms Websites **www.totaltele.com/links**
   A good starting point for telecommunications industry information.

Yellow Pages **www.yell.co.uk**

Tips and pitfalls

Don't be surprised not to find some businesses in the Yellow Pages: remember it costs to be included. Also, the majority of trade directories will provide telephone numbers, so don't assume that if you haven't found it in the phone book it doesn't exist. Using international telephone directories both in hard copy or via the internet can be frustrating because of the language barrier. Looking up terms in a language dictionary is one way to muddle through or you could try one of the translation services via the internet which allows you to type in phrases as well as single words. Try AltaVista's Babel Fish (*see* Languages & Translating).

312

TELEVISION *see* ACTORS & ACTRESSES

TEXTILES

See also Clothes & Clothing; Costume & Fashion

Typical questions
- Can you give me a list of chenille manufacturers?
- How can I find export data for the textile industry?
- What exactly is polyester?

Considerations

Textiles covers both natural and man-made fibres and fabrics/coverings. This type of information is quite specialist and consequently there are numerous directories and organizations providing information. It is, after all, a world industry. However, this does not rule out using general works such as *Kompass* or *Key British enterprises*, either for the UK or for any other country. *See* Companies. In addition, the textile industry has really utilized the internet; consequently, there are numerous excellent websites providing directory-type information, statistics and practical information. A number of recommended websites are listed below.

Where to look
Directories

Bailey, M. (comp.) *Wool trade directory of the world*, World Textile Publications
> Provides a country-by-country listing of companies involved in the wool and wool textile industries, an A–Z list of all companies by activity, a guide to textile machinery manufacturers and their agents, and mill supplies for the wool textile industry.

Davison's textile blue book USA, Davison Publishing Co
> Provides information on mills, dyers and finishers, yarn dealers, silk dealers, wool dealers, cotton merchants and agents in the USA, Canada and Mexico. In addition, there are yarn resource lists, fabric resource lists, testing and research laboratories, textile associations and textile schools. All listings are arranged by geographic location, first alphabetically by states in the USA, Canada, and Mexico, then alphabetically by city within the state and then alphabetically within the city.

313

Fashion and textile information directory, FATEC Fashion and Textile
Educational Consultancy
Lists company details by category with an alphabetical company index
provided. Useful for textile craft products. Also gives details of associations,
museums, etc. involved with textiles.

Bailey, M. (comp.) *Directory of UK textile industries*, World Textiles Publications
Covers all aspects of the textile industry. Provides company details arranged
alphabetically within categories with a general A–Z company index at the
back.

Kendal textile directory, Longwood Publications
A buyers' guide for the textile industry. All entries are listed alphabetically
and by process type. Also available on CD-ROM.

European index of yarns and fibres, World Textile Publications
Provides an A–Z listing of manufacturers of staple fibres and filament yarns
and spun yarns, as well as a categorized index.

In addition, leather is used throughout the clothes and upholstery trade and it is
worth including:

International leather guide, Miller Freeman
Providing a five-language index of all products and services listed, this is
an excellent directory with plentiful cross-references. There is also a master
index to companies and organizations.

Journals
There are a number of journals that are specific to the textiles industry.

Textile Horizons
World Textile Publications
Tel: 01274 378800 Fax: 01274 378811
Ten issues per year
Covers textile machinery, fibres, knitted, woven and non-woven fabrics and
apparel. Also carries features on chemical supplies, education and training.

Textile Month
World Textile Publications
Tel: 01274 378800 Fax: 01274 378811

Monthly

Covers the machinery and processes involved in the manufacture of textiles.

Textile Progress
> Textile Institute
> Tel: 0161 237 1188 Fax: 0161 236 1991
> Quarterly
> Articles on and about textiles.

Textile Technology International
> Sterling Group Publications
> Tel: 020 7915 9660 Fax: 020 7724 2089
> Annual
> Provides the latest information on raw materials, yarn, fabrics, printing and finishing, testing and quality control.

Wool Record
> World Textile Publications
> Tel: 01274 378800 Fax: 01274 378811
> Monthly
> Covers all aspects of the world wool-textile industry.

Statistics

PRODCOM Quarterly Industry Reports, Office for National Statistics
> Excellent source of UK manufacturer sales, imports and exports statistics. Available to download free of charge from **www.statistics.gov.uk/OnlineProducts/default.asp**

Dictionaries

FabricLink **www.fabriclink.com**
> This provides a dictionary of fabric terms. It is also excellent for its directory of fibre producers and trademarks. Well worth a visit.

Textile Dictionary **www.ntgi.net/ICCFandD/textile.htm**

Websites

British Textile Machinery Association **www.martex.co.uk/btma/**
British Textile Technology Group **www.bttg.co.uk**

British Wool Marketing Board **www.britishwool.org.uk**
British Wool Textile Export Corporation **www.bwtec.co uk**
Department of Textiles (University of Huddersfield) **www.hud.ac.uk/textiles**
Home Textiles Today (USA) **www.hometextilestoday.com/**
International Cotton Advisory Committee **www.icac.org**
International Textile Manufacturers Federation **www.itmf.org**
Irish Linen Guild **www.irishlinen.co.uk**
News and Analysis @TextileWeb **www.textileweb.com**
Textile and Clothing Network (Texclo) **www.texclo.net**
Textile Industry Link **www.mvmills.com**
Textile Institute **www.texi.org**
Textile Portal **www.textile4all.com**
Textile World (USA) **www.textileworld.com**
Wools of New Zealand **www.woolsnz.com**

THEATRE

See also Actors & Actresses; Plays

Typical questions

- What theatres are there in Leeds?
- What plays are on in the local theatre?
- Have you information about forthcoming theatrical events?
- How do I get to be an actor?

Where to look

For enquiries concerning local venues and events then there will be local publicity and contacts, such as the events pages in the local press, reception desks and telephone enquiry lines at the venue concerned, and various local websites. Probably numerous free leaflets in local libraries! First check which locality is required.

Printed sources

Banham, M. (ed.) (1995) *The Cambridge guide to theatre*, 3rd edn, Cambridge University Press
A major reference source of over 3500 entries.

Billington, M. (1982) *The Guinness book of theatre facts and feats*, Guinness Superlatives

Bordman, G. (1984) *The Oxford companion to American theatre*, Oxford University Press

Harrison, M. (1993) *Theatre*, Carcanet
A dictionary of words used in the theatre world.

Hartnoll, P. and Found, P. (1992) *Oxford companion to the theatre*, 2nd edn, Oxford University Press

Taylor, J. R. (1993) *The new Penguin dictionary of the theatre*, 3rd edn, Penguin

The Stage, The Stage. Weekly

Biography

Griffith, T. R. and Woddis, C. (1991) *Bloomsbury theatre guide*, 2nd edn, Bloomsbury

Directories

Amateur theatre yearbook; incorporating community theatre and training, Platform Publications. Annual
Directory of venues, specialist help, suppliers and organizations.

British performing arts yearbook, Rhinegold Publishing. Annual
A comprehensive directory of UK performing arts.

British theatre directory, Richmond House. Annual

Artistes and agents, Richard House Publications. Annual

Aloud.com **www.aloud.com**
Directories, events and reviews.

Events

Most weekend newspapers give theatre listings. See also:

Time Out
A magazine which gives reviews and listings for the London theatres.

Sunday Times Culture Section

News and reviews **www.whatsonstage.com**

UK Theatre Web **www.uktw.co.uk**

Acting and production

Fenner, J. (1998) *The actor's handbook*, 3rd edn, Bloomsbury
Cassin-Scott, J. (1979) *Costumes and settings for historical plays*, 4 vols, Batsford
Morrison, H. (1998) *Acting skills*, 2nd edn A & C Black
Buchman, H. (1989) *Stage makeup*, Watson Guptill

Other sources

Performing Right Society Ltd
    29/33 Berners St, London W1P 4AA
    Tel: 020 7580 5444 Fax: 020 7306 4054
    www.prs.co.uk
    The PRS administers rights, royalties, permissions and licensing on behalf
    of playwrights.

The Society for Theatre Research
    The Theatre Museum, Tavistock St, London WC2E 7PA
    www.str.org.uk

The various national Arts Councils also provide advice and (some) support for the
dramatic arts.

THERAPIES *see* HEALTH & HEALTHCARE

THESES & DISSERTATIONS

See also Bibliographies, References & Citation; Writers &
Writing

Typical questions

- What research has been published on …?
- I've been told to look at a thesis. Can you get a copy for me?
- What's special about writing a dissertation?

Considerations

Although both words are used loosely for the reports of research, more specifically, a (UK) 'thesis' is the written work done for a doctorate, which is a 'dissertation'
in the USA. A 'dissertation' in the UK generally refers to work done for a Bach-

elor's or Master's degree. However, since schoolchildren use both words for their 'research', care needs to be taken over what, exactly, the enquirer wants.

The point about checking indexes to theses and dissertations is that one can find what, if anything, has been already researched on a subject. Since they are, usually, unpublished, the many thousands of theses and dissertations that have been written represent a huge pool of knowledge not indexed by the standard indexes and bibliographies which relate to published work. Be warned, though, that advice may be needed from library colleagues who deal with interlibrary lending on any restrictions that may apply in obtaining or using this category of literature. A formal declaration may be needed and use will, almost certainly, be restricted to within the library.

Where to look

Printed sources

Allison, B. (1997) *The student's guide to preparing dissertations and theses*, Kogan Page

Turabian, K. L. (1996) *A manual for writers of term papers, theses and dissertations*, 6th edn, University of Chicago Press

Standards

British Standards Institution (1990) *Presentation of theses and dissertations*, 2nd edn, BSI

Lists

ASLIB (1950/1–) *Index to theses accepted for higher degrees in the universities of Great Britain and Ireland*
Arranged in broad subject areas, with author index. Abstracts.

The Brits index: an index to the British theses collection (1971–1987) held at the British Library Document Supply Centre and London University, (1989), 3 vols, British Theses Service

Comprehensive dissertation index, 1861–1972 (1973), 73 vols, Xerox University Microfilm
Over 417,000 dissertations.

Dissertation abstracts international, University Microfilms International.
Monthly, cumulated, 1938–

T TIMETABLES

Lists US doctoral dissertations available on microfilm or as xeroxed reproduction. Includes European theses from 1969. Arranged by broad subject with keyword and title indexes.

Electronic sources

ETD 'Electronic Theses and Dissertations' Digital Library **www.theses.org**
 Links to websites which list theses and dissertations.

University Microfilms International **www.umi.com**
 Over 1.4 million listed.

TIMETABLES

Typical questions

- I want to know the times of trains from Leeds to Blackpool.
- Do you keep local bus timetables?

Considerations

The main types of timetables people will ask for are for trains, long distance coaches, and local buses. Most main libraries should keep copies of the British Rail and National Express timetables. Some will keep local bus timetables too. However, these may not be available at smaller branches. Do not worry, though. This is where the internet can prove very useful, with every imaginable type of timetable on there somewhere.

For European travel, the Thomas Cook European timetables are available in some libraries, but are not, as yet, online.

Where to look

National Rail timetable, Railtrack, 2 p.a.
National Express coach timetable, National Express, 2 p.a.
Thomas Cook European rail timetable, Thomas Cook, 2 p.a.
Thomas Cook rail map of Europe (2001), 13th edn, Thomas Cook

Websites

Die Bahn Travel Service **http://bahn.hafas.de/bin/db.s98/query.exe/en**
 Provides timetables and routings plus graphs for the whole of Europe.

Pricing information is skimpy and in deutschmarks when available. It includes most of Europe's major rail, bus and ferry timetables.

Railtrack Train Timetables **www.railtrack.co.uk**

National Express **www.gobycoach.com/**

For local bus timetables, the following site is excellent. It covers all travel by rail, air, coach, bus, ferry, metro and tram within the UK (including the Channel Islands, Isle of Man and Northern Ireland) and between the UK and Ireland, plus all rail, ferry and coach travel between the UK and mainland Europe. This is *the* definitive index to timetables, fares, ticket types, passenger facilities and lots more: **www.pti.org.uk**.

TRADE *see* EXPORTS & IMPORTS

TRADE MARKS

Typical questions
- How do I register a trade mark?
- Can I check a trade name?

Considerations
A trade mark is a unique symbol, sign or logo used by a business to identify its product or service. The 1994 Trade Marks Act clarifies what constitutes a trade mark in law and it would be sensible to refer serious enquirers to this. There is an excellent book called *A practical guide to trade marks* by Amanda Michaels, published by Sweet & Maxwell.

Where to look
Registering a trade mark
Contact the:

Patents Office
    Concept House, Cardiff Rd, Newport, Gwent NP9 1RH
    Tel: 0645 500505 (Central Enquiry Unit)
    www.patent.gov.uk

The Patent Office also has an excellent site for understanding trade marks. Under 'Search our records' the user can search for brief trade mark information.

For trade mark information
Contact the:

Institute of Trade Mark Attorneys
    4th Floor, Canterbury House, 2–6 Sydenham Rd, Croydon CR0 9XE
    Tel: 020 8686 2052
    www.itma.org.uk
    Excellent site for those who need to understand what is meant by trade marks. It also links to world patent offices.

Trade mark/name searches
Waterlow Signature
    Tel: 020 7490 0049 Fax: 020 7549 8677
    www.waterlow.com/wishome.htm
    This is a subscription online information service for trade mark searching. It includes UK and European trade marks. Trade mark reports contain images and text on over 800,000 UK trade marks and 45,000 European Union trade marks.

Trademark World
    Informa Publishing Group
    Tel: 020 7553 1000 Fax: 020 7553 1100
    Ten issues per year
    Views and reports on law relating to trade marks

TRADE UNIONS

Typical questions
- Have you got the contact number for the local branch of my trade union?
- Can you tell me what ... trade union have said about ... issue?

Considerations
For enquiries that require trade union local branch contact details the local telephone directory should be sufficient. Most trade unions in the UK now have

websites which will provide further information. Otherwise, the resources listed below all provide excellent information.

Where to look
Directories
Trade unions of the world, John Harper Publishing
> The main trade unions are given for each country listed; in addition, some historical background information is provided.

Journals
Trade Union Review
> Trade Union Review
> Tel: 01228 592626 Fax: 01228 597880
> Ten issues per year

Websites
European Trade Union Confederation **www.etuc.org/**

International Confederation of Free Trade Unions **www.icftu.org**
> Excellent site that is packed with information including links to global unions.

TUC **www.tuc.org.uk**
> Excellent site for research publications and provides links to individual British unions.

TRANSLATING *see* LANGUAGES & TRANSLATING

TRANSLITERATIONS *see* ALPHABETS & SCRIPTS

TRANSPORT

See also Timetables

Typical questions
• Have you got the address of the local bus company?

- Have you statistics for rail usage in the UK and Europe?
- Can you tell me where the cycle lanes in the UK are?

Considerations

There is no end to the enquiries you could be asked regarding transport. Some are specific to timetables, contact details and how to get from A to B. In the main, most of these can be answered directly by the local bus or train companies. You can find contact details in your local telephone book or try **www.yell.com**. Other enquiries may relate to statistics and the state of the transport industry, or come from those interested in policy and campaigns. Fortunately, the transport industry does have available some good sources of information, which should offer answers or at least point you in the right direction.

Where to look

Directories

If you need information on the world's railway industry look no further than:

Bushell, C. *Railway gazette international*, Reed Business Information
This provides not only an alphabetical listing of the world's railways but statistics, maps, and manufacturers and suppliers of rail equipment.

For bus and coach information then:

The little red book, Ian Allan Publishing
Offers an alphabetical listing of suppliers and manufacturers, a section on tendering and regulatory authorities and UK operators.

Statistics

Annual bulletin of transport statistics for Europe and North America, United Nations Economic Commission for Europe
Covers general transport statistics as well as rail, road, inland waterways and maritime.

Transport trends, Department of Environment, Transport and the Regions (DETR)

You need look no further than the Transport Statistics website **www.transtat.detr.gov.uk**, which provides a wealth of transport statistical information including Transport Statistics GB.

Transport yearbook 2002, Transport Statistics Users Group
In addition to other information, this publication provides a directory to international publications and sources covering transport issues.

Organizations and websites

Air Transport Users' Council
CAA House, 49–59 Kingsway, London WC2B 6TE
Tel: 020 7240 6061
www.auc.org.uk

Chamber of Shipping **www.british-shipping.org**

Confederation of Passenger Transport
Imperial House, 15–19 Kingsway, London WC2B 6UN
Tel: 020 7240 3131
www.cpt-uk.org/cpt

CycleSource **www.cyclesource.co.uk**
Covers all aspects of UK cycling.

Department of Environment, Transport and the Regions – Roads, Vehicles and Road Safety **www.roads.detr.gov.uk**

Institute of Logistics and Transport **www.iolt.org.uk**

Office of the Rail Regulator
1 Waterhouse Square, 138–142 Holborn, London EC1N 2TQ
Tel: 020 7282 2000
www.rail-reg.gov.uk

Maritime.com **www.maritimenews.com/**
Excellent for links to all aspects of shipping.

National Federation of Bus Users **www.nfbu.org**

Rail Passengers Council **www.railpassengers.org.uk**

Transport 2000
The Impact Centre, 12–18 Hoxton St, London N1 6NG
Tel: 020 7613 0743
www.transport2000.org.uk
Campaign group aiming to reduce car dependency.

TRAVEL *see* AIRCRAFT & AIRLINES; COUNTRIES; HOTELS & GUESTHOUSES; TIMETABLES

UFOs *see* THE UNEXPLAINED

THE UNEXPLAINED

See also Myths & Mythology; Religion

Typical questions

- Have you any books on interpreting dreams? I want to know whether dreams can foretell future events.
- Where are the most haunted places in the UK?
- Where can I find something on the Bermuda Triangle?
- How can I work out my horoscope?

Considerations

The 'unexplained' covers a wide range of subjects from angels to zombies! Only a few of these subjects can be touched upon here. Broadly speaking, the subjects fall outside the boundaries of orthodox science and one of the first considerations the librarian has is to find out whether the enquirer is a 'sceptic' or a 'believer', that is to say, is the enquirer investigating the subject, or are they serious about the subject? The sources used may vary accordingly. For better or for worse, there is a great popular interest in these subjects and there is a need to be well supplied with sources, and information about them.

Where to look

General

Wilson, C. (1987) *The encyclopedia of unsolved mysteries*, Harrap

Bord, J. and C. (1996) *Dictionary of earth mysteries*, Thorsons

Picknett, L. (1990) *The encyclopedia of the paranormal: a complete guide to the unexplained*, Macmillan

Guiley, R.E. (1992) *Harper's encyclopedia of mystical and paranormal experience*, HarperCollins

Randles, J. (1996) *The paranormal source book; the comprehensive guide to strange phenomena worldwide*, Piatkus

Astrology

Parker, J. and D. (2001) *Parker's astrology: the definitive guide to using astrology in every aspect of your life*, 2nd edn, Dorling Kindersley

Goodman, L. (1968) *Linda Goodman sun signs*, Pan
  The classic best-seller.

Fenton, S. (1998) *How to read your star signs*, Thorsons

www.astrology.com

www.astrologygateway.homestead.com/

Dreams

The alleged 'meaning' of dreams can be addressed in a number of books compiled specifically for the purpose. The enquiries relating to such popular beliefs, like astrology, need to be distinguished from orthodox scientific enquiries about the physiology and psychology of sleep and consciousness. In terms of the Dewey classification, between the 135s and the 150s.

Numerous popular books are published on the subject, for example:

Miller. G. H. (1995) *Ten thousand dreams interpreted; or, What's in a dream*, Ernest Benn
Pelton, R. W. (1983) *The complete book of dream interpretation*, Arco Publishing
Raphael, E. (1996) *The complete book of dreams*, Foulsham

Most general books on psychology and sleep will contain information; encyclopedias too, e.g.:

Gregory, R. L. (ed.) (1998) *The Oxford companion to the mind*, Oxford University Press

Dictionary of dream symbols **www.petrix.com/dreams/**

Freud **www.freud.org/uk.index2.html/**
  A description of Sigmund Freud's famous book *The meaning of dreams*.

Prophecy

Nostradamus *The prophecies*. Many editions, e.g. *The prophecies of Nostradamus*, (1989) Spearman

The complete book of fortune (1988), Chatto and Windus
Includes numerology, tea-leaves, palmistry, omens, graphology, etc.

Ghosts

Spencer, J. and Spencer, A. (2000) *Ghost hunter's guide to Britain,* Collins
A popular and reasonably factual geographical guide to alleged sightings of ghosts.

Spencer, J. and Spencer, A. (1996) *The encyclopedia of ghosts and spirits,* Headline

Supernatural

Rickard, B. and Michell, J. (2000) *Unexplained phenomena: a Rough guide special,* Rough Guides

Tarot and runes

Garen, N. (1989) *Tarot made easy,* Simon & Schuster
Blum, R. (2000) *Book of runes,* Connections

UFOs

Randles, J. and Warrington, P. (1985) *Science and the UFOs,* Blackwell

UNIFORMS

See also Armed Forces; Costume & Fashion; Medals & Decorations

Typical questions

- Have you got a picture of the uniform of the Horse Guards?
- Which regiments wear the busby?

Considerations

There is a large literature related to the uniforms of the armed forces, much of it aimed at the specialist markets of the modeller, military historian and collector. Check which use is required, since the first will probably want coloured plates, the second well documented prose, and the third current price guides. Be aware, also, of the distinction between badges and insignia, which are part of uniform, and medals and decorations which may or may not be.

Where to look

Printed sources

Carman, W. Y. (1977) *A dictionary of military uniforms*, Batsford
    A to Z by feature.

Newark, T. (1997) *Brassey's book of uniforms*, Brassey's

Illustrated sources

Barnes, R. M. (1972) *Military uniforms of Britain and the Empire*, Seeley
    Line drawings.

Carman, Y. (1985) *Uniforms of the British army*, Webb and Bower

Knotel, H. and Sieg, H. (1980) *Uniforms of the world: a compendium of army,*
    navy, and air force uniforms, 1700–1937, Arms and Armour Press
    Line drawings, historical background.

Lason, C. C. P. (1996) *A history of the uniforms of the British army*, 5 vols, Kay &
    Ward

There a number of publishers' series featuring a particular country, period, type
of force or even particular regiments with coloured illustrations. These include:

Arms and uniforms series, Ward Lock
Osprey Elite series, Osprey Publications
Uniforms Illustrated series, Arms and Armour Press

Badges and insignia

Churchill, C. and Westlake, R. (1986) *British army collar badges, 1881 to the*
    present: an illustrated reference guide for collectors, 2nd edn, Arms and
    Armour Press
Davis, B. L. (1988) *British army cloth insignia, 1940 to the present: an illustrated*
    reference guide for collectors, 2nd edn, Arms and Armour Press
Short, J. G. (1988) *Special forces insignia, British and Commonwealth units: an*
    illustrated reference guide for collectors, Arms and Armour Press

All the above have price guides.

Hobart, M. C. (2000) *Badges and uniforms of the Royal Air Force*, Leo Cooper
Kipling, A. L. and King, H. I. (1978) *Head-dress badges of the British army*, 2nd
    edn, F. Muller Ltd

A two-volume definitive work.

Other sources

Imperial War Museum
    Lambeth Rd, London SE1 6HZ
    Tel: 020 7416 5320
    www.iwm.org.uk

UNITED NATIONS

Typical questions

- Have you got the Universal Declaration of Human Rights?
- What's the Charter of the UN?
- Who are the members of the Security Council?
- What is the UN doing about the refugee problem?

Considerations

General information on the UN is fairly easy to find: encyclopedias and books on international relations will have material. Harder to locate, or obtain, are detailed accounts of the proceedings and texts of resolutions of the UN as only the larger libraries stock this material and the UN itself is very slow at publishing. The best sources, are newspaper accounts and information on the UN's own website, which is extensive and helpful.

Where to look

Printed sources

Luard, E. (1994) *The United Nations: how it works and what it does*, 2nd edn, Macmillan

Rengger, N. (ed.) (1995) *Treaties and alliances of the world*, 6th edn, Catermill
    Has the texts of many of the international treaties and agreements that feature the UN.

United Nations *Yearbook*. Annual

United Nations (1998) *Basic facts about the United Nations*, UN Department of Public Information

United Nations (1998) *Image and reality: questions and answers about the United Nations*, UN
Slim booklet.

Osmańczyk, E. J. *Encyclopedia of the United Nations and international agreements* (1990), 2nd edn, Taylor & Francis

Try news databases such as the indexes to *The Times* or newspaper websites (*see* Newspapers) for recent events such as voting details in the Security Council.

Electronic sources
United Nations **www.un.org**
A large site giving a wide range of information and text.

Other sources
UN Office and Information Centre
Millbank Tower, 21–24 Millbank, London SW1P 4QH
Tel: 020 7630 1981 Fax: 020 7976 6478.
The UN publish a magazine called *UN Courier* and they also provide many 'freebies'.

Statesman's yearbook, *Whitaker's almanack* and many other current affairs sources will have information about the UN.
The United Nations is a serious publisher of statistics, along with enormous amounts of English-language material. Some material can be purchased/ordered through The Stationery Office outlets. There are also a number of linked organizations, e.g. UNESCO, WHO (World Health Organisation).

UNIVERSITIES & COLLEGES

See also Education

Typical questions
• Have you a prospectus for UMIST, Manchester?
• Which universities do courses on travel and tourism?

Considerations
Larger libraries may keep copies of university and college prospectuses. They may also keep copies of the UCAS (Universities and Colleges Admissions Service) book.

U UNIVERSITIES & COLLEGES

If your library does not have these then all is not lost. Nearly all colleges and universities are now present on the world wide web. There are also 'alternative' guides to these establishments, both in hard copy and on the net.

Where to look

UCAS, *The big guide*. Annual
> The official guide to university and college entry in the UK.

LASER compendium of higher education, Butterworth-Heinemann. Annual
> Lists courses and institutions which provide them. Also shows degree course offers and special requirements.

Hobson's postgraduate directory. Annual
> **www.hobsons.com**
> Lists over 20,000 postgraduate courses.

International Association of Universities *International handbook of universities 2001*, 16th edn, Palgrave
> Over 7300 entries in over 176 countries.

For a more 'independent' point of view try:

Dudgeon, P. (2001) *Virgin alternative guide to British universities*, Virgin

Electronic sources

For a list of all university and college websites try:

www.ucas.com/instit/index.html

For a more independent point of view try:

Redmole **www.redmole.co.uk**
> Alternative university guide. University ratings, cheapest beer, etc.

BigBlueSpot **www.bigbluespot.com**
> All-in-one student guide. City guides, jobs, accommodation, issues.

Tips and pitfalls

Try not to offer advice on choosing courses or universities. This is the job of careers centres and offices. Advise the enquirer to go there if they need more information. And remember that most colleges and universities are now online, so if you are in a small branch far away from larger libraries or careers centre, you can still

332

provide information on universities if you have access to the internet.

UTILITIES

Typical questions

- Have you got the contact details for ... electricity supplier?
- Who do I complain to about my gas supplier?
- How do I find out about water meters?

Where to look

Electricity

The main directory to use is:

Electricity supply handbook, Reed Business Information
> Established in 1948, this is a trusty handbook for the electricity industry, covering generation, supply and distribution and transmission companies along with government and regulation organizations, and research, trade and professional bodies.

Gas

The main directory to use is:

Gas industry directory, United Business Media
> **www.mfinfo.com**
> This directory has extensive coverage of over 2700 companies in 38 countries. It has sections on, among other things, industrial and domestic suppliers, who's who and trade names.

Water

The main directory to use is:

Who's who in the water industry, Turret RAI Plc

But try also:

Web4Water **www.web4water.co.uk**
> This includes an online directory and excellent links to everything to do with water and the water industry. Well worth a visit.

U UTILITIES

Drinking Water Inspectorate **www.dwi.gov.uk**

OFGEM (Office of Gas and Electricity Markets) **www.ofgem.gov.uk**

OFWAT (Office of the Water Services) **www.ofwat.gov.uk**
Useful for water companies' contact details.

Water UK **www.water.org.uk**
Provides a huge amount of information covering all aspects of the water industry.

WATER *see* UTILITIES

WEATHER

Typical questions
- What will the weather be like in Madeira next week?
- What is the average summer temperature in Boston, USA?
- What was the weather like on 23 September 2000 in Lytham St Annes?
- Have you any information about tornadoes? I want to know how they are formed.

Considerations
There is much to consider here. Enquirers may want forecasts for holidays, or want to check previous weather for insurance purposes. They may be doing school projects on the weather. The possibilities are endless. However, with a few select resources, you should be able to manage most enquiries.

Where to look
General
Watts, A. (1994) *The weather handbook*, Waterline
> A good general introduction to our weather systems.

Whitaker, R. (ed.) (1996) *Weather: the ultimate guide to the elements*, HarperCollins
> A comprehensive and accessible guide to meteorology.

Meteorological Office (1991) *Meteorological glossary*, 6th edn, HMSO
> The definitive glossary.

Electronic sources
There are some great weather sites around on the internet. Here are a selection:

Weather gateway **www.weather.co.uk**
BBC Weather **www.bbc.co.uk/weather**
The Met Office **www.met-office.gov.uk**
Yahoo World Weather **http://weather.yahoo.com**

There is a useful site for flood warnings:

www.environment-agency.gov.uk/subjects/flood/floodwarning

Tips and pitfalls

Many libraries keep weather figures from their local meteorological offices. Check to see whether yours does or not. These figures are very popular for people putting in insurance claims for storm damage, etc. If you do not keep these then check local newspapers or contact your local meteorological office.

WEDDINGS *see* ETIQUETTE & FORMS OF ADDRESS

WEIGHTS & MEASURES

Typical questions
- What's 80 degrees in centigrade?
- How much does a pint of water weigh?
- When do children's shoe sizes change to adult ones? Are they the same in the USA?

Considerations

Simple conversions from, say, imperial measures into metric, can be found in most desk diaries, even pocket diaries. Staff should learn what is in theirs! More complex conversions, such as those used in engineering, may well be beyond the librarian's comprehension, but possibly within that of the engineer who asks!

Printed sources

Whitaker's almanack, A & C Black. Annual
    Has conversion tables.

Diagram Group (1997) *Collins gem ready reference*, HarperCollins
    Over 130 quick conversion tables.

Economist (1998) *The Economist desk companion. How to measure, convert, calculate and define practically anything*, 3rd edn, The Economist
    272 pages and index.

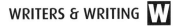

Beyer, W. H. (ed.) (1991) *CRC standard mathematical tables and formulae*, 29th edn, CRC Press

Bolton, B. (2001) *Newnes instrumentation and measurement and measurement pocket book*, 3rd edn, Newnes
Technical data.

Tips and pitfalls

Different countries use different sizes for clothes.

The UK and USA still use some imperial (non-metric) measures, the USA more so, but not always the same ones! An example is paper sizes.

WHITE PAPERS *see* GOVERNMENT

WRITERS & WRITING

See also Biographies; Books; ISBNs and ISSNs; Literature; Proofreading; Pseudonyms

Typical questions

- How do I write a dissertation?
- I've written a book. How do I get it published?

Considerations

It is natural that people interested in writing should ask a librarian. Many people, though, have a naive view of how easy it is to get published. Don't feed these expectations!

Printed sources

Germano, W. (2001) *Getting it published: a guide for scholars serious about serious books*, Chicago University Press

The writers' and artists' yearbook, A & C Black. Annual
Sub-title is: 'A directory for writers, artists, playwrights, writers for film, radio and television, designers, illustrators and photographers'.

Turner, B. (ed.) *The writer's handbook*, Macmillan. Annual
Both this and *The writers' and artists' yearbook* contain pretty well everything

the aspiring writer needs, from information on how to present work, agents and publishers to advice on copyright, rights and contracts, and much else in the literary and media marketplaces.

Bolt, D. (2000) *New authors handbook*, 2nd edn, P. Owen

Kane, T. S. (1988) *The new Oxford guide to writing*, Oxford University Press

Legat, M. (1998) *An author's guide to publishing*, 3rd edn, Hale

Hoffman, A. (1999) *Research for writers*, 6th edn, A & C Black
Includes many directory sections.

International authors and writers who's who, Melrose Press. Bi-annual
A comprehensive directory to living authors worldwide.

Writers' News.
A monthly magazine giving advice on techniques and contacts published by Writers' News Ltd. Has a helpline.

The Author: Journal of the Society of Authors
As well as feature articles it includes adverts for courses, prizes and agents. Good for 'official' news such as legislation and legal matters.

Ritter, R. (2000) *The Oxford dictionary for writers and editors*, Oxford University Press.
One of many handy works which lists words and abbreviations writers need to check for meaning and spelling.

The writer's directory, St James Press. Annual
Biographical, bibliographic and contact information on 17,500 living authors from English-speaking countries.

Text preparation

Grossman, J. (2001) *The Chicago manual of style*, 14th edn, Chicago University Press
The essential guide for writers, editors and publishers.

Butcher, J. (1992) *Copy-editing: the Cambridge handbook for editors, authors, publishers*, 3rd edn, Cambridge University Press
The classic handbook.

M[odern] H[umanities] R[esearch] A[ssociation] (1996) *Notes for authors,*
editors and writers, 5th edn, Maney Publishing
Details on copy preparation, proof correction, etc. More basic than Butcher.

BS 5261–1: 2000 Copy preparation and proof correction
Covers document layout, arrangement of headings and footnotes, choice of
typography, etc.

Strunk, W. and White, E.B. (2000) *The elements of style*, 4th edn, Allyn & Bacon

Reports, etc.

There are numerous popular, low-priced guides to writing 'papers'. Examples are:

Berry, R. (1999) *Research project: how to write it*, 4th edn, Routledge
Oliver, P. (1996) *Teach yourself writing essays and reports*, Hodder & Stoughton
Jurabian, K. (2001) *A manual for writers of term papers, theses and dissertations*,
6th edn, Chicago University Press

Indexing

BS 6529: 1984 (1991) Recommendation for examining documents,
determining their subjects and selecting indexing terms.
Collison, R. L. (1969) *Indexes and indexing: guide to the indexing of books*, 3rd
edn, E. Benn
One of several guides to indexing.

Electronic sources

Author.co.uk **www.author.co.uk**
A website supported by The Arts Council of England which provides
contacts, reviews, news, discussion groups and other web-based services.

Other sources

The Society of Authors
84 Drayton Gardens, London SW10 9SB
Tel: 020 7373 6642 Fax: 020 7373 5768
E-mail: authorsoc@writer.org.org.uk
www.writers.org.uk/society

Tips and pitfalls

Talking to authors can be enormously pleasurable, talking to wannabe authors usually less so. Beware of getting drawn into doing their research, or passing opinions.